CARDINAL BARONIUS
OF THE ROMAN ORATORY

FOUNDER OF CHURCH HISTORY

BY

LADY AMABEL KERR

Author of "Life of Blessed Sebastian Valfrii," etc

𝔐𝔢𝔡𝔦𝔞𝔱𝔯𝔦𝔵 𝔓𝔯𝔢𝔰𝔰
MMXV

ISBN: 978-0692471715

Originally Published by
Benziger Brother, 1898

NIHIL OBSTAT :

HENRICUS G. S. BOWDEN,
Censor deputatus.

IMPRIMATUR:

HERBERTUS CARDINALIS VAUGHAN,
ARCHIEPISCOPUS WESTMONAST.

Die 25 Nov., 1897.

T HE object of the following pages is to present to the reader a life of Baronius, from a purely personal and individual point of view, no attempt being made to study him critically as a historian, or even to pause on any of the vexed questions which may have been raised by his writings. With this object in view the materials have been drawn mainly from his correspondence with intimate friends, contained in the collection of his letters edited by Raymund Albericius (Rome 1759), from his Life by the same writer, and that by G. Ricci (Rome, 1745), and also from the accounts of his life at the Oratory, incidentally made known to us by the biographers of St. Philip.

NOTE TO THE MEDIATRIX PRESS EDITION

We have, as much as possible, preserved the 19th century English spellings of the original. Still, it has been necessary to update some of the language where it is too archaic, or prone to misinterpretation as well as rephrase some of Lady Kerr's rendering from her original Italian sources. We have also taken pains to translate the numerous Latin quotes throughout the book, as well as add pictures of the subjects in the book.

Table of Contents

THE LIFE OF BARONIUS

CAESAR BARONIVS SORANVS TIT.SS.NERELET ACHILLEI CARD.SACROSANCTAE APOSTOLICAE
SED.BIBLIOTHEC.ANNALIVM ECCLESIAST.SCRIPTOR EXIMIVS AETAT SVAE ANN.LXIIII.
Historia, et pietate micat Baronius alter
Lvmen ab alterius lumine lumit honos.

Friderchio Villamena fe Romae Anno 1602 Cum priuilego. Sumtis Petrolas r. Sigenorum authoritat.

CHAPTER I
Boyhood

H AD Baronius chosen, he could have traced for himself a noble pedigree and a line of ancestry of which he might have been proud. He himself cared nothing for such things, but some of his relatives were far from sharing his indifference, and sought to kindle a pride of race in his soul by relating to him how, in the century preceding his birth, his family had stood in such high favour with the then sovereign of the Two Sicilies as to create jealousy in the hearts of other nobles. These, in enmity, made a raid on the family of Baronius, and well nigh exterminated it. No male representative was left, save one infant, unborn at the time of the raid and from him had descended the race of Baronius in its three branches, in Naples, Sicily and Spain. This retrospect is not without interest, for it shows on how slender a thread at one time depended the existence of the writer of the Ecclesiastical Annals.

Born, then, of noble but by no means affluent parents, Cesare saw the light of day at Bora, in the kingdom of Naples, on the 30th of August, 1538. His father, Camillo, who was in those days much given to the things of this world, was possessed of unusual vigour of character; for his conduct to his son when, in the early days of his manhood, he crossed his will, was that of a veritable Brutus. No doubt Cesare inherited his own energy of character from his father, while from his mother, Portia, he drew that tender love of God which made his life's

1

work holy. When he, her long-wished for and only son was born, Portia regarded him as Our Lady's gift; and, in accordance with a promise made before his birth, solemnly dedicated him to the Mother of God in the neighbouring chapel of Santa Maria in Valle, so called from its position in a nook among the hills. In this same little church, about a year after his dedication, Portia and her mother-in-law, Philomena, made a fervent triduo for the child's recovery from a fever which threatened his life. At the end of the triduo, Portia heard a voice, which, as she affirmed, told her to take heart and be joyful, as her prayer was heard. Nothing doubting, the two women hastened home, and were scarcely surprised to find the little Cesare sleeping peacefully in his cradle, delivered from his fever.

This cure was always regarded as miraculous by Cesare's family, and as such he himself accepted it when he reached the age of reason. It was, presumably, the first cause of his very marked devotion through life to the Mother of God. The chapel of Santa Maria in Valle was inseparably mixed up with the memories of Cesare's childhood, and so great an affection had he for it, that when in the middle of life he saw the Oratory take definite form at Santa Maria in Vallicella, his joy was increased by the connection by name between the new church of the Congregation and the humbler and more unknown Santa Maria in Valle.

The incident of her little son's cure, and the remembrance of her previous gift of him to our Blessed Lady, made Portia very quick to perceive the germs of sanctity and genius latent within him; and she was ever on the look out for visible signs of God's favour. While Cesare was still a child, an uncouth mendicant pilgrim

2

came to the house to ask for alms. So rough was he in appearance, that Portia, who was always fearful of possible harm to her boy, hid him behind her but her mother-in-law, scolding her for her nervousness, drew him forward. The mendicant looked kindly at him, and made the sign of the cross on his forehead. "Take care of this child," said he, turning to Portia. "Bring him up well, for he will live to do great things for God's Church." These words drove from her heart all fear of the stranger, and she hastened to fetch an alms for him; but when she returned he had disappeared. She always believed this pilgrim to have been a supernatural visitor. She may have been right, or it is possible that he possessed the gift of reading character by its outward impress, and may have seen signs of future excellence in the boy's noble brow and thoughtful countenance.

It needed not the mendicant's advice to make Portia devote herself to the careful training of her boy and many were the early lessons in charity which he learned from his mother. She took him with her to visit the sick in the hospital, a ministration to which she entirely devoted the last twelve years of her life. Moreover, so anxious was she to foster pity for the poor in his heart that, whenever she had an alms to give to the maimed, sick, or blind beggars, who abounded throughout southern Italy, she invariably gave it by the hands of her child. If Cesare's piety delighted his mother, his proficiency in learning and his eagerness for study satisfied the ambition of his father. Until he was eighteen, he was educated at Verola, a town about nine miles from Sora. But so bent was the boy on acquiring knowledge that he was not content with what he could learn in the classes, but obtained, as a favour from his father, permission to have private lessons at home in addition. Having learned all that the schools at Verola could teach him, he was sent at the age of eighteen to Naples, full of bright prospects and high hopes, to study and take up his doctor's degree in jurisprudence. There he remained for a year, and there, no doubt, he would have remained to finish his course of study, had not God held in His hand other designs for him.

Perhaps there are few more dreary passages of history than the records of the constant little sixteenth-century wars and quarrels between France and Spain for supremacy in Italy. At the period when Baronius was approaching manhood the differences between the two nations had slumbered for a while; for each had cares of its own which fully engaged its attention. Spain was resting in peaceful possession of such Italian territory as she had secured, when Pope Paul IV stirred up the old rivalry. It was the dream of the earlier part of his pontificate to drive the foreigner altogether from Italian soil, and to restore his native country to that state of national freedom which he himself could remember as existing three-quarters of a century before. His desire was, according to his own expression, that Italy should once more be like a well-tuned instrument, the four strings of which should be the Papal States, Venice, Lombardy and Naples. With this end in view, and as a preliminary measure, he instigated the King of France to attack Spain in her Italian dominions. The attempt, however, was not attended with success, and served only to strengthen the Spanish hold on the Two Sicilies; and the disappointment of the failure changed the tenor of the Pope's thoughts, and made him devote the remainder of his life to ecclesiastical reforms instead of politics.

This attempt to drive Spain out of the Italian peninsula, and its failure, would be of little interest to us were it not for the effect of the expedition on Cesare's career. After he had been a year at Naples the French invasion caused such disturbances, and threatened to upset everything so completely, that Camillo decided on sending the boy to Rome at once to finish his studies there. He little dreamt how entirely this concession to expediency would destroy the brilliant hopes he had built for the future of his gifted son.

Cesare's heart had always leapt within him at the very thought of Rome, the centre of learning; and now that circumstances took him there so many years before he had anticipated, he readily adopted the capital of Christendom as his home. With very rare and unimportant exceptions he dwelt there all his life; and within the walls of the Eternal City, the centre and pivot of ecclesiastical history, he found ample food for every mental want. "Although Rome may have been harmful to some," he wrote, paraphrasing St. Gregory Nazianzen's words about Athens, "to me she has been all gain and blessedness. She received me when I was wandering without curb or rein; she made of me a disciple under the yoke of Christ, and was my teacher and mistress in morals as well as learning."

Cesare was only nineteen when, full of high hopes and with life before him, he entered the gates of Rome as a stranger, and went to lodge in the Piazza Branohia with Nardo Marta, a native of Sora, intent on the pursuit of his studies under Cesare Costa, a well-known master of jurisprudence. Study was his passion, and his principal recreation lay in the composition of Italian verses. We know from himself that these two engrossments

5

represented the sum total of the hold which the world had gained on him. Nevertheless Mario, a citizen of Sora, a friend of his, and a devout frequenter of the S. Girolamo exercises, was anxious about his young fellow-countryman's spiritual welfare, and, in a moment ever blessed to him, made him known to St. Philip Neri.

We know not what took place at that first meeting between the Saint and Cesare. Even our surmises are based only on what we know to have occurred in the case of other young men, when they also first came under the spell of St. Philip's influence. We can, however, form a fair conjecture of what took place from the results which followed the interview; for, whatever it was that passed between the Saint and him, it changed the whole of Cesare's life. St. Philip looking on him loved him; and the young man opened his heart to the grace which that glance of love carried with it. Unlike his prototype in the Gospel he did not turn away sorrowful because he had great possessions, but there and then, in intention, he gave to God all his rare possessions of soul and brain, and all the great gifts latent within him.

Almost his first act after the Saint's words or look had pierced his heart was to destroy every one of the poems he had taken such delight in writing. There could have been no harm in these verses, for there was no harm in Cesare himself; nevertheless they were the first sacrifice he offered. Perchance the absorption he had felt in writing them was incompatible with a life given entirely to God; or else the action denoted, unbeknownst to himself, that the pen destined to do such great work for the Church was not to be sullied by its connection with any lower object. Be his motive what it might, the sacrifice was very real. He was greatly attached to these effusions of his

6

boyhood, and owned to a friend that he had never had a harder fight with himself than when he destroyed them.

All his acts of self-sacrifice in those early days of his conversion were characterized by the same generous impulse. The lessons in charity given him by his mother had been very practical; so, now that his heart had turned to God, he sought to prove his love of Him by ministering to His poor. At that time a famous Capuchin preacher, Fra Alfonso Lupo, was giving a course of sermons in the Church of S. Giacomo of the Spaniards. In one of these he described in vivid language the destitute state of a certain poor family, and appealed to his hearers for assistance. Cesare, who was present, would gladly have responded to the appeal; but he had no money, for even while still in his father's favour his allowance from home was of the scantiest. However, he suffered no such lack of means to stop him, but, hastening to his lodgings, he fetched thence some new shirts which he had that morning received from his mother, and gave them to Fra Lupo for the poor family. The Capuchin, struck by such a gift coming from a young man of the class to which Cesare evidently belonged, drew from him his name and history, and, we are told, recounted the incident next day from the pulpit. Once converted, it was not in Cesare's ardent nature to stay where he was. It was something indeed to have made the sacrifice of his early compositions, and to give more than his superfluities to the poor; but such partial gifts as these could not satisfy him. The time soon came when his soul became possessed by the desire to offer himself entirely to God in the religious life. He purposed to give up his studies and enter the Capuchin Order, then in the first fervour of its reform and treading very literally in the footsteps of St. Francis. He would not, however, take such

7

a step without consulting him to whom he owed his conversion; and he opened his heart to St. Philip, and placed himself in his hands.

St. Philip Neri

CHAPTER II
Vocation

A T this point of Cesare's life, when it flowed into and was for awhile merged into that of the Saint, we find ourselves in a difficulty, for our subject is overshadowed and in danger of losing its individuality. In fact, the early disciples of St. Philip, pillars of the Oratory though they were, have no existence apart from him. Take him away, and they are not; for they were what they were on account of him. Remove him from their lives, and, if known to the world at all, it would be as totally different men. This may be to a certain extent less true of Baronius than of the other companions of St. Philip, on account of the great work to which, at the Saint's initiative, he devoted his life, and which has immortalized his name. Yet, during the earlier portion of his life—until, indeed, his holy Father was taken from him—he had no life apart from him; and the chief interest of his early biography lies in tracing the process by which, under the touch of the Saint, he became what he was. So true is this, that it is scarcely rash to assert that Cesare was the work of St. Philip's hands in a more eminent degree than any of his companions.

But this rightly belongs to the life of St. Philip rather than to that of Baronius; and in every life of the Saint the methods by which he moulded the great historian have been used as an illustration of his own gifts. Here, however, in a biography of Baronius, the case must be reversed, and the lower must be put in the higher place.

He who was fashioned must stand forth in the front, and the master-hand which fashioned him must be relegated to the background; the light of the lesser luminary being in a sense made to shine with a light superior to that of the greater. So must it be; but still it must be borne in mind that "one is the glory of the sun and another the glory of the moon," and that, radiant though the latter may be, all its brightness is borrowed from the greater splendour of the sun.

When Cesare, full of his fervid desire to embrace the religious life, put himself in St. Philip's hands and asked his counsel, the Saint bade him wait. He whom St. Ignatius likened to the bell which, while it remains outside the sanctuary, calls others to go in, knew by divine intuition that it was Cesare's part as well as his own to remain outside. A glance at St. Philip's own life shows us that it was in that same year, 1557, that his zeal for God's glory and his thirst for souls filled him with a desire to spend himself among the heathen. He had recognised the voice of God in the words of him who told him that Rome was to be his Indies; and the same Holy Spirit who spoke through Ghettini told him, in his turn, that the young man before him was to be his companion and fellow-worker in that sphere.

Cesare, even then docile to his touch, waited, or rather tried to wait; for during three years he could not succeed in mastering his desire for the religious life. St. Philip knew of his inward struggle, and by legislating for the complete employment of his time, helped him through the period of suspense which he had imposed on him. With the constant prescience of the great things Baronius was destined to do for God, the Saint bade him continue his studies with redoubled energy; but, careful meanwhile of

10

his soul, he drew him towards the Oratory. Cesare threw himself completely under the influence of the Saint in the exercises of S. Girolamo, which were at that time changing the face of Rome. He went to confession every day and to communion frequently, and spent the hours not devoted to prayer or study at the Hospital of Santo Spirito, which he visited morning and evening.

Meanwhile, rumours reached his father's ears of the mode of life led by his only son, in whom he took such pride. He wrote angrily to remonstrate with him against neglecting his studies and throwing away his chances in life; and, with indignation, repeated the reports which he had heard of his having embraced a semi-religious life, with the further intention of entering the priesthood, and of his going about clad in old clothes which were a disgrace to his name. Cesare wrote back temperately and assured his father that he had by no means given up his studies, and that he dressed in a manner befitting his state. As, however, his son took no notice of the main accusation, namely, his intention to leave the world, Camillo wrote a still more angry letter, and told him that, unless he assured his parents that he would give up his present mode of life, he need look for no more help from home. To this Cesare impetuously replied that he must take more care of his soul than of his body, and that he would rather be disinherited than change his purpose.

His father's words were no empty threats; and, on receipt of his son's reply, he at once withdrew the allowance he had hitherto made him, and left him penniless and without a profession in the city of Rome. Nor do we hear that this allowance was ever renewed, even after Camillo had forgiven his son and had been converted to a better life by his letters. He certainly did not leave him anything when he died. It is evident from several allusions and incidents in his life that Baronius possessed no private means of his own; nor is there any mention of such in an enumeration of the various sources of his income which he made in a letter to Father Talpa, of the Naples Oratory. The fault may not have rested entirely with his father, and Cesare, following in St. Philip's footsteps, may have refused to receive his inheritance even when it was offered to him. There are, however, grounds to think that his want of private means was in some way attributable to Camillo, for when Baronius bade farewell on his death-bed to his nephew, Baldino, he told him that he left to him the same legacy he had himself received from his father, namely, poverty.

Cesare might have found himself in that grave predicament in which his father had meant to place him, with the view of reducing him to submission by depriving him of all external aid, and exposing him to danger of starvation. God, however, suffered this design to be frustrated. He whom from henceforth Cesare regarded more than ever as a father provided a home for him for at St. Philip's request, Michele Paravicino opened his house to him, supplied him with everything, and made him as one of his own family. This generous man did not go without a special reward. Ottavio, his son, the future Cardinal, was at that time a little child, and learned to know Baronius under his father's roof, being trained and educated by him, so that he ever afterwards regarded himself as his disciple in learning. The boy's childhood was spent among blessed influences, and at a very early age he was brought into close touch with St. Philip and the Oratory. "It was given me by the grace of God," he himself writes, "to know Philip Neri when I was about six

12

years of age; and from that time I enjoyed his conversation and intimacy for twenty-one years." The little Ottavio, precociously clever though slightly deformed, lived as much at the Oratory as in his own home; and years afterwards, when he was Cardinal, Baronius, in a letter which accompanied a presentation copy of the fourth volume of the Annals, reminded him of those early days at S. Girolamo.

"As you may remember," he writes, "you as a boy plucked with your little hands the first young shoots of these my Annals, as, in my daily discourses, I poured into your young and innocent mind the acts of the holy Fathers of the Church. And you, as was your wont, so as to help our Oratory, used to recite these acts with a grace and charm which won applause from your hearers, who wondered that one of your tender years should speak with the dignity of an old man, and combine eloquence and prudence with your simplicity."

So entirely was Ottavio a child of the Oratory that when, as will be told in its place, St. Philip sent five fathers to S. Giovanni of the Florentines, young Paravicino, then a boy of twelve, accompanied them, and used to read in the refectory. While there he continued his studies under Baronius, who stood sponsor to him at Confirmation when he reached the years of manhood. Confirmation was at that period usually given to adults, for it was only after Cesare was received into the home of Michele Paravicino that he himself received the sacrament.

There are not many records left of the years when Cesare was passing from youth to manhood. Study and works of charity combined filled his life between the ages of nineteen and twenty-six, during which time he lived with Paravicino and little else is told of him except that he gave himself over more fervently than ever to the life of mortification which had kindled the ire of his father. He slept on a bare board, fasted several days in the week, spent hours of the night in prayer, and did his best, sometimes to an heroic degree, to overcome the flesh and its passions. He yielded himself completely to St. Philip's guidance, and, even before he bound himself by the vow which remains to be spoken of, paid him unhesitating and entire obedience.

There is one incident related of Cesare's discourse with the family with which he had found a home, which proves that Michele had at times to pay somewhat dearly for his act of hospitality. He possessed some pictures on his walls, of some merit as works of art, but the subjects of which offended his young guest's sense of decency. With impetuous zeal Cesare obtained some colours and painted over all the objectionable parts. This made Michele very angry, and an unpleasant scene ensued. However, Paravicino's wife acted as peacemaker and took up Cesare's defence, protesting to her husband that far from injuring the pictures he had removed from them their special defects.

Morning and evening Cesare visited the hospital, where he made the beds of the sick, fed those who were helpless, and devoted himself to the care of their bodies and, as far as he could, to that of their souls. This work, undertaken at St. Philip's bidding, was blessed to him. One day, though prostrated by an attack of fever, he managed to drag himself to the hospital by sheer force of will rather than omit his morning visit. As, however, he passed from bed to bed the fever left him, and he returned home quite cured.

14

Sometimes it was for others that his obedience was blessed. A certain poor man was received into the hospital in a dying state who, by some unwonted negligence on the part of the chaplain, was put to bed without any inquiries being made as to whether he had received the sacraments, or wished to receive them. A candle was then placed at the head of his bed—the usual token that its occupant was in a dying condition, and that nothing more could be done for him. All this was made known to St. Philip by internal light; and when Cesare came to him to make his usual daily confession, he stopped him, and sent him off without delay to the hospital. It was in the middle of the day, and the hour when the inmates, their wants having been ministered to, were left to rest, while the attendants took their own siesta.

Cesare knew this perfectly well, but he instantly obeyed the Saint's command.

For some time he wandered about the silent wards of the hospital, seeking him to whom St. Philip had sent him and, though he could find no one in apparent need of assistance, he persevered, feeling sure that the Saint had not sent him there for nothing. At last his eye lighted on the poor man who lay in extremis, and he asked him whether he had received the last sacraments. In reply the dying man earnestly begged for a priest, that he might make his confession before he died. Cesare went in all haste to fetch the chaplain, who arrived in time to give him all the sacraments. Then the poor man gave up his soul, having been kept alive by the prayers of St. Philip long enough to enable him to receive them.

It was just at this time that the new Oratory had been built over the aisle of S. Girolamo, and there the exercises began to take shape. Baronius, on whose life these

15

exercises had such a powerful influence, has described them in the first volume of the Annals, and there compares them with the gatherings of the early Christians. "By God's favour," says he, "we have seen here in Rome in our own day a renewal of those things recommended to the Corinthians by the Apostle St. Paul and have with our own ears heard the things of God told in a way profitable to all. These meetings were instituted by the Reverend Father Philip Neri of Florence, with the help of Messir Francesco Maria Tarugi of Montepulciano, who may well be called the *dux verbi*, so unequalled is his mode of preaching. To these two is it primarily owing that those who seek perfection may when they choose go to the Oratory of S. Girolamo—whence the Congregation of the Oratory takes its name—and there hold pious conferences.

"The method followed is this: After mental prayer one of the brothers reads from a spiritual book, and one of the fathers discourses on what has just been read, and expounds it in a manner which goes home to the hearts of the hearers. Sometimes Father Philip calls on one of the brothers to give his opinion and, in that case, the instruction takes the form of a dialogue. At another time Father Philip commands one of his own disciples to seat himself on a raised stool, and discourse in simple language on the life of some saint, illustrating his words by passages from Scripture and the fathers. Then another takes his place, and speaks in the same way on some other subject; and, after him, a third discourses on ecclesiastical history, each of these discourses being limited to half an hour. Then, when all have finished, a spiritual canticle is sung, and the exercises are concluded by more prayers."

Among his lay disciples who, as described by Baronius, were set to preach by St. Philip, was Cesare himself, though at the time he was barely twenty years of age. He preached in the simple way introduced and commanded by the Saint; but his own nature stamped his sermons with a sternness and earnestness which made them very impressive, all the more as in the heat of his early fervour his favourite subjects were death, judgment and hell. His discourses stirred the souls of his hearers, and were the cause of several conversions. On one occasion four men of standing, one of them a prelate of the Church, were present, and were so moved by the young preacher's words that then and there they made up their minds to leave the world, and shortly after entered religious Orders.

Throughout all this, Cesare's own soul was far from satisfied. He had obeyed St. Philip, and put from him all immediate thought of embracing the religious life; but the longing still lurked within. Again and again he pleaded with the Saint, and as often the latter told him that such was not his vocation. At last, seeing that though Cesare gave up his will, he was unconvinced and in a state of suffering, and having let his disciple's anxiety and struggle of mind last three years, St. Philip sent him to ask counsel of Costanzo Tassone, who had been one of his earliest disciples, and was a member of the household of St. Charles Borromeo. So one morning, after hearing Mass at S. Girolamo, Cesare put the whole matter before this priest; but Costanzo refused to answer him at once, or even soon. He found the decision of this vocation, thus left entirely to him, no easy matter, for some divine instinct told him that much depended on it and he kept Cesare in a state of suspense for five long months. Early, however, in

17

the year 1560, on the vigil of the feast of the Conversion of St. Paul, when St. Philip with several of his disciples, among whom were Tassone and Cesare, had gone to the Apostle's Basilica outside the walls, light was vouchsafed to Costanzo, and he felt his mind made up on the weighty subject. Taking Baronius by the hand and leading him apart, he said: "Know, Cesare, that God has heard the prayers which I and others have offered, and He wills that you should serve Him as a secular priest, and not in the religious state."

Cesare had put his vocation into the hands of Tassone too honestly and whole-heartedly to hesitate any longer. He repeated Costanzo's decisive words to St. Philip, who ratified the verdict. Having found his vocation, Cesare finally put all thoughts of the religious life out of his mind, and resolved to cast in his lot with the Saint in the, as yet, unmatured Congregation of the Oratory. But with his permission, and in compensation for the renunciation of his desire, he took three solemn vows of poverty, chastity, and obedience to St. Philip, a fourth, that of humility, being added at his urgent request. His whole future life has to be looked at in the light of these four vows.

San Giralomo
The side altar where St. Philip said his first Mass.

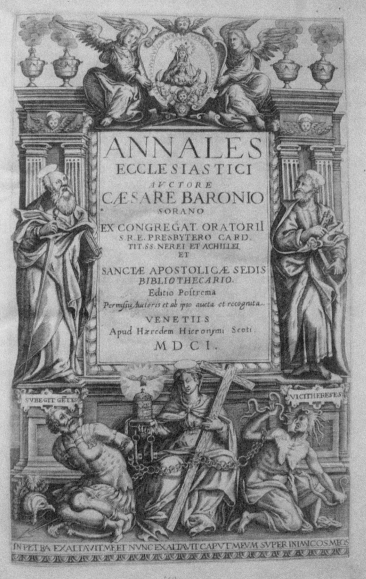

ANNALES
ECCLESIASTICI
AVCTORE
CÆSARE BARONIO
SORANO
EX CONGREGAT. ORATORII
S.R.E. PRESBYTERO CARD.
TIT. SS. NEREI ET ACHILLEI.
ET
SANCTÆ APOSTOLICÆ SEDIS
BIBLIOTHECARIO.
Editio Postrema
Permissu Auctoris et ab ipso aucta et recognita.

VENETIIS
Apud Hæredem Hieronimi Scoti
MDCI.

SVBEGIT GETES

VICIT HERESES

IN PETRA EXALTAVIT ME ET NVNC EXALTAVIT CAPVT MEVM SVPER INIMICOS MEOS

CHAPTER III
The Origin of the Annals

S OON after Cesare accepted Costanzo Tassone's decision about his vocation, he received the tonsure and minor orders; and then, in token of his entire renunciation of the world, he tore up his certificate as doctor-of-law, a degree which, in spite of his youth, had been conferred on him. As soon as he had received the subdiaconate, and felt himself armed against all pressure from without, he broke to his parents the news of his irrevocable choice of life. His father, being more angry than ever, reproached him bitterly for having taken such a step, especially without his knowledge; and loudly bewailed the inevitable extinction of his race. After a time, when the first heat of his anger was over, Camillo tried the force of persuasion, and, accepting the fact that his son had pledged himself to the sacerdotal state, he vainly tried to extort a promise from him not to commit himself to what he considered eccentric and austere ways. The father and son did not meet, and the whole argument was carried on by letter, in a correspondence which lasted for several years, with the final result that Camillo turned to God from the world, and devoted his means and the remainder of his life to good works, especially that of visiting the sick.

Cesare's mother had, no doubt, followed him to Rome with her prayers, and, considering her gift of him to God at his birth, it is difficult to imagine that she absolutely regretted the step he had taken. However, she joined her remonstrances to those of her husband, though it is evident that her objections sprang from human affection rather than from thwarted ambition. Her son's reply to her expostulations has been preserved, and is especially interesting, as showing how blameless his life had been as a young man in the world, before God called him and bade him go up higher.

"I must indeed congratulate you, my mother," he writes, with a touch of irony, "if you think that in my present state I am less able to repay you than before for all the tears you have shed for me, and the labours you have endured for me. Until the end of your life it will be better for you that I should be as I am, than that I should be in any other position. Remember that as soon as you had given birth to me, I was taken to the holy font of baptism, where I renounced the world, the flesh and the devil. Though, indeed, I never once broke my baptismal vows, still, as soon as greater light and understanding were given to me, I conceived a desire to leave the world, so that I might keep them more perfectly. What reason had you for wishing me to be a Christian except that I might comply with the laws of Christ, and try to imitate His life? Well, it behoved me as a Christian to leave the world and follow Christ. This I have done, so that I might spend my life in a way worthy of a good Christian. Do you therefore pray for me that I may have the grace to carry out those things which I promised to God in holy baptism."

Portia responded to this and other letters written in the same strain, and eventually aided him instead of putting obstacles in the way of his vocation. Years afterwards, we find Baronius replying to human suggestions by quoting maxims with which his mother supplied him when he was raised to the priesthood. From the time that she made the sacrifice of her son, Cesare's mother devoted herself to good works, setting an example to her husband, and leading the way to his conversion. For the last sixteen years of her life she gave herself over entirely to the service of the sick and poor, so that the inhabitants of Sora regarded her as their mother.

On the feast of St. James, 1580, while Baronius was sitting in his confessional at the Chiesa Nuova, he saw, as in a vision, his mother's soul being taken to heaven. He at once despatched a messenger to Sora, who brought back the news that Portia had in fact breathed her last at the very moment of his vision. Cesare took this manifestation as a very hopeful sign of his mother's salvation, and wrote about it with consolation to his father; though at the same time he urged him to be most careful to have masses said for the repose of her soul, and to offer up good works for the same purpose. Camillo, however, did not live long to put his son's injunctions into practice, for he died the death of the just a very short time after his wife.

But little has been recorded of Cesare's life between the time when Tassone enabled him to decide on his vocation, and his elevation to the priesthood in 1564. Even to form surmises as to what it was likely to have been, it is necessary to turn both to St. Philip's life and to contemporary history for events which in all probability left their mark on his life.

At the time when Baronius was first set to preach, St. Philip had obtained permission from the deputies of S. Girolamo to build a room over one of the aisles of the church, in which to have his assemblies and exercises; and to this room the name of the Oratory was given. It was also in the early days of Cesare's connection with St. Philip that the processional visits to the seven churches

23

started by the Saint were fully organized. During one of these, Cesare, still a layman, came to a stand before the ruins of the church of SS. Nereus and Achilleus, the church selected by him as his title when he was raised to the purple. Shocked and grieved by its dilapidated and desecrated condition, he exclaimed, "Here is a fine state for a church to be in! And yet it was once a cardinal's title. It is enough to scandalize heretics who visit Rome. O Lord, Thou knowest what I would do if I could!" Probably the painful impression produced by the ruins remained in Cesare's mind with sufficient force to influence him in his choice of his title, and in his subsequent restoration of the old church.

In 1559, Paul IV, misled by calumniators, stopped the public visits to the seven churches, and even suspended the Saint. It does not require much imagination to picture the state of Baronius's loving, loyal heart, as he lived beside St. Philip through that dark time. When Paul died soon after, though not before he had reinstated the Saint and made what amends he could, the populace, whom he had ruled with a rod of iron, rose in rebellion against his memory. His statue, set up on the Capitol, was overthrown and mutilated; and other outrages were committed.

The reopening of the Council of Trent by Paul's successor, Pius IV, a step mainly instigated by St. Charles Borromeo, the close friend of St. Philip and of the Oratory, is another epoch which must have affected the life of the young Baronius, by turning his mind towards the question of heresy and the means of combating it, and, perhaps, by filling his soul with enthusiasm by the visible consolidation of the Holy See which rose up out of the confusion. By these and similar occurrences, we can in a

24

measure bridge over what is lacking in the records of his life.

One event, which caused at the time some small stir and which was all powerful in its influence on the future career of Baronius, was the publication in 1569 of the Centuries of Magdeburg, a book which professed to be an ecclesiastical history from the earliest times, and was full of garbled facts intended to justify the Protestant revolt against the Catholic Church. The appearance of this book caused some apprehension in the minds of Catholics but, as a matter of fact, it was badly planned and badly executed, and, as is the usual fate of things that are not true, it produced no permanent effects. Doubtless its very name would have been forgotten by this time, had not St. Philip, and he who so perfectly carried out his designs, made the work memorable.

The dangerous effects produced for a time by the Centuries put it into St. Philip's head that the only effectual antidote to their poison would be an exposure of the enemy's disingenousness, by means of an opposition history of the Church, in which nothing but the truth should appear. He knew well enough that the Catholic religion has nothing to fear from the revelation of real facts, and that, at the time of the great revolt of the sixteenth century, even as now, souls were kept from the Church not by historical truths as they are, but by the same truths half told, misrepresented, and removed from their context. This much was plain to the Saint; but the right method by which to teach ecclesiastical history so that all might understand it, was a subject of anxious thought to him. He finally decided on employing for this end the same instrument which had in his hands proved so efficacious for turning the souls of the Roman citizens

25

to God, and resolved to teach Church history from the Oratory pulpit. St. Philip had no thought of doing this with his own lips, but determined to effect his end by means of one whom he knew, with gifted foresight, to be well fitted for the task.

Some dozen or more years previously, the mendicant pilgrim had discovered the gifts latent in the boy Cesare; it lay with St. Philip to gauge the depth of his disciple's intellect, and turn it to account. If we look at Baronius as he was then, we may wonder at the Saint's prescience. We behold a fervent, impetuous son of Southern Italy who, once he turned from the world, knew not how to do things by halves, and who, as soon as he had tasted the goodness of God, desired to give himself over entirely to His service in the highest way. That ardent and generous desire was still burning unquenched in his soul, for, at the time of which we speak, Cesare was not yet twenty-one. His zeal, though restrained, found its vent in impetuous and severe mortifications, and he emulated the saints in some of his acts of self-conquest. When he was put to preach at the Oratory, the strength of his convictions and the fervour of his love of God were so powerful that they lent an eloquence to his simple discourses which spoke straight to the souls of men, and made them renounce the world at his bidding. Some prophets might have seen a future Savonarola in the young Neapolitan. St. Philip saw only the historian —the man who till premature old age was to consume his life in libraries and among archives, and quench his fervour among the difficulties and dryness of ages, searching throughout the civilised world for facts with the same absorption with which his fellow men were at that same time seeking for gold in the New World. This is what St. Philip saw in Baronius, and in him, in spite of

26

his erstwhile repugnance to the task, he found an instrument responsive to his touch.

When first bidden by the Saint to give up preaching about those great truths on which he and his hearers delighted to dwell, and to deliver instead, from the same chair, a series of discourses on ecclesiastical history, Cesare's heart failed him, for he had no attraction whatever to the subject. So strong was his conviction that he could not do any work for the salvation of souls in the novel way prescribed, that he let his repugnance to the imposed task overmaster him, and urgently protested against it. His resistance was vain, nor did he persist long in it, but bent his back to the burden, as he always did when St. Philip commanded, even before he bound himself to him by a vow of obedience. The manner in which he—a youth but scarcely emerged into manhood—undertook the gigantic task can be related in no other words than those in which, nearly forty years later, he apostrophised his holy father, then reigning with the saints in glory.

"Burning with zeal for the cause of God, no sooner did thy mind, illumined by Him, and full, if I may so speak, of the prophetic spirit, behold those Centuries of Satan issue out of the gates of hell, than thou didst rise up to combat them on behalf of the people of God. But thou didst not set thyself to raise an army greater or even equal to the number of the enemy. Thou knewest that God chooses the weak things of this world to confound the strong, and so thou didst select one of thine own sons, the least among his brethren, and of the meanest ability, and sent him forth alone and unarmed to do battle against the numerous and well-equipped ranks of the enemy. Feigning a different project, thou didst not send him at once into the wider field; but, in order to make trial of his

27

strength, thou didst choose a small room, the Oratory of San Girolamo, and didst command him to relate in daily discourses the whole history of the Church. This I began in obedience to thee, and, persevering for thirty years, I went through the entire history of the Church seven times."

The last sentence is, as it were, an epitome of the life of Baronius during its prime, though like all epitomes it leaves a good deal to the imagination. At the end of three years, while still in the spring-tide of youth, and probably not yet in holy orders, he finished his first course and doubtless, that obedience being satisfied, he thought he would be free to resume some more congenial work for souls. But not so : instead of being set free from his burden, he had to take it up again, and tread anew the same ground, with even the interest of novelty removed. Yet five times more was the same command renewed, till all hope of other more direct work for souls died within him, and he knew that his road to heaven had to lie in the monotony of unchanging repetition. We know, however, that in time obedience brought its own reward, and that the work from which he had at first turned with repugnance became a matter of absorbing interest to him.

The manner in which the foundations of the Annals were laid kindled the admiration of the Protestant Bishop, Montacute, though he was at the time doing his best to stir up Casaubon[1] to try to demolish the book itself. "His

---

[1] Isaac Casaubon was a French Protestant, the son of Huguenot exiles. He was a classical historian and brilliant philologist, noted for his scholarly work on Roman texts. His critique of Baronius is generally considered the poorest work of his otherwise great literary career. -Editor.

work was great, nay, I may rather say, prodigious," he writes. "He actually went through this mountain of ecclesiastical history seven times, and only when he had finished this repeated course, did he begin to build up his written work with the matter he had pondered over and prepared before he put his hand to his pen-verily a new example, unheard of from the furthest antiquity." Truly might he say so, for the ways of the saints are not like the ways of other men.

Probably the extent and magnitude of the work on which he thus forcibly entered before he was twenty-one years of age was hidden from Cesare, nor, perhaps, was it quite realised by his holy father. Baronius himself describes the unexpected development of the work from its slender beginnings at San Girolamo, and how gradual and almost imperceptible was the growth in his brain of the idea of the Annals as a book. In his dedication to Sixtus V of his first volume, published just twenty-nine years after he began his simple discourses, he thus describes the process by which he arrived at writing the book.

"In writing my Annals, I have, Holy Father, experienced the truth of the words of Blessed Paul the Apostle: 'Neither he that planteth is anything, nor he that watereth, but God who giveth the increase.' About thirty years ago I entered on the production of this book, neither deliberately nor even consciously. I did not rely on my own powers, I should have known to be wholly inadequate for surmounting the difficulties in the way of such an undertaking as narrating the history of the universal Church; for I was not bold enough when I began even to contemplate such a work. However, God, from whom all good gifts proceed, so governed events that, little by little, almost without my knowledge, while He, giving the increase, this no inconsiderable work grew out of the very small seed.

"Your Holiness is aware of our old custom at the Oratory of breaking the bread of the word of God for His little ones every afternoon, not by means of that elevated kind of eloquence usually displayed in sacred orations, but by means of humbler and more familiar discourses calculated—as is proved by daily experience —to move the hearts of the hearers, the things of God being treated, as it were, face to face and on terms of equality, in a manner suitable to every class of hearer. Among other subjects thus treated, the writings of the Fathers are adapted practically to the Christian life, and lives of the saints and ecclesiastical acts are related, these being found most efficacious for exciting piety and a desire for virtue in the hearts of the hearers. In order that I might be able to discourse on the lives of the saints and the events of Church history, I began to devote myself to the diligent and accurate study of such matters, being moved thereto by the persuasion and authority of him who, in Christ, stands in the place of father to me and my brethren. Still moved and spurred on by him, I lent myself to the study of the ancient writers on ecclesiastical history; and, taking delight in the subject, I persevered and made notes of many documents, sifting them and distributing them according to their proper places. Thus slowly and bit by bit I collected a very storehouse of copied material, useful for the confutation of the innovations of our time, and for maintaining the sacred traditions of antiquity, and the authority of the holy Roman Catholic Church. In the course of nearly thirty years I narrated the history of the Church seven times in succession, and not till I had done

30

this did I, at the instigation of others, though of my own free-will, set to work to compile the Annals."

We can see from this that no slight labour was required for the preparation of even such simple and familiar narrations of Church history as were prescribed by St. Philip. Baronius knew but little or nothing of his subject to begin with and, as accuracy was not only the chief object St. Philip had in view for combating the falsifications of heresy, but was also the invincible bent of Cesare's own mind, every statement he made had to be verified. Thus, even in his earlier experiences as a historian, he became familiar with the Vatican and other libraries and learnt how to search for documents, how to study them and how to utilize them. Probably, as he undertook each of his seven courses in succession, he worked in the light of the greater knowledge obtained in the last, went deeper into his subject, and sought more widely for information. Among the many letters written and received by him concerning matters of historical detail, are some of a date prior to the actual compilation of the Annals, showing how early he began to seek materials beyond the walls of Rome. He sought verifications of his facts in every direction, and even dead stones came to life under his touch and had their tale to tell. There was scarcely a building or ruin in Rome, scarcely a monument, pagan or Christian, which did not speak to him. Every inscription was studied and dissected; and the relics in the churches, their history, antecedents and authenticity were gone into and made use of for his work. Thus, during those long years of preparation, his insight grew more keen and his perception more unerring, till the day came when the harvest was ripe, and ready to be stored in the written volumes.

31

CHAPTER IV

St. John of the Florentines

T|HERE had existed for some fifty years, at San Giovanni of the Florentines, a brotherhood of hardworking secular priests, natives of Florence. For several years they had cherished the desire to have St. Philip—their own countryman—at their head, but the Saint had steadily refused their invitation. In 1564, being reduced in number and more than ever bent on carrying out their wish, they had the wisdom to seek the intervention of Pius IV, and pointed out the great good for Rome which would follow, could the Saint be over-persuaded. The Pope was convinced, and commanded St. Philip to accede to the Florentines' request, though he consented to his governing the house without leaving San Girolamo. It resulted from the Pope's command that the Congregation, without in any way ceasing to be one, was divided into two, and five of the fathers were sent to live at San Giovanni. Among these five was Cesare who, at the age of twenty-five, was ordained priest, preparatory to being sent there.

When St. Philip detached the five fathers from him he established for their benefit something approaching more nearly to a rule than had hitherto prevailed at the Oratory, and from this the Constitutions, as they now stand, were gradually developed. The fathers sent were not to consider themselves as in any way severed from the Oratory at San Girolamo, but spent half of each day there. Every morning they went there to confession to the Saint. After dinner they returned there a second time for the usual sermons, and again in the evening for the Oratory exercises. The rest of the day they attended to San Giovanni and to the work for souls connected with that church. On Sundays, Baronius and Father Bordini, who had been ordained with him, preached by turns, a cotta being worn in the pulpit for the first time, in compliance with the wishes of the Florentines. Cesare had never yet preached a real sermon, and but scant preparation was allowed him; for, late one Saturday, he received a message from St. Philip that he was to preach in the church next day. The date of his first sermon, April 30, 1565, was considered of sufficient importance to be recorded by his contemporaries. He was more gently treated in this matter by his holy father than was Bordini, who was allowed only an hour's notice before preaching his first sermon.

Each father served at table in turn, and they took it week by week to cook for the others. Such was the rule, but Baronius had a disproportionate share of the cook's duties. So constantly did his term of office in the kitchen recur that at length he wrote these words over the chimney-piece: *Baronius coquus perpetuus.*[2] This exception to the weekly rule was made by St. Philip for the obvious purpose of keeping his gifted son humble. Hidden as was his life, his genius was making itself known, and already many personages of importance sought interviews with him and, when such went to San Giovanni in search of him, it was in the kitchen that they found him, with his cook's apron on, washing the dishes. That this could occur and did occur shows us plainly why St. Philip kept him so

---

[2] Baronius, perpetual cook.

severely in the kitchen. Cesare's soul rose to the mortification, for, when notable personages found him washing dishes, it is especially mentioned that he was washing them joyfully. Mortifications of this sort inflicted on him by his holy father increased in severity in proportion with the growth of his renown as a historian.

While Cesare was at San Giovanni, exposed to such mortifications and to other really inevitable hardships, his father took the opportunity to try to tempt him away from the Oratory. Camillo had become reconciled to his son being a priest, but he wished him to be in a different position. Hence he persuaded the Bishop of his diocese to offer him a rich canonry, which would have enabled him to make his home with his parents. Cesare, however, had not followed the finger of God in his vocation for such an end as that, and refused all bribes and offers.

During this time Cesare's life was one of great austerity, hidden indeed, but none the less severe. He was always most keenly sensitive about the needs of the Church, and felt public calamities more acutely than he could have felt any private misfortune, and whenever Christendom was threatened with special danger, he redoubled his penances. He began in his youth a practice, which he continued to latest old age, of wearing a hair shirt on such occasions, until the danger was averted. "Blessed Mother," he would say to our Lady when he put it on, "I will not remove this hair shirt until thou hast removed this present calamity."

The year after Cesare's ordination Suliman the Magnificent, Sultan of the Turks, hoped, in the pride of his power, to make himself master of Christendom, and in 1565 made his famous attack on Malta, his designs being checked and foiled by the heroic defence of its Knights. So

intense was Cesare's pain of soul produced by the
imminence of the danger, and so severe were the
austerities he practised to avert it, that he fell seriously ill.
Such attacks, brought on by anxiety of mind and severity
with himself whenever Europe was in danger, were by no
means infrequent. One such illness was occasioned by the
intense anxiety for the public safety which filled the
hearts of many besides himself in 1571, before the glorious
victory of Lepanto restored security to Christendom.
While lying ill, Cesare had, as it were, a vision in which he
thought his soul was being taken straight to heaven after
his death. But he earnestly prayed the Divine Majesty to
suffer him to pass first through the fires of purgatory,
such terror did he feel at the thought of appearing before
God with any unperceived stain of sin on his soul.

All through his life we find Baronius believing in and,
in a measure, guiding his actions by the light of dreams
and visions. There is scarcely an epoch in his career which
was not heralded by some such manifestation; which in
several cases at least, appeared to be undeniably sent to
him by God either in warning or for counsel. After the
above vision of his state after death, Cesare recovered; but,
having resumed his labours and penances too soon, he
suffered a dangerous relapse. So ill was he that he received
the last sacraments, and the doctors held out but slight
hopes of his recovery. St. Philip, however, obtained his
cure in a way which reveals to us how deeply he could
love his disciples and how human his heart was. The
manner in which the Saint interceded for his recovery was
shown to Cesare in a vision, while he lay hovering
between life and death and that what he was then shown
did really occur is manifest from the tacit admission of the
Saint. Baronius saw our Lord seated on a throne. On His

right hand was His blessed Mother, and at His feet St. Philip, who cried out instantly: "Give me Cesare, Lord give me back Cesare. This I desire, this I will, O Lord." But it seemed to Baronius that the petition was refused. But then St. Philip, turning to the Madonna, asked her intercession, by means of which the desired boon was obtained. When the sick man came to himself, feeling strength and life returning, he told his vision to the Saint, who scolded him, and passed it off and told him not to put faith in dreams. But from that moment Cesare recovered his health, to the astonishment of the doctors, who attributed his cure entirely to St. Philip.

A story belongs to this portion of Cesare's life which illustrates his zeal for souls, and shows what leisure of heart he possessed for the needs of others, in spite of his daily increasing brain-work. Gregory XIII was on the Chair of St. Peter; and during his pontificate brigandage reached terrible proportions in the States of the Church and the neighbouring parts of the kingdom of Naples; and the evil went on increasing till it was swept off the land by the relentless rigour of Gregory's successor, Sixtus V.

One of these brigands was distinguished for his audacity even among his fellows. He belonged to the kingdom of Naples, in which most of his depredations were committed. Baronius set his heart on the conversion of this man, and engaged a Capuchin father to seek him out and read to him a letter composed by himself and Tarugi. The letter was accompanied by some rosaries and other objects of piety, carefully selected by Cesare for their gaudiness and tinsel, which he thought likely to attract the man. Meanwhile, he fasted and prayed, and we are inclined to think that he attained his end by his prayers rather than by the simple means he employed.

37

But, by whatever means, the end was gained. The brigand was moved to deep compunction by the Capuchin's visit and by the letter which was read to him, and so completely was he converted that he abandoned his evil ways and took to saying his prayers devoutly. But his old nature was in him. Hearing that his enemies had taken advantage of his peaceable dispositions to attack and slaughter some of his kinsmen, he was seized by a frenzy of revenge, and committed some fresh deeds of violence; for which, being arrested in the act, he was brought to Rome to be put to death. As soon as he was cast, chained, into prison, he sent for Father Cesare, to whom he attributed his conversion, and was attended by him to the end. The last night of the poor man's life was spent by Baronius, shut up with him in his dungeon, praying with him. In the early hours of dawn he said Mass in the cell and gave the criminal Communion; and then, going forth with him, stood by him on the scaffold till he gave up his penitent soul to God.

Even in the early days of his priesthood Baronius was distinguished by that fearless liberty of spirit which was the most marked characteristic of his later life. An anecdote has been handed down which, though the incident involved nothing of any importance, illustrates his entire absence of human respect. One day Cesare found some young nobles playing at ball against the walls of the church. The sight stirred up his naturally hasty temper, and, snatching the ball from their hands, he upbraided them somewhat sharply for their want of reverence. He was unknown to the young men, nevertheless they accepted his rebuke, and, with an apology, went their way.

On another occasion his fearlessness in rebuking evil led to more unpleasant consequences. Seeing a gentleman audaciously misconducting himself in the church, Cesare laid hold on him for the purpose of turning him outside. But the man, with no respect for place or person, resisted with violence, and turning on Baronius, abused him in no measured terms. Tarugi, seeing the commotion from the other side of the church, came across and interposed. "I have nothing against you," cried the gentleman, wresting himself from F. Francesco Maria's grasp, "but only against that priest there;" and, so saying, he shook his fist furiously in Cesare's face. But Baronius stood his ground unmoved. "Get you gone," he said pointing to the door; "God will avenge this insult." The man, thinking, perhaps, that he had gone far enough, left the church, muttering fierce threats. As he mounted his horse outside, his foot slipped, and falling heavily to the ground, he broke his leg. The story does not end there. During the long and severe illness which followed the accident, Baronius frequently visited the man, till he succeeded in bringing him to better ways, and back to the sacraments from which he had kept away for years.

Baronius and the other fathers lived at S. Giovanni for about eleven years. In 1574, owing to certain difficulties arising from false accusations brought against the fathers residing there, St. Philip was most strongly urged by his companions to establish the Congregation in a church where it would be independent, and formed on a firmer basis. So great, however, was the Saint's dread of being regarded as the founder of a Congregation, that it was some time before he would consent to the move and when, forced by circumstances, he did consent, it was only on condition that he was suffered to remain as before, hidden in his room at San Girolamo. Thus, he vainly hoped that his share in the work would be ignored.

Now that the change, even under these conditions, was agreed on, it was necessary not only to fix on a new abode, but also to obtain the formal approval of the Congregation by the Holy See. This was joyfully given by Gregory XIII, together with the choice, freely left to St. Philip, between several churches wherein to establish the Oratory. He at once decided on Santa Maria in Vallicella. The new and present church was commenced with slight delay, and on February 3 the first Mass was sung in it by Cardinal Alessandro Medici, afterwards Leo XL, ever a devout disciple of St. Philip, and ever to the front at every new phase in the development of the Oratory. When the Congregation was formally established at the Vallicella on July 15, 1575, the life of Baronius at San Giovanni came to an end.

It is necessary to pause for a few moments and see what was the actual position in the world of Baronius at the period when he took up his abode at the Vallicella, being then thirty-seven years of age. His name was by this time well-known in Rome; indeed so noted was it that the Florentines put up a tablet when he left San Giovanni to testify that he had preached there. Small as was his scope, his reputation for learning was considerable, and he was the intimate friend of, and in many cases consulted by men of note. His fame had spread beyond the walls of Rome. There is a letter from one Charles Sigonio, a man of well-known erudition at the University of Bologna, who, as early as 1579, assumed the attitude, when writing to him, of a disciple before his master.

"For years," he says, "I have heard of your name in connection with your researches into ecclesiastical history and I have borne you that affection which we usually bestow on learning. Now, the chains which bound me to you before have been drawn closer, for I am told that you have commended my writings, unworthy as they are to be mentioned by you. . . Having such high esteem for your opinion, I wish you would ask Mgr. Sirleto in my name to give you my three volumes on ecclesiastical history. Read them, and I pray you to let me know in general and in detail what you think should be changed in them. Do this, and I shall be eternally grateful to you."

Such was Baronius's position before the world; and from his room at San Girolamo his holy father watched him closely and anxiously. For St. Philip still lived in the home of his choice, and, till the end of 1583, resisted all the petitions and persuasions of the fathers to come and dwell in their midst. At last, however, he granted their desire, but solely in obedience to the command of Gregory XIII, to whom as a last resort the Congregation appealed. To live once more under the same roof with St. Philip was an epoch in the lives of all his sons but the influence of the change was greater on Baronius than on any other. It was soon after the Saint moved to the Vallicella, and probably as the result of living in closer contact with his great disciple, that the idea of utilizing Cesare's wealth of historical knowledge, and turning it to a wider and more permanent account, took practical shape in St. Philip's brain. And with this project began those more crucial trials of his son, by which he was to be moulded to the service of God.

CHAPTER V
Tempering the Weapon

IT is with diffidence that we approach the subject of this chapter, and study the method whereby St. Philip fashioned him on whom he had laid his hand to carry out the great work which he had conceived, and how he tempered the weapon wherewith the enemies of the Church were to be overthrown. The ground we stand on is manifestly holy, and it behoves all men to tread cautiously when tracing the footsteps of the saints, which often lead us along strange paths and by-ways not always easy to understand. The manner in which St. Philip trained his disciple for his work by means of mortifications and humiliations has been often told, but none the less it must be re-told in these pages, for no life of Baronius could be attempted without relating the process by which, under the touch of his holy father, self was driven out, and he became what he was.

There is something very wonderful about the slowness and patience of the saints. It is peculiar to them, and has become part of them by their contemplation of this eternal attribute of God. The idea of a true and Catholic history of the Church, to be used as an antidote to the reformers' garbled work of a similar description, had been in St. Philip's mind for a long time, though it had not yet matured. He could not have failed to know that such an undertaking would be the work of a lifetime, nay, of more than a lifetime; yet, when he had fixed on a man fitted to carry out his scheme, he devoted thirty years of that man's life to fashioning and tempering him as his instrument. It took Baronius not quite twenty years to write the twelve great volumes completed by him, but it took thirty years to prepare him for the work; and not till the Saint was in all ways satisfied with his instrument would he allow the actual work to be begun. It needs the very closest study of the character of Baronius to understand what this hurried and utilitarian age might rashly call the lavish waste of time exhibited by the Saint.

We know Baronius only as he was, not as he might have been. We behold in him a mixture of exquisite childlike simplicity and absence of all worldliness, of utter disregard for the opinion of man, and total dependence on the will of God. In spite of the praise of men and of the flattering appreciation of those whom he revered, in spite of the consciousness he must have possessed of his own abilities, and of the unrivalled success which attended his labours, we see in him the most profound and spontaneous humility, which made him turn for advice to those immeasurably his inferiors and accept their corrections and suggestions without a latent thought that he was thereby humbling himself.

All this he was, but such he might very easily have not been. We can at times see touches of the nature which was sanctified under St. Philip's touch; and we can see how easily he might have become a mere student, with jarred and irritable nerves, entirely engrossed in his work for its own sake, impatient under contradiction, and fretful under hindrances and interruptions. In a word, he might have been a book worm, a genius without sanctity, as void of higher life as the very documents among which he spent his days. All this he was not, but might have been had not St. Philip spent those years in forming him.

44

Cesare was as wax in the hands of his holy father, and lived a life of most perfect obedience to him, begun almost as soon as he placed himself in his hands, and ratified, confirmed and strengthened by the vow he took after his vocation was decided. All the four vows he then took had a marked effect on his life, but, though the vow of obedience was efficacious only as long as St. Philip was alive, it was perhaps, while it lasted, the most potent of all.

In the general bent of his life as well as in its minutest details the Saint most studiously mortified him. He knew Cesare's ardour for study and growing interest in his historical researches, and, though he kept him steadily to his work with one hand, with the other he introduced every sort of distraction from it, employed him in constant active works of charity, or, as at San Giovanni, such manual employments as confined him to work in the kitchen. It seemed as if his intentions were to distract him from and hinder him in his great work yet, whenever his ardent nature and zeal for souls led him to wish of his own accord for more active work, the Saint imperatively restrained him. When St. Charles urged St. Philip to start an Oratory in Milan, Baronius fervently desired to be sent to a place where there was, apparently, more scope for his apostolic zeal than in Rome where labourers abounded; but St. Philip would not have it. St. Charles, who could not accept the Saint's decision as unquestioningly as did Cesare, more than once wrote to urge him to send the latter to Milan but St. Philip was immovable, and in his wonted manner refused the demand half jestingly, and called the Saint of Milan a daring robber of souls.

The same thing happened a little later, when in 1584, Baronius would gladly have been delegated to found an Oratory at Naples. He was sent there by Gregory XIII to enquire into the case of a heretic, the same year that St. Philip came to live at the Vallicella. While in Naples, the Theatines and others, who were anxious to have an Oratory in their city, persuaded him to use his influence with the Saint. At first St. Philip was unwilling to grant the request; but when, after two years, he gave way, it was Tarugi he sent, and not Baronius. Cesare's work for God was not to be active, nor was his work for souls to be carried on in a direct way.

In order to destroy self-love and self-consciousness in his disciple—who was, as the Saint knew full well, pursued even into the kitchen by those who valued his opinion, St. Philip made him appear ridiculous on every possible occasion. He sent him out into the streets to beg for food and clothes like a mendicant. At another time he sent him out with a two-gallon flask to buy a few spoonfuls of wine, with the injunction to see that it was correctly measured; and then, having made all this fuss, and tried the temper of the wine-seller, he had to pay for the drops he had bought with the change out of a gold piece; with the result that the man lost all patience and drove Cesare out of his shop with abuse. With the same desire to destroy self in his son, St. Philip made him carry the cross at a funeral, usually the office of the neediest in the social scale, and, with still more crucial ingenuity, bade him sing the Miserere at a wedding-feast. How much Baronius suffered was his own secret; but he never flinched, till at last all thoughts of self were in very deed destroyed. So intensely did Cesare hate being praised that St. Philip, taking hold of whatever was natural in his dislike, made a point of praising him before others, with the sole purpose of mortifying him. But he took everything with exquisite simplicity; and, seeing this, the Saint, even to the end of his life, used tenderly to call him his novice, though Baronius was at the time in his fifty-seventh year; and he often gave him caressingly a box on the ear, which ever filled Cesare's heart with the deepest consolation.

Instances are given of miraculous rewards being vouchsafed to Cesare's implicit obedience to his holy father. When the cook of the house, a very holy man, was dying of some infectious fever, the Saint bade Baronius nurse him; which he did till he was attacked and laid low by the same fever. St. Philip, on hearing this—for it was before the Saint had left San Girolamo—sent him word to command the fever to leave him. Full of confidence and simplicity, Baronius no sooner received the message than he said: "Fever, I command you on behalf of the Father, to go away," and at once he got up and dressed himself, being completely cured.

In spite of the constant mortifications which he inflicted, so tenderly and humanly did St. Philip love Cesare that he kept a ceaseless watch over his needs. This was wanted, for far from abandoning or even relaxing the austerities he had adopted in early manhood, Baronius rather increased them with his advancing years, though from humility he rarely let them appear. Father Pateri, of the Oratory, affirmed that during the thirty years he had known Baronius he satisfied neither hunger nor sleep. So unostentatious were these mortifications that his humility might have deceived many; but it could not deceive his holy father St. Philip, who at times sent him back to sup over again after he had gone through the farce of a meal.

Even in his earlier days, partly as the result of his austerities, and partly from over brain-work, Baronius suffered from that weakness of digestion which caused him at times agonies of pain, and was the immediate cause

47

of his death. When these attacks came on, the Saint forbade him to fatigue his mind in any way; and even while he turned Cesare's malady into an occasion of obedience and mortification, he touched him with his healing, hand. One day Cesare, in a state of acute suffering, went into St. Philip's room. The Saint knew the condition he was in as well as its cause; but, nevertheless, taking up a large roll of bread and a lemon, which were on the table, he bade him eat them on the spot. Notwithstanding the horrible repugnance he felt to any food and to this kind in particular, and notwithstanding the conviction that it would add much to his suffering, Cesare obeyed unhesitatingly, with the result that he was, for that time, cured.

All the best known of St. Philip's mortifications of his great disciple are in one way or the other connected with his historical work. At the time that the Saint took up his abode at the Vallicella Baronius must have been either completing his sixth course of lectures on Church history, or he may have been commencing the seventh. Already he had made a name for himself as a writer on ecclesiastical subjects, and many saw in his little life of St. Gregory Nazianzen an earnest of greater things. When St. Philip moved to the Vallicella, Cesare had just completed a Life of St. Ambrose, written at the request of Cardinal Perretti, afterwards Sixtus V. Probably, this growing reputation, as well as his own closer and more personal acquaintance with the extent of Cesare's researches and quantity of collected material, made the Saint decide that the moment had come for the actual commencement of the Annals as a book. We know from Baronius himself that he had begun to write them in 1584, when another task was imposed on him, which delayed the greater work for about two years.

Owing mostly to the reform of the calendar effected in the pontificate of Gregory XIII, but partly to the tendency to romance and embroidery which endangers every work, various errors had crept into the Roman Martyrology. The Pope, wishing that it should be entirely revised and partly re-written, consulted Cardinal Sirleto, one of the greatest scholars of the day, who had rendered him the greatest assistance in the reform of the calendar, and who had, moreover, studied the subject of the Martyrology. Probably, the Pope hoped that the learned Cardinal would himself undertake the work; but he, warmly supported by St. Philip, suggested that the task should be given to Baronius. The Saint hoped great things of his son as a historian, but he had no certainty that his hopes would be realised. He was glad, therefore, that this lesser work should be given to him as a test whether he were indeed capable of carrying out the greater scheme formulated in the Saint's brain.

The labours of Baronius had increased enormously. In his latter courses of history he had entered more deeply into his subject, and required all his time and skill to handle the mass of material which he had gathered round him. He was, moreover, engaged at this period in shaping the idea of the Annals as a written book. He was diffident of his own powers—always rated more high by others than by himself—and, knowing that he was, at the best, untried, he quailed under the responsibility of undertaking a work so important to the Church as the revision of the Martyrology. Other and more personal motives also held back his will from consenting to the task; for he shrank from the thought of adding a new burden to that which was already exhausting his vital powers. When, therefore, he found the work imposed on him beyond the power of refusal, he suffered under a sense of injustice, for, he knew that, even without this additional labour, he had more to do than had any of the other fathers. Thus, he first tried to decline the new duty, and, when obedience compelled him to accept it, he begged that he might be relieved from some of his ordinary duties, or, at the very least, permitted to say his Mass at the hour most convenient to him. But St. Philip, knowing what he was about, refused every concession, showing himself now to be that "stern exactor" as which Cesare, later, so lovingly described him.

Baronius said no more, but bent his back to the burden, being aided, during the short remainder of that prelate's life, by Sirleto, and in a more material manner by a monthly pension of ten crowns given him by the Pope to cover his expenses. He tried at first to refuse this allowance on the score of his vow of poverty; but he was compelled by obedience to accept it. Gregory XIII was no more when Baronius finished his task, though it took him barely two years to complete it; and it was at the feet of his successor, Sixtus V, that he laid it with this humble letter, which is full of interest, both as showing, from his own point of view, the immense area of his researches during the past twenty-seven years, and also as pointing out beyond dispute that he was actually engaged in writing the Annals when he undertook the revision of the Martyrology.

"Last year," he says, "I revised the Roman Martyrology with much labour, illustrating it by notes on the early history of the Church. With my poor abilities I undertook to clear away the many difficulties which obscured it. However, you appointed to help me, a man of singular piety and great learning: I mean Cardinal Sirleto of happy memory; and, moved by his encouragement, I undertook

50

more than, perhaps, I was able to accomplish; and I accepted the duty, relying solely on God's help. I did not approach the work quite unprepared, because for many years I had been engaged in treating the subject of ecclesiastical history, and in thoroughly sifting the acts of the early ages, not only by reading histories written by other men, but by turning over and examining the writings of the fathers and a great many other documents, especially the mass of manuscripts hidden away in your Holiness's library, many of which are of great antiquity. To these labours I hope my ecclesiastical Annals will testify later, for I have not ceased to work at their compilation with that modicum of talents given me by God."

Baronius's work on the Martyrology was an undeniable success, and was met on all sides with the approval which it still receives. De Marquais, the Abbot of St. Martin's, Tournay, a scholar of repute, who was always warmly sympathetic with and interested in everything written by Baronius, saw in the Martyrology the promise of greater things to follow, and wrote to beseech him not to put his light under a bushel, but to get on with his Annals and give them to the world with the least possible delay. The same note ran through all the congratulatory letters which Baronius received from the erudite men of the day.

No doubt St. Philip rejoiced more than any at the success of the experiment he had been instrumental in making, and now felt confident in the success of the greater work already conceived. But his love for his highly-gifted son filled him with anxiety about him, and he questioned himself as to whether Baronius would be able to stand success without falling from his high estate.

51

Of his love for Cesare was born the desire to purify him by trial, and prove whether success had in any way tarnished his humility and simple spirit of obedience. Thus it was that the Saint made the work of the Martyrology, imposed on Cesare against his will, into the occasion of the most crucial trial to which he ever subjected him.

When Baronius presented the completed Martyrology to Sixtus V, that Pontiff, in recognition of the work done, added a monthly pension of fifteen crowns to that granted to Cesare by his predecessor, the allowance being made for the express purpose of expediting his work with the Annals. This time, Baronius welcomed the Pope's gift for the sake of its object, for though, as will be seen in the next chapter, he resisted the idea of writing the Annals when it was first propounded to him, no sooner had he really given himself to the work than it became a matter of absorbing interest to him. When therefore he went to St. Philip to tell him of the Pope's generosity it was with no hidden desire to refuse the pensions as had been the case on the former occasion of the allowance made him by Gregory XIII

No doubt the Saint not only desired to mortify Cesare, but also dreaded his growing absorption in a work begun by pure obedience. Therefore, in reply to the announcement, he told Baronius that now he had this money he must contribute—as did the rest of the fathers—to the expenses of the house; for owing to Camillo's Brutus-like severity, he had entered the Congregation penniless. This injustice, as he thought it, to himself, to the book and to the Pope, stung Cesare to the quick; and for the first time his will rose up in rebellion against that of his holy father. How could he, he protested, give what was not his to give, what had been granted to him for the sole and express purpose of facilitating and expediting the work of the Annals? How could the book ever be completed by the appointed time, if all aid were taken from him? He was, probably, already smarting under the absence of help from the Roman fathers, as well as the number of hindrances placed in the way of his work, and this new command of the Saint was, as it were, the last straw. But in answer to all his arguments St. Philip only told him to obey at once without a word; and Baronius left him, unconvinced and rebellious. He put the case before Father Bozio, who saw it in the same light as he did, and undertook to convince the Saint of the impossibility of spending the money as he directed. But St. Philip's only response was: "Tell Cesare he must either obey or go. God has no need of men." This message stirred Cesare to the depths. What were the whole world or the Annals to him in comparison with the house of St. Philip? He hastened to his holy father, threw himself at his feet, and, bewailing his fault, offered him the pension and all else beside. This submission was all St. Philip wanted. "Keep everything you have," he replied, "the Pope's pension and all else. I desire nothing but the sacrifice of your will. It is enough. Learn always to obey, for in obedience is your salvation."

St. Philip Neri with Baronius

CHAPTER VI

St. Philip's Part in the Annals

IT must have been after this crucial trial that St. Philip bade Baronius proceed systematically with the compilation of the Annals, with which he had already made a beginning. He was no doubt content with the result of his trial of Cesare, and satisfied that the man who was to do the great work was sufficiently trained in humility and self-forgetfulness to embark on the perilous sea of absorbed study and human praise.

The very humility and self-contempt which the Saint had spent years in instilling into him made Baronius unwilling at first to carry out the great scheme of St. Philip's mind. He pleaded want of ability, want of experience, and also want of time, for every available moment was taken up with the multifarious duties of the Oratory, such as preaching, hearing confessions and so forth. St. Philip listened to all his remonstrances and then quietly repeated his suggestions under the form of a command. It was not in Baronius to refuse to obey, but he put clearly before the Saint how much better fitted for the task was Ottavio Panvinio, a man renowned for his learning, and especially versed in ecclesiastical history, whose posthumous notes on the subject were, after his premature death, of the utmost use to Baronius. The Saint listened silently and patiently to the praises of Panvinio poured out by Cesare, but when he had finished speaking, he quietly said, "As to the Church history it is you, Cesare, who have to write it."

Baronius said no more, but retired to his room filled with perplexity. Taking his trouble with him into his sleep, he had one of those dreams which often decided his actions when he was in a state of doubt. He thought he was in the company of Panvinio, and earnestly besought him to undertake in his stead the task of writing an ecclesiastical history. But Panvinio refused to listen to him and walked away, while Baronius followed him about from place to place, arguing and entreating. Then he was arrested by the sound of St. Philip's voice. "Hold your peace, Cesare," he said, "do not wear yourself out with these argumentations for as to the Church history it is you who have to write it, and not Onofrio." Next morning Cesare related his dream to St. Philip, who knew of his faith in such manifestations. "Get you gone with those dreams of yours," he said, "and do just as I tell you." And after this Cesare resisted no longer.

St. Philip's part with the Annals was by no means over with the command to write them; rather might it be said that it only began then. During the first half of the work, or, to speak more accurately, during the progress of the first seven volumes, he was ever by Cesare's side, if not to make suggestions, at least to encourage and keep him to his task by exhortation and command. We should have never known either the kind or degree of the part taken by St. Philip in the work had not Baronius, in the fulness of his heart, revealed it in the dedication to the Saint of the eighth volume, the first which he wrote after his holy father had left him. In the presence of him who would never listen to a word said in his praise Baronius held his peace; but now the Saint was gone, and he gave vent to his love by telling the story to the whole world.

"What shall I say," he bursts forth, "of that Father who, ever near me, ever aiding me, has so often begotten me with the apostolic spirit, and by the same spirit held me in check from my boyhood, and kept me from falling on those slippery paths along which the young travel. Being so beholden to him I desire that this my thanksgiving to him should speak for ever through my Annals, and I dedicate this volume to him, as an eternal remembrance of all I owe to him. For it is but just, and the mark of a humble mind to acknowledge what we owe to others, even as it is unjust to attribute it to ourselves. He who of old took too much to himself and said, 'By the strength of my own hand I have done it, and by my own wisdom have I understood,' received this answer from God: 'Shall the axe boast itself against him that cutteth with it, or the saw exalt itself against him by whom it is drawn?' And lo, the vengeance of God followed these words, and the miserable man because of his pride, was cast down from his throne and sent to dwell among the beasts.

"I therefore freely confess of the blessed Father Philip that which was said by Christ our Redeemer when speaking to the Apostle Philip: 'My Father who is in me doth the works.' I do not mean by this that I give glory to man rather than to God, but I say it to show that he from whom I received so much worked with God, and thus testify my gratitude to God and man at the same time. For it was the blessed Philip who, by divine inspiration commanded me to perform this work, and, like another Moses, employed the workman to build the tabernacle after the model which he himself had seen on the Mount. I set myself to work very much against my will and only after repeated commands from him; for I distrusted my ability for such an undertaking. I accepted it solely out of

57

obedience to the will of God and, for the same reason, blessed Philip constantly urged me on whenever, overcome by my burden, I paused in my work, and with sharp rebukes compelled me to resume the task immediately."

Having related in the passage quoted in a previous chapter how the work originated in the task assigned to him of narrating the history of the Church in familiar discourses, he goes on, apostrophizing the Saint:

"Thou wert continually by me, spurring me on with thy presence, and urging me on by thy words. Thou wert—pardon me what I say—always a stern exactor of the daily task thou didst require of me, so that if ever I turned aside to something else, it seemed to me as if I had committed a sacrilege; for thou couldst not endure that I should swerve by even a hair's breadth from my work. Often, I confess, I was half scandalized, and it seemed to me that thou wert dealing tyrannically by me; for I measured things by my own strength, and did not perceive that thou wert first treating the matter silently with God. Not only was no companion given me to help me, but, as it was of old with the children of Israel, my labour was increased and yet no straw was given me. Many other duties were required of me. To the weighty task of the Annals was added the burden of the care of souls, of preaching, of the government of the house; and many occupations were daily imposed on me, now by one, now by the other.

"By thus treating me and letting me be treated by others it almost seemed to me that that which thou didst desire least was that one thing at which thou wert in reality aiming. It seemed to me as if thou wert imitating Elias, who, when calling down fire from heaven to

58

consume the sacrifice, first drenched it with water to make the power of God more manifest. But, on the other hand, in thy protection of the work thou didst imitate Eliseus, who, laying his hand on the hand of the king, made him ruler over Syria by the flight of his arrow. In like manner didst thou act by me. Thou didst join thy strong hand to my weak one, and change my blunt pen into an arrow of the Lord. Thou wert ever working miracles, yet striving not to appear wonderful; for above all things thou didst seek not to be made much of, and didst often cover thy wisdom by a mantle of folly, bearing in mind that paradox of the Apostle, 'Whoso wisheth to be wise let him become a fool.'"

After extolling the virtues of the Saint and foretelling the glories with which his shrine would be surrounded, Baronius in his dedication addresses his brethren and begs that his words may be hung before it as a perpetual thank-offering. Then turning once more to his holy father, he implores his aid from heaven, in words which will live for ever.

"Come then, O father—for I speak to thee as though thou wert present, for thou beholdest Him who is omnipresent—come and protect this work of thine; and that the victory may be thine alone, I will say to thee as Job said to David, 'Come and finish what remains of the battle,' and by thy prayers send an army from heaven to utterly discomfit the enemy. And now look down on me, thy son, to whom while on earth thou wert ever a protector, whom thou didst guard by thy vigilance, whom thou didst govern by thy counsel, and with whom thou didst bear in thy patience. Now from heaven where thou dwellest give me still stronger aid, and let thy perfect and consummate charity succour me still more. And further, grant unto me, only in a greater degree as needing it more, that which St. Gregory Nazianzen declared that he received from St. Basil, even to have thee as my monitor and corrector after death, so that, still holding the reins of my life, thou mayest guide what remains of my old age, that it stumble not, so that when my labours are finished, I may at length attain to that blessed rest which thou enjoyest now in the Father, Son and Holy Ghost, to whom in perfect unity be glory, praise and honour now and for evermore. Amen."

It must strike every one that St. Philip's action, as described thus lovingly by his son, was unique even in the annals of the saints. We at the distance of three centuries from the time that Baronius wrote that dedication can, to a certain extent, understand the Saint's intention, for what was future then is past history now, and we are better able to discern the guidance of the Holy Ghost. Yet still it startles us, and it is easy to enter into Cesare's feelings when he confesses how puzzled and well-nigh scandalized he was. He owns that he thought his holy father was dealing tyrannically, and perhaps, though he does not say so, capriciously, with him when he hindered the work about the accomplishment of which he was on the other hand so rigidly exacting. Even when he wrote, with all the light which the death of the Saint had shed on the past, we can see that the sense of wonderment was still on him, and he reproaches his holy father as much as he dares. Truly the ways of the saints 'are not like those of other men!' The very humility of Baronius prevented him from understanding the process by which he was moulded, as one with more vanity in his composition might have understood it, for he did not perceive the special perils which would beset one of his mental calibre; and it did not

60

occur to him to draw the comparison which is obvious to us who come after him, and comprehend that the loftier and greater the building, so much the stronger must be the buttresses which prevent it from falling.

Who cannot picture to himself Cesare's imperative desire for a rest, for a short cessation of his weary toil, if only to clear his brain in the midst of the confusion of material he had collected, to break the dull monotony of the work, and let in new light on it by distracting his thoughts? But it was not to be. The daily grinding measure of work was exacted, until he looked on it as almost a sin if he failed in it. It was only after St. Philip had gone to his eternal reward that his son even began to understand his apparent inconsistencies. For with the still painful memory of that daily relentless task there were mingled other memories yet more painful, of how, while he was straining every nerve to accomplish the measure demanded, he was hindered in his work in every possible way by sermons and their preparation, by frequent calls to the confessional, and by various miscellaneous community duties for which he was at the beck and call of others. One privilege he asked; namely, to be allowed to say his Mass at whatever hour was most convenient to him. St. Philip did not absolutely refuse this concession as he had done when Cesare was suffering under the lesser strain of his work on the Martyrology, but he granted it only so far as to let him choose his hour, provided that, once chosen, he kept to it; and he gave stringent orders to the brother sacristan to summon him at the appointed time.

The strain of the exterior work imposed on him weighed on Baronius as an injustice, and made him at the time pour out his soul to Father Tarugi, who was then in charge of the house at Naples—not however, as its superior, for Rome and Naples though divided formed but one Congregation. Baronius had a special and very reverent love for Tarugi, which was, as it were, the echo and offshoot of his love for St. Philip himself, and such as he had for no other father, however great an affection he might bear hint. The letter alluded to was written in May 1588, just after the publication of the first volume of the Annals, and while their author was weighed down by the work of compiling the second, which he had promised—probably by command of the Saint—to complete a twelvemonth after the first. The absolute impossibility of fulfilling this promise vexed and disturbed him.

"God knows the multiplicity of my occupations," he writes. "It is not the will of God but the concerns of others which hinder me in my laborious studies. I declare to you, my father, that if the Congregation cares that I should finish the work I have undertaken, it will be necessary that I should be relieved from hearing confessions. Not only do they take up my whole morning, but they bring with them an amount of business connected with them, such as visiting the sick, acting as peacemaker, going before tribunals or to the prisons, and other like engagements, which occupy my time to such an extent, and cause so many distractions, that the greater part of my day is consumed, and I have to deprive myself of even such sleep as is necessary to me. I have therefore asked God, if it be His will, to relieve me of this duty. I will not withdraw from it of myself, nor will I seek relief in any extraordinary way, such as by obtaining a command to that effect from His Holiness, which I could do at any moment I wished. *Sed absit.* If God so will it, He will inspire hint on whom it depends to govern me. Many men of singular piety have raised scruples in my mind about attempting to do the two things together, but God forbid that I should hearken to anyone but my Father Messir Philip, who has hitherto been firm on this point.

"When I read that part of your letter in which you say it is against your conscience that you trouble me, I felt as if I must write to you about this matter. I am fifty years of age, and even with health and strength it would take me twenty years to finish this work. There! Now I have said all I mean to say. I will not say that I ought to be taken from the confessional, nor will I say that I should be left to it. *Sicut est voluntas in cœlo, sic fiat.*[3] I do but submit the matter to you for your consideration, for I am not willing to trust my own judgment, which might most easily deceive me. This being the actual state of things, and the facts being precisely as I have written them to you, I have thought good to make you acquainted with them. I will cite you the example of Father Bellarmine, who has accomplished so much work. Not only is he exempted from hearing confessions, but he is even spared the trouble of reading over his printed sheets so that once what he has written has gone to press, he has nothing more to do with it. Though I know that I ought not to compare myself with him, nevertheless my labours are, as you know, greater than his. He treats of a subject which has been treated by many before him; for there have been already about two hundred works written against heresies. No one has paved the way for me; or, if any have previously trodden the ground, they have only added to

---

[3] "Just as his will in heaven, let it so be done."

my labours by obliging me to point out and confute their errors.

"This being so, it strikes me that with the additional work of preaching, my writing would be sufficient employment for me, and that by confining myself to this I should put no one in the Congregation to inconvenience. May God inspire you and the other fathers to decide what will be purely for His honour and the good of souls. I beg you to read this letter to the other fathers, and then to write with one consent to our Father Philip. I promise to be satisfied with whatever you, illumined by God, shall decide to be best for His service. Pray for me and bless me, and ponder over what I have written, with prayer and counsel, so that nothing may be done except what is God's will."

We do not know precisely what the Naples fathers decided; but the substance of their advice can be gathered from a letter written by Baronius to Father Talpa about three weeks later:—" I am quite satisfied with what both you and Father Francesco Maria say and I feel sure that if God desires that the actual state of things should be altered He will cause it to be so commanded without my having to make any request. I will attend to and, as far as possible, carry out, your advice about withdrawing from the confessional. I cannot, however, send away any of those who now come to me, for if I heard the confessions of some and refused others it would create gossip; but I will do my best to accept no fresh penitents." Thus matters went on, and, as a matter of fact, the burden of external work was never removed from Baronius until he himself was torn from the Oratory. He had a confessional in the church and heard confessions for more than thirty years—for so long, in other words, as he was in the Congregation.

Though Baronius cordially wished to be relieved of some of his offices, he was, in the daily routine of his life, much averse to any peculiarities or exemptions, except in the one respect of the hour of his Mass; though some such would have been approved of and were perhaps urged on him by the Saint. Thus, when Cesare steadily refused the aid of any of the Congregation in putting his profusely littered room in order, St. Philip, in his solicitude for him, had a duplicate key of his room made, and, when he was out, sent Father John Ancina, brother of Blessed Juvenal, to sweep it.

CHAPTER VII
The Scope of the Annals

H AVING reached that point in his life when, though reluctantly and full of diffidence, Baronius had actually put his hand to his great work, it is well to pause before considering the success that attended it, and try to form some slight idea of its immense scope and the difficulties with which it was beset. To us who look back across three centuries, it requires an effort of the imagination to realize the difficulty of compiling a book like the Annals, and the obstacles which their author had to surmount; but the following extract from the *Pinacotheca* of Nicius Erythreas gives us a good idea of the light in which the immense work was regarded by Baronius's quasi-contemporaries.

"He bent his back to a burden so great that the strongest might have succumbed under it; but to his everlasting praise be it said that once he took it up he bore it without flinching to the end of his life. Before Baronius undertook this work, he was a man of mediocre knowledge, but slight classical education, and no facility in writing Latin. But from the little seed cast into the soil of the Church and watered by the rain of heavenly grace, there sprang up such a mighty trunk with such spreading boughs that no tree ever planted has equalled it for height, foliage or fruit.

"The style of the book, though not eloquent, is by no means familiar, being truly grave and devoid of puerile artificialities or tricks, as is becoming both to a Christian writer, and to the great and serious subjects of which he treats. This great compilation originated in the performance of a duty assigned to him by St. Philip of relating from the pulpit of the Oratory the acts of the Church from the earliest ages. Among the many excellent customs of the Congregation there exists that of devoting one of the four daily sermons to the expounding of ecclesiastical history to an audience whose presence is never failing. By quotations from authors, Greek and Latin, sacred and profane, ancient arid modern, taken from printed works or manuscripts, the history of the Church is narrated in such a way as to be grasped by the understanding of all. From these simple discourses Baronius, by the help of God and St. Philip's prayers, built up an everlasting monument.

"I shudder when I try to fix my mind on the amount that he wrote; for I cannot understand how a man occupied with hearing confessions, preaching sermons, offering the Holy Sacrifice, saying his office, and doing other necessary and natural things, could have found time to collect together, as he did, such an infinite quantity and variety of material, scattered throughout a multitude of books; and still more, how he was enabled to understand what he had gathered together, or to discriminate between, classify, and then commit to paper, the results of what he had collected. In fact, my mind succumbs under the thought of what he did, and I can but arrive at the conclusion that this work, which was so necessary for the Church, could never have been completed had he not been guided by a divine instinct, miraculously bestowed. Many things—follies, trivalities and inaccuracies—have, partly by the malice of human nature, and partly by the perfidy of pagans and the frauds of heretics, crept into the history of the Church, greatly to the injury of religion. Baronius, with his wonderful gift of confutation, has demonstrated and exposed all these results of ignorance, fraud and romance, and has brought into true light the whole history of the Church from the birth of Christ down to the pontificate of Innocent III."

The method pursued by Baronius in writing the history of the first twelve centuries of the Christian era was to relate events in exact chronological order; and he carried out this principle so closely as to give the year, month and sometimes the day of every fact recorded. The one object he had in view was to bring to light by this chronological chain of ungarbled facts the evident and undeniable existence from the beginning of one unfailing Church, under one visible and supreme head; and he accomplished his object so effectually as to rouse the ire of his opponents, who, however, could not withhold their admiration of his accuracy and powers of research. Starting from the earliest acts of the Church, he laboriously traced the origin of all ecclesiastical laws, canons, ceremonies, traditions and discipline, and thereby demonstrated the various Christian doctrines in their infancy. Every authentic tradition was turned to account for the same end, and the words and acts of the martyrs were as familiar to him as the history of his own time.

In Rome he trod on holy ground, saturated with the blood of those who had shed it for their faith, and this consciousness bred within him a spirit of reverence which made him depart from his usual severely chronological style whenever he had to write about their sufferings. "It is impossible to please everyone," he writes to Father Talpa in allusion to such portions of his work. "When I come across acts of the martyrs written at the time, I

69

quote them at full length out of reverence for such antiquity, though I know that I run the risk of being accused of prolixity." In the same way that, in his own desire for martyrdom, he himself lived and died in the lives and deaths of the martyrs, so did he speak with the tongues and think with the thoughts of the great doctors of the Church, in whose company he lived and whom he made his familiar friends. All the saints of the early centuries were more living realities to Baronius than those of later ages.

So thorough was his knowledge of Scripture that as his life went on he could rarely discourse except in its words. He saw the Church mirrored on its pages even where others, with their spiritual instincts less quickened, had discerned no trace of her. Seeing her there founded upon Peter, he traced her course with an unerring certainty of touch right through the succession of events, down to that period of history where he had to stay his pen. He saw and proved the oneness and undying vitality of the Church through all the early destructive heresies, even those which, like Arianism, threatened to obliterate her. He saw her shining brightly through the invasions of the barbarians which well-nigh crushed her, and through the still more perilous times of the later empire, and those days so dark for the Holy See, before Gregory VII was raised up, when it is more difficult than at any other period to trace Peter in the Church. In his fearless love of truth and horror of anything defiled entering the holy place, Baronius, as has been decided by more modern investigators, overcoloured the darkness of that always dark time. But through all this, not in spite of it, but because of it, Baronius brought out the supernatural existence of the Church of God. He had, moreover, to carry his researches beyond the limits of strictly ecclesiastical annals, and unearth from the documents of centuries the true facts of the secular history of the Christian world, as it affected the Church. He had to trace with his faithful pen the course of wars within and wars without, and the careers of emperors and kings, either as they fulfilled the end for which their power was destined, and protected and adorned the Spouse of Christ, or else, when they forgot that end and did their utmost to mar her beauty by their vices or enslave her by their despotism.

Thus, bit by bit and step by step, with no eloquence save in his perorations and some stray passages, did Baronius toil through the centuries, severely letting facts speak for themselves. "The profession of an historian differs from that of a defender of dogmas," he wrote when he was beginning his work on the second volume. "Traditions and even doctrines must be demonstrated by the historian in such a way that the intention of the writer is not manifest. He must leave the reader, whether Catholic or heretic, to gather the truth from the well authenticated facts put before him, and from these to form for himself arguments for the destruction of heresy."

All critics of the Annals, whether friendly or hostile, acknowledge Baronius's paramount love of truth; though from the confused nature of the material which he had to sift, it was impossible but that some errors should have crept into his pages. On no account, however, would he allow the slightest inaccuracy to remain uncorrected once it was pointed out to him and proved. He spared no pains to investigate the truth of a statement, and gave his reasons for every conjecture. If any doubts on the subject remained after investigation, he asked help and advice from those in a position to give it; and if these were living at a distance he took no account of either time or trouble in his correspondence with them. "Our century being so erudite," he writes to Camillo Severino, who was helping him with the Hebrew text of the eleventh Psalm, which he wanted to quote, "nay being, I may say, so hypercritical, we must be armed at all points against detractions and calumnies. It is thus necessary that I should have the whole of the various translations, and a complete knowledge of the Hebrew text. I do not say this to frighten you, or make you draw back from the work, but only to induce you to mature it by careful study. It has been said, though very thoughtlessly, that as the Psalms will bear any interpretation, it ought to be easy to write on them and apply them in any way convenient."

He ruthlessly rid history of anything like fable or imposture, and rejected every attempt to improve on the simple truth, however much it might tell in favour of his argument. A favourite prayer often on his lips was: *Domine, ne auderas de ore meo verbum veritatis usquequaque*—a prayer offered up against temptations to swerve in any way from the simple truth.[4] "I have put nothing in my book which is not most solid, and most authentic," he says to Father Talpa; "and I have been most careful to guard against obscuring the pure truth by putting in anything doubtful. One single thoughtless entry might destroy confidence in the writer."

It may be said that he was greedy for suggestions and corrections, and thanked those who pointed out errors more genuinely than he did those who paid him

---

[4] Literally, "Lest thou might hear from my mouth anything but the word of truth." -Editor.

compliments. He freely accepted emendations from those who, as his common sense must have told him, were incapable of making them. Many of the letters written and received by him are on the subject of such suggestions, and in every case there is to be found the same simple gratitude, and the same humble request for more help of the same kind. This humility can be traced in a message which he sent to one of the Naples fathers, who, as will be seen in a later chapter, was pre-eminently incapable of criticizing such a book as the Annals. "As to Father Camillo," he writes to Talpa, "far from being annoyed by his corrections and advice, I thank him for them; and I hope that not only you but every one in the house will try to find out everything which is not right."

He was always displeased if his critics showed any reluctance to find fault, and at once wrote to beg for a more explicit correction. Nicholas Faber, Regius Chancellor of Paris, a most learned man and among the first critics of the age, was one of Baronius's most frequent correspondents. There was a statement in the Annals which he wished to challenge, but with the diffidence inseparable from real learning he merely hinted at it in his letter to Baronius. The latter promptly replied:

"As to your praises of my book—which I blush to have published—they manifest your generosity, for you praise that which you admit to be displeasing to you; and you touch the matter with a hand as light as that with which you might touch a man laid up with the gout, in other words you write as if you feared to hurt me. But touch boldly; speak freely; and know that you will thereby give me real pleasure. I have ever on my lips those words of St. Augustine: 'I delight in a true and severe corrector.'"

73

He never varied in this desire for candid and even severe criticism, and even when he knew that censures passed on his writings proceeded from a spirit of mere opposition, he declared they were not to be despised on that account, for, in spite of the motive, the emendation itself might very likely be of use.

As he was approaching the end of his labours, he laid down plain rules as to how corrections and criticisms should be taken; and what he there describes as praiseworthy was in fact nothing but the principle on which he had himself always acted.

"First," he says in this passage, "a writer may be congratulated if he never tramples on the truth. The greatest doctors of the Church affirm that it is given only to the Sacred Books to be free from all error; and this being so, the only thing that an ordinary writer can do is to correct any mis-statement which may have crept into his work, either by a wrong understanding of documents, or by the carelessness of copyists. He may, secondly, be congratulated if he freely acknowledges and corrects the errors caused by his own incompetency. If he have in view solely the end which he wishes to attain, he should be ready to regard his monitors in the light of benefactors.

"From such he should not exclude those who oppose him from personal enmity, or who revile his writings in an unfriendly spirit and, like harpies when they have feasted, leave behind them an evil odour of detraction. As St. Jerome says, no one is safe from the sharp wit of the detractor, so let no writer expect to escape it. Let us, however, turn the censures of others to our own profit. If the objections be unsound, let us refute them; if there be any obscurity, let us elucidate it; and if there be anything omitted, let us add it.

"Nothing is perfect in its beginning; neither can we expect to accomplish a long and difficult journey without sometimes stumbling. But by dint of great vigilance we need never be overcome by that deep oblivion to which human nature is prone."

It was in all this that the fruit of St. Philip's inspired training of Baronius was manifest. Self was so nearly annihilated that not only did Cesare give all the glory of the Annals primarily to God, but he attributed the rest to those who helped him. He himself was nowhere; and he did not feel even a flicker of wounded vanity when mistakes were pointed out to him. He wrote the Annals at the call of obedience, solely for the glory of God and His Church, and it did not occur to him to think of himself if anything suggested would make the work more perfect, and therefore more likely to fulfil the end for which it was undertaken. This paramount love of truth was so well known that no one, even among those whom he attacked and whose want of veracity he showed up, ever attempted to retaliate by bringing a similar charge against him. Casaubon, who, after the death of Baronius, was stirred up by the enemies of the Church to write against the Annals, was warned not to try to charge their author with any attempt to garble the truth, as such a baseless accusation would but serve to destroy his own credit.

Baronius's work in compiling the Annals was therefore tremendous. To realize the greatness of his task it is necessary to bear in mind that the ground on which he was labouring was as yet untilled. He had, as he reminded Tarugi in the letter already quoted, to begin at the beginning. Mere fragments of Church history had been written before, and each of these, instead of helping him, opened a new field of labour; because whatever had

75

been written previously had to be sifted and examined, for it was not in Baronius's nature to take any written statement for granted. The field covered by his researches was manifest to those chiefly whose own literary labours enabled them to appreciate it. "I am filled with admiration by the great variety of subjects with which you appear conversant," wrote the Archbishop of Gnesen, after he had studied the first volume of the Annals; "as also by your great knowledge of so many languages, and your familiarity with all history whether sacred or profane. I am also amazed at the exactitude and accuracy with which you have examined antiquity, whether in the form of old manuscripts and coins, or in that of inscriptions on ancient buildings, triumphal arches, columns, temples, &c." Such was the result as it struck the erudite men of his time; and now it remains to glance rapidly at the process by which that result was achieved.

Even making out what he had to do and how to do it was in itself a gigantic work. Baronius, it is true, lived as it were in a gold-mine of historical treasures, for the Vatican Library and the priceless archives of St. Angelo were thrown open to him. But even as a worker in a real gold-mine must learn the art of quarrying and crushing before he can turn the precious metal to account, so had Baronius to learn how to make use of the wealth of material put into his hands. Long before he completed his last volume he probably knew every book and manuscript in the libraries but there is a beginning to everything, and in the earlier stages of his task, when be first began to search and sift and turn over what was before him, his work must have been bewildering enough to turn his brain. His material was of the most confused description. No printed books, containing in fair and clear type the fruit of other men's labours, were ready to his hand, for even in his day printed books were still comparatively few in number and, what was worse, the copies varied from each other. When therefore he had written a portion of a volume from notes taken from one edition, and was constrained by circumstances to finish it from another, he was at a loss. "I should be grateful," he writes to Father Talpa, when he was but beginning his first volume, "if Father Francesco Maria would lend me his St. Basil. Here we have only the Venetian edition, in which some parts are left out and which, moreover, does not correspond with the text quoted by me from the edition which I have studied. As I had put the references to the passages I quoted, I find the copy I have is of no use, and it gives me much trouble to hunt for the page to which I have referred, and which I have noted down quite differently." Such matters may be called trivial nevertheless they serve to bring home to us the annoying difficulties with which he had to contend even in gathering together the material with which the structure was to be built.

The greatest obstacle which had to be overcome in the way of this great work imposed on him by his holy father arose from his very slender knowledge of Greek and practical ignorance of Hebrew. A very large portion of his material, especially that belonging to the earlier centuries, must have been written in Greek and it does not require much imagination to picture to ourselves the tension of the historian's brain as he pored over ancient and half-illegible manuscripts, written in a language of which he had a very imperfect knowledge, but by means of which alone he could glean accurate information on subjects absolutely indispensable to his work. Baronius did all he could himself at the same time, in the matter of

77

deciphering and interpreting Greek manuscripts and the writings of the Greek fathers, he had to trust a great deal to the help of such friends as Nicholas Faber of Paris, Henry Gravius of Louvain, F. Soria of the Society of Jesus, Fronto Ducceus, Peter Morino, and others. Often a whole correspondence; devoted to the meaning of a single passage, passed between him and these learned men; and some of his answers are treatises in themselves.

His correspondence, which later in his life attained such proportions as to be altogether beyond control, formed a large part of his work before even the first volume of the Annals was published; and the onus of its increase, at least in those earlier years, lay with himself. No point of history was too minute to be verified by him, even at the cost of many letters. If he heard of some manuscript, some inscription, or some relic in any part of Europe which he could not himself visit, he at once got into communication with a competent person living on the spot, willing and able to investigate the matter for him, and furnish him with details. Nor was he satisfied with slight or partial information, but, regardless of the additional labour involved, was insatiable in his further demands. In writing to Fronto Ducæus—one of those on whom he mainly depended for help, and whom in his ninth volume he publicly styled as "that man of remarkable piety and learning"—he says: "I thank you gratefully for the fragment of the letter on St. Gregory's Dialogues; but why did you not send me the whole? You feed the hungry in such a way that instead of satisfying his hunger you do but irritate it. Do not imagine I am content with this fragment. Look on me if you will in the light of the importunate friend who went at night to borrow three loaves, and if you will not give me what I consider a necessity for the sake of friendship, give it on account of my importunity." Baronius was most grateful to his friends for the trouble they took on his behalf, and wrote to this same Fronto Ducæus that he did not know how he should have got on at all without him, and reminded him that "a brother who is helped by a brother is like a strong city."

Under this strain and bewilderment of work, hampered by his constant correspondence on the one hand, and his relentless routine of community duties on the other, Baronius must have found his days impossibly short, even though he limited his hours of sleep first to five and then to four and a half. He had to own as an old man that for thirty years he had not once satisfied his desire for sleep. This deprivation told on his health, and when, after his long hours of work in the night and early morning, food was placed before him, what wonder that he could not touch it. Under this treatment of his body his nervous system grew strained. He was often hasty in his dealings with others, though he invariably humbled himself profoundly after every inadvertent loss of temper. His biographers excuse these ebullitions by reminding the reader of his habitual overstudy and want of sleep and indeed, when we realize what his life was, the only wonder is that he should have had any temper left at all, and that it should have betrayed itself in only the very mild examples of hastiness cited. Small wonder that when St. Philip, for the good of their souls, let the boys play at ball outside his room, Baronius should have remonstrated and declared that the noise was unbearable. We ask ourselves whether, in addition to the sanctification of the boys, the Saint had that of Cesare also in view.

79

CHAPTER VIII

The One Safety-Valve

B ARONIUS received next to no help in his great work from the Roman Oratory. It might be almost said that he received none at all, for the only exception was that given by Brother Andrea Brugiotti, to whom was afterwards consigned the management of the printing-press belonging to the Oratory, which St. Philip set up in the piazza of the Vallicella. This brother is mentioned as having helped Baronius, but his aid must have been of a most casual kind, for it is expressly said that every word of the Annals from beginning to end was written by their author's own hand. Not only did he correct every sheet himself as it came from the printer, but he often made fresh copies of his manuscript sheets, so as to include the corrections and suggestions which he received from outside. All this he did alone; and when a foreign bishop came to see him after the publication of the first volume of the Annals, and asked him how many assistants were appointed to help him in his great work, he smilingly replied:

"*Torcular calcavi solus*—I have trodden the winepress alone."

"There is no thought of relieving me here, or of in any way helping me with the work," he wrote to Talpa in 1589, while he was struggling with his second volume, vainly working against time to get it finished by the time he had promised it to the Pope. "All hope of help lies in you, who from the beginning have sympathised with the work. But there, let the matter rest. There is much more that I could say, but not with pen and ink. Pray to God for me." "I am now writing at the rate of one sheet per diem, which is very severe work," he says in another letter. "I know not whether I ought to complain of receiving no help from here. However, I make no remonstrance, for I know that all are busy with other things."

We can gather from some of Baronius's letters to the Naples fathers that as part of St. Philip's method of dealing with him—a method described by himself as causing him to make bricks without straw—the Saint not only forbade all help from the Roman Oratory, but made certain regulations which necessitated great caution on Cesare's part in profiting by the help so freely offered by the Naples fathers. "Now," he writes to Tarugi, while still engaged on the first volume, "as soon as the volume is printed, an index must be made and as I cannot do this myself, I should like to hand over the work to Messir Tomaso Galletti, and Messir Francesco Bocio." Evidently, however, obstacles were put in the way which arose from no want of will on the part of the fathers mentioned; for later in the year he wrote again, this time to Father Talpa: "I have decided to do the index myself; not because Messir Camillo with a little advice could not do it very well, but in order to remove all idea that he is kept at Naples only to do my work. It is evident that this is not approved of. As God has given me the grace to endure the fatigue of the greater work without the help of any one in the house, I hope He will not fail me now, and will enable me to bear this extra burden, which is little or nothing compared with what I have already borne."

Whatever it was that St. Philip said or did in connection with this affair, to which Baronius alludes in the veiled and guarded way in which he always wrote when referring to his holy father's actions towards himself, it was probably only one more instance of the Saint's way of exacting obedience, and removing the trial after it had been given. Father Camillo made the index after all, though, owing to his incompetency, Baronius may have regretted having permitted him to undertake the task. "The index made by Messir Camillo is by no means perfect," he writes later in the same year, 1588; "but he will learn to do better another time."

Thus gently does he allude to Father Camillo's blunders, which were the cause of some of the smaller trials which accompanied Baronius's work.

No one can live at high pressure without some safety-valve. Certainly Baronius could not have done so, for his nerves were strained to their utmost tension, his soul was depressed by his solitary work, and his heart was wounded in spite of himself by the Saint's attitude towards him, which he could not understand, and which "almost scandalized" him. He found his safety-valve in the Naples Oratory, from the fathers of which he obtained not only all the help he had, but—still more precious—the sympathy without which he could scarcely have got through his work. There was no point about the Annals too minute for him to lay before them, and he took and acted on their advice about all such minor matters as the size and arrangement of the type and marginal notes, as well as the weightier subjects connected with the writing itself. His letters to Father Talpa, which he sent by courier regularly every week, while the first volume was in process of construction, are full of the most graphic touches, illustrative of his own absorption in his work, as well as the equally sympathetic absorption of his correspondent and the other fathers.

There were at that time three fathers at Naples to whom Baronius was much attached, Tarugi, Talpa and Blessed Juvenal Ancina. To Tarugi, the *dux verbi* as he called him, he was especially bound by affection, and his feeling towards him amounted almost to veneration. Though Baronius was younger than himself by eleven years, their lives ran on very parallel lines. They were two of the Saint's earliest disciples, and were those whom he chose in an especial manner to carry out his ends. None of his sons are so closely connected with his memory as they. They were both made Cardinals on the same day; and they died within a year of each other, and lie side by side in the sanctuary of the Chiesa Nuova.

Of Blessed Juvenal it is not necessary to speak at present, but of Father Antonio Talpa a few words must be said, for the weekly correspondence between him and Baronius, in which the latter related every little event as it occurred and noted down the passing thoughts of the moment, is almost like a diary, and entitled their recipient to a special place in Baronius's life. This father—*il prudente*, as the saint called him—was St. Philip's right hand, and he would never come to a conclusion on any important matter without consulting him. Compared with many of St. Philip's sons, Father Talpa led an unknown life; and though possessed of a mine of knowledge he never initiated any literary work. His fund of information, however, made him very appreciative of the work of others; and probably without his wise sympathy, by which he was able to encourage even while he criticized, the Annals of Baronius would have lacked some qualities which they now possess. Cesare thoroughly valued his assistance, and when he completed the Martyrology he declared in the preface that the whole credit of the work was due to Father Talpa, the librarian of the Congregation. It is characteristic of their intercourse, and of Baronius's trust in his judgment, that though every man, however learned, might have praised what he had written, he would not allow one word to appear in print without Talpa's approval.

To Father Talpa, then, Baronius sent every portion of the first volume of the Annals, page by page, sheet by sheet, as they came to him from the Vatican printing press, set up by Sixtus V and placed under the management of Domenico Basa. This printer, however, did his work so unsatisfactorily at first, and was so dilatory, that Cardinal Caraffa, the Apostolic librarian, "flew into a great rage with him on account of the multiplicity of errors," till he cried for mercy and implored the Cardinal not to report the matter to the Pope, who would certainly dismiss him. Basa was not dismissed, and printed some of the later volumes, but the second volume was taken out of his hands and printed at Antwerp by "*Plantinus accuratissimus*," as Baronius loved to call him in his letters of thanks for the manner in which he had done his work.

This excellent printer, however, died soon after the publication of the second volume, and Basa was employed again. By that time Baronius was in a position to dictate his terms, and gave him the work only on condition that he hired a house and set up his press near the Vallicella.

Baronius had to correct all the proof-sheets with his own hand, which added immensely to his labours and put him at a disadvantage compared with Bellarmine, who, as he had pointed out to Tarugi, was entirely relieved of all such work. After correcting them himself Cesare sent the printed sheets to the Naples fathers for revision. The principal help, however, which they gave him was with his own manuscript sheets, which he sent to them week by week to be revised, commented on and corrected, before they were put into the hands of the printers. So keen was the sympathetic interest in the Annals taken by the Naples Congregation that Baronius found as many censors as there were fathers, and there is nothing more beautiful in his life than the way in which, true to his vow of humility, he accepted the corrections made by men who probably knew little or nothing about what they were doing. Talpa's corrections he always accepted most cordially, and to them he attributed any merits the book was pronounced to have. "It is difficult for me to take to myself the fruit of the labours of others," Cesare writes, "for I thus rob them of their glory and reward." With Talpa's criticisms as well as Tarugi's he was genuinely and reasonably satisfied, but some of the self-appointed correctors caused him a great deal of trouble.

Father Camillo made corrections which were like a conundrum to him. "Ask him," he writes to Talpa, "to write more slowly when he makes his corrections, so that I may understand them better and at the cost of less labour." "Thank Father Camillo," he says again in another letter, "thank him for his trouble, but do beg him to write more slowly, so that I can read what he has written." Father Camillo, though most obliging, does not seem to have been very intelligent. In the index which, after the hesitation mentioned above, he undertook to compile, he made the strangest mistakes, which offended Baronius's accurate and methodical mind. The latter cites one startling error by which the indexer placed all the different persons bearing the same name under one head, and mixed up the different Jameses and Herods as if they were all one and the same person. Another pin-prick came from Father Tomaso, who, once he got hold of the sheets for revision, kept them so long that some pretext had to be found to extract them from him. Another trial came from Father Antonio Carte who undertook to make a scriptural index. In the case of his blunders Cesare lost patience, and he sent him a sharp message through Blessed Juvenal. "Tell him," he says, "that the index will not do, because *non est habitus delectus.* He should have begun by the Old Testament, and he should have mentioned only those passages quoted in the text, and no others. Thus, in addition to all my other labours, I have to remake this index from the beginning." The very unintelligent way in which Father Antonio did his task gives us a good idea of the sort of assistance Baronius received, which, as a rule, he accepted humbly and gratefully.

But most of his trials—and very real they were to a man as busy as he—came from B. Juvenal Ancina, who constituted himself corrector and reviser in chief, and in whose judgment Baronius had not the same implicit confidence as he had in Talpa's. Ancina was a most severe censor, and, though Cesare thanked him repeatedly for his severity, he could not help finding fault with its undueness. Nor could he refrain from complaint at his dilatoriness in making his promised corrections of the sheets, of which he held fast possession. In letter after letter are to be found passages such as these: "Try to hasten Father Juvenal. Beg him, if he wishes to be in time, to make more speed. If he does not send by the next despatch, his labours will be in vain. . . . If Father Juvenal undertakes to do the revision, he must do nothing else. For

I tried him here in Rome, and he kept one sheet nearly a month, which was intolerable, seeing what speed is required." Baronius wrote thus confidentially to others, but even when writing to B. Juvenal personally he did not spare him. In a letter to him in which he complains of the waste of a very good eulogy on St. Silvester promised by Ancina long before, but sent at last two days after the part of the Annals to which it referred had gone to press, he concludes by this sharp reproach: "It is wonderful that anyone can take things so leisurely. Good God! I believe a crane would not make you move any faster, in spite of my impatience which keeps spurring you on! "

The uncalled-for severity of Father Juvenal's criticisms, and the "undue importance" which he attached to trifles irritated Baronius, and occasionally made him depart from his humble rule of never defending himself. In an intimate letter we find him thus sarcastically scolding Ancina for his tendency to hypercriticism: "Thanks be to God that learned men such as Cardinal Paleotto, Cardinal Caraffa, Messir Silvio, and the Abate Maila who all insisted on reading the volume through from beginning to end, have found means to praise it though, I admit, too highly. They, being intent only on the matter treated, are pleased, and pay no attention to mere errors in printing. It is not that they approve of these errors, but they make less fuss about them than you do. It is sufficient for them that gold should be gold, in whatever way it may be worked. I do not wish to infer by this that you have not got good—nay, exquisitely good—judgment, but you are so scrupulous that you note things which you might just as well pass over without censure, as, for instance, *intus* for *intra*, and *proximior*, which words, though open perhaps to criticism, are none the less used by ancient and good authors. Now, however, make haste, for Plantino is begging to have the corrected sheets, and I would not think of sending them to him without your precise and painstaking emendations. So I beg you to let me have them with least possible delay, so that the printer may have in his hands some samples of those grave errors. I beg you not to do by these sheets as you did by the others, which, though I reminded you about them time after time, were never sent at all." Fearful, however, lest Juvenal should be offended by what he had said, Baronius added a postscript to this letter: "I pray you to attend to this with that diligence which you always bestow on my affairs. I shall be better pleased if you are scrupulous in your corrections than if you are remiss."

However much Baronius could afford to tease Father Juvenal about his undue severity when he wrote to him personally, there is no doubt that he was at times stung by it. One of his letters to Talpa finishes with these words : "To God from whom all good things come be honour and glory, but to me be confusion, of which I receive abundance by the errors noted by Father Juvenal."

But, unfortunately, neither Ancina's severity nor his dilatoriness were his worst offences against his friend. He had decided views of his own both about ecclesiastical history, and the way it should be treated. This made him overstep the limits of even severe corrections and meddle with the text itself. Baronius sent repeated messages to him through Father Talpa, and begged him to at least note down his corrections on a separate piece of paper, and let Talpa, who wrote a clear hand, copy them on to the sheets, "for," added he, "it is his habit to fill even printed books with his writing." To anyone who has seen Baronius's own neat and beautiful caligraphy, it is easy to understand how much his human nature must have writhed under the defacement of his faultless sheets. All his remonstrances were, however, fruitless, and in letter after letter he had to repeat his request to his too zealous friend not to touch the text. "Try," he says in a letter to Talpa, "try to put a curb on Father Juvenal. He is too impetuous, and is possessed of such a sharp gift of criticism that I believe he would like to change every period." And again: "Father Juvenal suggests to me that every page should be re-written at his dictation. I would willingly accept the suggestion, but I fear it would quite change the style, because his reverence, being so exquisitely particular, never contents himself with slight alterations. It would, therefore, be a dangerous experiment, and there would be great risk of changing the sense with the words. However, I submit myself in this matter to your judgment. If you think it well to do it, I will pay the writer; but, anyhow, do not waste time." This last sentence shows how deep was Baronius's humility. It is wonderful that he should have even considered a proposal, the audacity of which might have well made him angry.

"I am more than satisfied with Father Juvenal's corrections," he writes again most patiently, "even though he does meddle with the text, which, if possible; I had rather he did not do. But I must put up with it so as not to offend him. I will cite you an instance of what he does. Whenever he comes across the word god, he takes the trouble to change it and re-write it with a capital G; which is not correct, as it is the name of God only which should have a capital." "Father Juvenal," he writes again, "though he has been most zealous in his corrections, gives me a great deal of extra work, for in many places he puts his pen right through the passage he is correcting, and adapts it to suit his own ideas of latinity; and, to fit the text to his own views, he has changed quotations taken from various authors. Wherefore I have had to revise these passages and place them back as they were before. It is always considered a sacrilege to alter the text of any quotation, unless there be an evident misprint, or else more than one reading of the passage, and even in the latter case the alternative ought to be put in the margin. Beg of him not to do this any more; and let him confine his corrections to what I say myself, and there I will submit myself to his judgment. Put this to him gently, lest I appear ungrateful."

The same tendency to change the text remained with Ancina in spite of this gentle and courteous remonstrance; and Baronius found it necessary to write to the offender himself, begging him to be especially careful in his corrections of quotations, and giving him for his guidance three pregnant rules which he was never to transgress: "What I say now must serve you on all future occasions. 1. If the quotation be a text from Scripture, it must not be touched: *sacrosanctum est, cave.* 2. If it be a quotation from a Latin father, do not touch it unless the text be inaccurate: *alias temerarium est.* 3. If it be a translation from a Greek father into Latin, you can use some discretion, *servato sensu auctoris.*"[5]

At length the manuscript sheets over which Baronius had spent such time and care were so defaced and injured by the many solicitous correctors that, in spite of his deep humility and acquired patience, he had to make a stand

---

[5] 1) "Beware, it is sacrosanct." 2) "Anything else would be rash."
3) "While preserving the sense of the author." -Editor.

and lay down certain fixed rules, the carrying out of which was to be left to Talpa. No one but the latter was to touch the sheets, on which he alone was to insert the corrections made by others. "Correct evident solecisms," he said, "and all barbarisms inadvertently committed by the author. 2. If the orthography of a word is doubtful, do not correct unless there be a manifest mistake. 3. Quotations from other authors are to be left untouched. 4. Never transpose passages, or change sentences for the sake of greater elegance, for this would necessitate the work of re-writing on the part of the author. 5. When correcting use all diligence, but be also merciful to the author by not defacing the page unnecessarily; and write the corrections slowly, and in characters resembling as nearly as possible those of the text. To this end let each corrector note down his suggestions on a separate piece of paper, and let Father Talpa copy them into their proper place. Let all corrections be inserted by him only. Finally, if any difficulty arise, or if anything in the text require elucidation, refer the matter to the author, whom you will not find at all obstinate."

Difficult as it may be to believe, even these definite rules produced no effect, and the ardent revisers could not keep their hands and pens off the sheets. Baronius was, therefore, compelled to devise another plan, which, in its turn, proved as futile as all preceding ones. He asked Talpa to number all the lines of his manuscript by fives or tens, like the stanzas of a poem, and then to collect the various corrections of the fathers and note down the line to which they referred, leaving it to Baronius himself to make the necessary changes. For a time this plan worked very well, and the fathers, with certain notable exceptions, conformed themselves to the rule. "Go on with the corrections as they have been begun," he writes, "for things really begin to look well. You might, however, remind Father Juvenal to note down the number of the line to which his correction refers, for by so doing he would save me the trouble of searching for it. Be you, as you always have been, the protector of the work; and, as for me, I will be always guided by your judgment." Soon, however, Baronius's new rule, or, rather, the inobservance of it, led to worse confusion and greater labour on his part than ever, for the Naples fathers sent him list after list of their emendations, without any reference at all to the numbers of the lines, and he very naturally complained that in addition to all his other overwhelming work he should have to search through his sheets for the place where the correction fitted. The one obvious thing which never occurred to him was to pay no attention whatever to the corrections and suggestions which were poured in upon him.

At length daylight broke through the confusion, and Tarugi, who probably understood his friend's trials better than even Talpa, offered to be sole corrector of the sheets. Baronius evidently breathed a sigh of relief. "Father Francesco Maria will be a delightful reviser," he writes; "and I really think it would be well to give no further trouble to Father Juvenal. However, about this I will do exactly as you and the other fathers think best." Much as the over-worked and over-tired historian suffered under the fret of the additional labour imposed on him by his friend's want of judgment, he never let himself forget the fear of seeming ingratitude, and even, in the midst of all the worry Ancina was causing him, he could write to him as follows : "It is impossible ever to thank you enough for the continuous trouble you are taking in my affairs. I must leave that to God."

When we read the account of all these, perhaps petty, hindrances and grievances with which Cesare's weekly letters to Talpa make us acquainted, and to which he was subjected by those who most warmly sympathised with him, we are half inclined to think that his work would have been facilitated had the Naples fathers kept the same rigid silence about it as was observed at the Roman Oratory. But it was not thus that he judged their interference with his concerns, riddled with pin-pricks though it might be. In the solitude of his room at the Vallicella, ceaselessly spurred on by his holy Father, allowed no rest, hindered in his work, yet censured if it were not accomplished, bewildered and staggered by the methods of him for whom he would have gladly laid down his life, he might have altogether succumbed under the weight of his burden had it not been for his human intercourse with the Naples fathers. Their warm sympathy and the deep interest in his work, which betrayed itself even in their ill-judged assistance, were to him like a glimpse of the sun in a cloudy sky and probably his weekly, confidential, unrestrained outpourings to them were what made his life's work possible.

CHAPTER IX
Success

A T length, early in 1588, the first volume of the Annals was completed and given to the world. Being the first, the labour was disproportionately great, and its subject covered more ground than that of any subsequent volume. In spite of the pains he had taken, and the deliberation spent on each page Baronius, was not satisfied with the result, for he felt the publication of the volume to be premature, and evidently had an uncomfortable sensation of being hustled. With this conviction fixed in his mind he prefaced the book by a semi-apologetic address, or rather appeal, to his readers. "Though," he says, "it may contain no misstatements, the volume is given to the world too soon. It has been printed at the magnificent Vatican Press, which, however, having been but recently started, is manifestly in its infancy, and the volume produced by it is not perfectly finished. We seriously recognise its deficiencies, and when a second edition—at which we are working with all possible speed—is published, we will make all defects good with interest, not by corrections so much as by additions. Meanwhile, reader, we pray you to give more attention to the matter than to the execution of the work."

Cardinal Caraffa, the Apostolic Librarian, had always been the powerful friend and patron of Baronius, and it was he who overcame his hesitancy, and persuaded him to give his book to the public without further delay. "To you is due the present publication of this volume, which I had wished to postpone awhile," Baronius wrote to Caraffa when sending him a presentation copy. "When I contemplate the greatness of my subject I cannot ignore the difficulty of fulfilling the promise contained in the title which I have given to the book; nor can I fail to see how hard it will be to satisfy the erudite men, so deeply versed in ancient history, with whom this century abounds. I fear the acuteness of your criticism more than that of any, for with rare erudition you combine a special knowledge of ecclesiastical history. However, I am reassured by your kindness, and I hope you will attribute the meagreness of the results to my incompetency and not to any want of industry; for whatever may be the demerits of the book, it is undeniably the fruit of much labour and many vigils."

Though, in obedience to his injunction to the public, we are bound to regard the subject matter of Baronius's great work rather than the manner in which he compiled it, it cannot fail to be interesting to learn from himself the process by which the memorable first volume was built up, even though his account is to a certain extent the recapitulation of that to which allusion has been already made.

After relating to Sixtus V, in the passage quoted in its place, the manner in which the great work had grown out of the small seed sown by his simple discourses at the Oratory, Baronius, in the letter which he laid at the feet of the Sovereign Pontiff with his first volume, goes on to say: "Having at length embarked on the ocean, I have, by God's grace, sailed safely over its immense depths. It required much labour, diligence, and study to surmount the great and almost indescribable difficulties which met me in my efforts to trace the sequence of events and fix the order of chronology, which is always obscure in ancient documents. It was not sufficient to read those histories

96

which were ready to my hand, but I had to search through the writings of the fathers, to pore over the old manuscripts in the libraries, and often to investigate the hidden sense of the documents. In order to weigh everything with its exact measure, I had to use the scales of judgment; for there is no greater snare in history than to put faith in every stray writer who treats a subject : I do not say all this, Holy Father, in order to boast of my extensive reading, or from any desire that others should hold that opinion of me. On the contrary, I write as I do with the object of obtaining indulgence at the hands of fair judges if, on account of the great difficulty of the task, I have treated some parts less happily than I might have done. I do not know whether my work will prove to be of any use, or whether it is worth the labour bestowed upon it: for where does there exist a writer who is not filled with misgivings by those words addressed to Sabinus by St. Ambrose, who had such contempt for his own works: 'A man's writings deceive and mislead him. Even as deformed children are objects of love to their parents, so are even unseemly words flattering to their author?' All that I do know is that I have laboured indefatigably, though, more truly, it is not I who have laboured, but the grace of God on which I depend."

At the end of this letter Baronius expressed his intention of completing and laying at the feet of the Sovereign Pontiff a new volume each successive year. In this almost impossible design we can scarcely fail to see the hand of St. Philip, who was always urging his son on to greater and greater efforts. But the work was too heavy, and to Baronius's annoyance the second volume was published quite a year and a half after the first. "The first volume was scarcely finished before I was at work on the

97

second," he says to the Pope in apology for his failure to keep his promise of an annual volume "and even while I was at work on the second, necessity drove me to gather material for a third. With my labours thus succeeding each other, I had not breathing time even to condense my matter. I trust that your Holiness will hold me worthy of forbearance if I have found myself compelled to overstep the prescribed period of completion. Far from having had time to complete the work, I have not had sufficient time even to begin it as it should be done. It is a known fact that weighty structures cannot be moved rapidly by a crane.

We saw this with the obelisk recently set up by your Holiness. Many contrivances had to be used, in order that it might be moved slowly and let down gradually and gently, so as to be placed straight on its foundations. I will in future work so hard that with the remaining volumes I hope not to exceed by much the promised time. I have no wish for delay, for I am spurred on by many learned men; and, moreover, my advancing years warn me to complete the work speedily; for my impaired strength might easily fail under the weight of the burden."

The time lost by Baronius in the production of the second volume was, by his great exertions and the constant spur applied by St. Philip, never lost further; for the next four volumes were published in the four following years. The seventh volume was nearly completed at the time of the Saint's death in 1595; but, owing to all the after occurrences and the dignities conferred on Baronius, its publication was delayed for more than a year. Afterwards, for reasons told in their place, the five remaining volumes appeared at longer intervals.

It is, however, time to return to the first volume. It is no exaggeration to say that the success with which it met was tremendous; and its praises poured in from all quarters. There was scarcely a learned man who did not write his congratulations to the author; and its dry pages were devoured with an avidity more frequently bestowed in this century on sensational novels. Abbot Rescius, of Poland, declared that never did glutton devour his supper with more greed than he devoured the first volume. Never had he known a pleasanter travelling companion; and he read it all day in his litter and half the night at the inns where he lodged. The Bishop of Evora wrote that he had read it over several times on end; and the Bishop of Cracow said that its perusal was a solace to him, and a diversion in the midst of his business worries. The Bishop of Antwerp, who had earned an European reputation as an ecclesiastical historian, declared that all that he had written was mere child's play compared with Baronius's work. De Marquais, the learned Abbot of Tournay, wrote to implore him to take care of his health, as his life was too precious to be risked; and the praises of the writer which he wrote to a third person were so lavish that Cesare blushed when they were repeated to him. Papirius Massonus, one of the lights of the century, publicly called him the glory of Italy. Louvain made him an honorary member of its University, while the southern University of Coimbra prayed for the honour of his friendship.

Nearer home, all those whose opinion Baronius most valued, such as the Holy Father himself, the future Pontiffs Clement VIII, Leo XI, and Gregory XIV, Cardinal Caraffa, Cardinal Cusano, and others too many to be enumerated, uttered but one unanimous expression of approbation and satisfaction. Cardinal Sfondrato, afterwards Gregory XIV, read the volume sheet by sheet as they came from the printers, being too impatient to wait for the volume as a whole; and Cardinal Aldobrandini did the same. Of the latter, when he was raised to the See of Peter under the name of Clement VIII, Baronius writes thus to Talpa: "The new Pontiff has always shown the greatest interest in the Annals. He has already insisted on reading them line by line, and has made notes on the margin. He would never wait for the volume to be published, but sent for the printed sheets as they were done; and he has continued to do this up to the present moment."

So great was the fame of the Annals, and so completely did they promise to supply the great want of the day, that a request came from three different quarters for permission to translate the first volume into other languages. The Archbishop of Gnesen asked that the Jesuit fathers might translate it into Polish; and the learned Mgr. Panicarola and Marco Fuscaro made personal application to Baronius for leave to translate it respectively into Italian and German.

"I have lent my copy to Mgr. Panicarola," Baronius writes to Talpa. "He has just finished his translation of the first volume, and rejoices in having accomplished it. He has praised the book even from the pulpit. *Non nobis, Domine, non nobis, sed nomini tuo da gloriam.*[6] "Mgr. Panicarola is already publishing his translation," he says in a later letter. "You will believe me when I tell you that I have prayed him to omit all the praises of me which he

---

[6] "Not to us Lord, not to us, but to thy name give glory." -Psalm 113 (114).

proposed to put in the preface. He has already said too much, for in his preface *ad lectorem* he says that public prayers ought to be offered up, and processions organized for the preservation of my life. This makes me blush; and I have begged him to withdraw the words. However, what he says is worse than what he has written; and even when he was preaching on the feast of St. Lawrence he could not refrain from praising the Annals. Therefore, over and over again do I repeat, *Non nobis, Domine, non nobis*, and I try to humble myself and recognise my vileness. I beg you of your charity to help me by your prayers, that I may take heed and not let myself be blown upward like a straw in the wind of vainglory. I beg this of you, and also to obtain the prayers of all others in the house."

For the sake of the souls whom it would benefit, Baronius was especially pleased with the offer made by Fuscaro to translate the Annals into German, and thus open the way to a more popular refutation of the errors of the Centuries of Magdeburg and the eradication of other poisonous weeds sown by the German reformers. "For the glory of God I will tell you a piece of news," he writes to Talpa. "The chamberlain of Signor Marco Fuscaro, a most learned man, tells me that this gentleman is so pleased with the first volume that he has begun to translate it into German for the benefit of the people both Catholic and heretic, and is anxiously awaiting the second volume. So you see that I, who can speak neither Latin nor Italian properly, am to be made to speak German! I like the idea of this translation, because of the good that may result from it, and because it is being done by one whose library is famous all over Christendom. I am writing to tell him that I approve of his undertaking."

Baronius's letter to Fuscaro himself shows his anxiety lest any errors or inaccuracies should creep into the book in the process of translation, and he lays down rules which any translator must have found it very hard to adhere to. "If you read the volume," he says, "you will see that the work of translation will cost you no small labour. Indeed, it will be necessary for you to read it through attentively more than once, and study it with accuracy and intelligence. It should be translated not so much sentence by sentence, but, as far as possible, word by word. This must be, as anyone will understand, the work of the Spirit, for the interpretation of tongues is one of His gifts."

The childlike pleasure taken by Baronius in some of the praise he received, and the evident surprise which it caused him, speaks almost more for his humility than had he quite disregarded it. "I am doubtful," he wrote to Talpa soon after the publication of the first volume, "whether I ought to send you some letters which have been written to me by certain learned men in praise of our affair, and especially the last which I have received from Henry Gravius, the President of the University of Louvain, who is a distinguished and well-known man. I am on the one hand restrained by Christian modesty on the other hand, gratitude forbids me to withold this consolation from you, defrauding you thereby of the fruit of your labours, seeing how much you especially have interested yourself in my affairs. I have let this last consideration outweigh the other, on condition that the letters I send shall not be considered common property, nor shown to anyone except in confidence. Do as you please about keeping them or sending them back. I am not sending you those which I have received from learned men in Italy, as I do not lay so much store by them and have not kept them. Pray understand why I send these others to you, and let everything be for the honour and glory of God from whom all good things come."

Another time, in reply to certain reproaches on the part of Talpa for witholding some laudatory letters, he writes thus: "I did not mean to do wrong by keeping back those letters received by me in praise of the Annals; for to God, the real author of the work, must be given the praise and not to me. I have received commendations beyond all expectation from many men of letters. Deo gratias, Deo gratias! To Him be honour and glory, but to me confusion." "With this," he again writes, "I enclose an eulogy from the Bishop of Antwerp, who, as you know, has written to me before. It has given great pleasure to everybody, and is, in my opinion, far more than I deserve. Show it to Father Juvenal who, being of the legal profession, may receive encouragement from it." This last sentence was added, we may conclude, in order to bring home to Father Juvenal that the severity of his criticisms was not borne out by the judgment passed on the book by one of European reputation as a historian.

Baronius's innate modesty and humility forbade him to make even an allusion to the admiration excited by his book to any save Father Talpa, his alter ego; and it was only when writing to him that he allowed his own pleasure at such approbation to leak out. The struggle which went on within him, between his modesty and the joy which the praises of his beloved work caused him, gave rise to certain mental scruples and difficulties which he thus put before Talpa: "It has occurred to me that I had better ask you to solve a doubt which troubles me. Would it be a good thing to put into the next volume those letters

103

referring to the translations into other languages which have been made? On one hand they might be useful to posterity; but on the other I shrink from anything which might have the appearance of boasting. What I say applies also to the Bishop of Antwerp's eulogy."

While some men of note contented themselves with laudatory letters, others tried to testify to their admiration of the Annals in a more substantial manner, by offering money to the author. The Archbishop of Cracow was the first who vainly pressed gifts on him, and many, including the King of Portugal and the Duke of Bavaria, followed his example. It was not only to do honour to the great historian or to express their appreciation of his work that men pressed their gifts on him, for the rumour was spread abroad that Baronius was in a state of real penury. Those who came from afar to visit him were slow to understand that the extreme poverty and simplicity in which he lived were the result of sanctity and not of indigence.

The Bishop of Coimbra was the most importunate of all the would-be benefactors, and many letters passed between Baronius and him before he would be convinced that his generous efforts were quite in vain. "I beseech you," wrote Cesare in 1592, "to allow me to cherish holy Poverty, from whom I have received so many good things. Do not compel me to be ungrateful and forsake her from whom all treasures flow as from a fountain. To have enough is to have abundance and wealth. You will understand that there is no contempt in my rejection of your gift; for I have to put pressure on myself to refuse it, and none the less do I return you heartfelt thanks." The Bishop, however, would not take "No" for an answer, and in spite of the refusal to accept it sent a policy for five hundred crowns to a merchant in Rome. "What!" wrote

Baronius in reply, "Do you still seek to wound me with these golden shafts? It is quite unnecessary to make all these warlike preparations to overcome me, for I yield myself unconditionally to you, and without striking a blow. Cannot I be yours without your having recourse to these golden weapons, and without being vanquished by money? Is my devoted service of no value to you unless you bind me by chains of gold? But for your comfort I will tell you that I have received an accession of means from another quarter, and am in no need of any further assistance."

Though the Bishop allowed this to be the last word to pass directly between him and Baronius, he was not convinced, and obtained the intervention of Father Sottomayor of the Order of Friars Preachers, one of the most learned men of the day, and the author of a profound commentary on the Bible. Baronius had often corresponded with him about various Hebrew and Greek manuscripts, and the Bishop hoped that the great historian would listen to reason from such an advocate, though he turned a deaf ear to himself. Sottomayor threw himself into the task and spared no pains to induce Baronius to accept the Bishop's gifts, quoting from Aristotle's Ethics that it befits a generous man to accept the generosity of others, and that it is ungenerous always to refuse. However, his learned friend's pleading was ineffectual, and produced no further result than to draw out more explicit reasons for his refusal. Having heard rumours that the Pope, Clement VIII had expressed his pleasure at his rejection of all gifts, he thought it expedient to lay the blame on him. "I would accept the Bishop of Coimbra's generosity," he wrote, "were I not sure that it would displease His Holiness. As soon as he was raised to the See of Peter, he made it his business to look into my affairs, and supplied me with what was necessary to meet the expenses of the Annals. He would consider himself defrauded were he to hear that I had accepted assistance from anyone else. I hope this will convince you and will enable you to plead my excuses with the Bishop. If, all the same, he would send me some trifle, more as a memento than a gift, I would accept it gladly."

Some who offered gifts to Baronius were more fortunate than those who have been mentioned, though to the end he never accepted anything of his own free will. Some who were most anxious that he should accept a token of their gratitude thought his resistance might be more vulnerable if the gift took the form of an object; but he would never give way until his will was coerced by those to whom he owed obedience. He had a particular objection to receiving the smallest gift or favour from secular princes, or from anyone in power—and this not only because of his love of poverty. He feared lest his acceptance of anything from them should fetter his liberty of speech and action in political matters. In reply to those who argued that such a persistent refusal of gifts savoured of pride, he was fond of quoting the words of Moses to the people of Israel: "Thou shalt not accept persons nor gifts, for gifts blind the eyes of the wise and change the words of the just." He would therefore have refused everything indiscriminately had not Clement VIII, thinking that he carried his principle to an extreme, insisted in certain cases on his accepting what was offered.

There was an unfortunate silver credence table which Henry IV of France, through his ambassador, begged him to accept, even writing to him with his own hand to pray him to keep it as a memento of him and a testimony of his affection. Baronius had almost a devotion for the French King, and, had he let himself be moved by human affection, might have been willing to receive a gift accompanied by such very complimentary language. But, unfortunately for Henry's object, he supplemented his expressions of attachment and gratitude by a request that Baronius would continue his good offices on his behalf with the Sovereign Pontiff. This betrayed but too plainly the ulterior object of the King's munificence, and three times did Cesare return the valuable present to Henry's ambassador, the Count de Sillery. At length the Pope, anxious that the French King's susceptibilities should not be wounded, commanded Baronius to accept the gift, adding the permission, of which Cesare promptly availed himself, to present it to the Chiesa Nuova.

Something of the same sort happened many years later, when the Emperor Rudolph II sent Baronius a costly crystal crucifix as an acknowledgment of the dedication to him of the tenth volume of the Annals. Being compelled to accept the gift, he at once sent it to the Capuchins at Sora, whom he had helped to establish there.

Pope Clement VIII
He received spiritual direction from both St. Philip Neri
and Baronius, as well as made the latter a Cardinal.

CHAPTER X
Behind the Scenes

B UT where was St. Philip all this time? We find no mention of him in the records of the success which attended the venture which he had initiated; and unless Baronius had himself told us of the share taken by his holy father in the compiling of the Annals, we might be led to imagine that, having once given Cesare the command to write, and "launched him out on the immense depths of the sea," he had left him to complete the task without him. But, thanks to his son, we know that he was ever by his side, "spurring him with his presence, and urging him forward with his words"; though of this Cesare said nothing at the time, even to his most intimate friends. The part taken in his life by the Saint belonged to his inward soul, and was too like the movements of interior grace, too sacred a thing altogether, to be manifested to others as the motive power of his exterior actions. Thus when, in his confidential letters, necessity obliged him to allude to some action of the Saint towards him, he did it in such veiled language as to require the light of actual circumstances for its interpretation.

St. Philip, after spending thirty years in preparing it, had launched his weighty missile into the camp of the enemy. Now, however, he trembled, not lest it should fail to do its work, but on account of the great dangers to which his venture was exposing Cesare, whose soul was so inexpressibly dear to him. The work begun so unwillingly and sanctified by obedience had become a matter of engrossing absorption to Baronius; and the fear, lest this should become wholly natural gives us the key to the Saint's action in so perpetually checking it, even at the risk of hindering the work itself. Over-absorption was one danger which made St. Philip tremble, but this was harmless compared with that consequent on the success of the book, and the torrent of praise, seasoned with flattery, with which it had met; and out of St. Philip's love for his son there grew the desire to safeguard and sanctify him by crucial mortifications. None rejoiced more than the Saint at the success of the book and the effect it was producing on the age; yet he alone had no words of praise for it. He kept its author at his daily task, and seemingly had no care except for its performance; and as Baronius came and laid the volumes one by one at his feet as he finished them, the Saint's only response and need of thanks was the command to serve thirty masses, as if he were an altar boy.

Under St. Philip's influence, probably by his direction, the Roman Congregation, with whom Cesare lived his life, was studiously unsympathetic towards the work and the sympathy which came to him by the weekly mail from Naples could not make up for the coldness of the atmosphere which he was breathing every hour.

As if he feared that such a system of repression should not suffice to keep his son humble, St. Philip prepared for him a truly crucial test, which brought out the reality and depth of Cesare's humility. Still avoiding on his own part any word of approbation—a silence which no doubt created very uncomfortable misgivings in Baronius's breast as to the real merits of the book—the Saint set Father Antonio Gallonio, then quite a young father, to examine, criticize, and pass judgment on the work which the intellectual monarchs of the age failed to find words eloquent enough to praise. The mortification was ingeniously chosen, and Baronius felt the sting of it acutely, all the more as the Saint carefully spread about the news of what he was doing. The youth of the censor thus deliberately chosen wounded him, and added to the suffering caused to his human nature by the contempt it evinced on the part of him for whose approbation alone he really cared. The most painful part of the business was the doubt in his mind as to whether he ought or ought not to defend himself against the accusation of errors cited by Gallonio, which he himself considered groundless. As usual, Baronius made Talpa the confidant of his trouble, and declared that he would rather die than defend himself against his brother; for possibly the Father was acting in this way only to prove his love by wounding his (Cesare's) vanity, and to protect him against the dangers of self-complacency. "That I have written the Annals at all," he says at the end of the letter, "is, as I know, solely and entirely the gift of God. To Him, therefore, be all glory, and to me humiliation." In all probability these words never met the eye of St. Philip, and towards him Cesare's attitude was one of simple silence.

There can be no doubt that the shaft sent out by his holy father was well driven home into the heart of Baronius, nor was the cause of his suffering and humiliation soon removed. In a later letter to Talpa he again alludes to his trial, aggravated by a growing conviction that Gallonio himself had not behaved quite honourably towards him. "Believe me, father," he says, "I do not at all object to my writings being criticized, as I know on what I have based my facts, and that all my statements have been well discussed outside by both

111

friends and enemies. What weighs upon me is the thought that, this rivalry is neither good, nor was it entered on with that candour which should exist between brothers. I fear that in order to blow away the flies I may have to defend myself, which, all the same, however necessary it may be, I will not undertake to do without the counsel of you all. Pray God it may not come to that."

As soon however as St. Philip had assured himself by observation that the crucial trial had had its effect, and was satisfied that, in spite of the suffering, the humility of his disciple had stood the test to which it had been put, the cause of humiliation was quietly withdrawn, and Gallonio was required to pass no more censures on the Annals. It was never the Saint's way to repeat his mortifications when they had proved effectual, as was exemplified by Baronius's experiences relating to a pension granted to him by Clement VIII, when the affection and sympathy shown him by St. Philip formed a striking contrast with his severity on a former and similar occasion. The third volume of the Annals, dedicated to Philip II of Spain, was on the point of being given to the world when Cardinal Aldobrandini was raised to the See of St. Peter under the name of Clement VIII He was a most devoted disciple of St. Philip, and knew Baronius well, having followed the progress of his great work with deep interest. One of the first things he did after he was made Pope was to settle an annuity of two hundred crowns on Cesare and what happened on that occasion and the Saint's attitude about this pension are best told in the following letter to Talpa, written by Baronius soon after that in which he had poured forth his trouble about Gallonio, and while the latter's work of criticism was still in progress.

"I must tell you what has befallen me since I last wrote, in order to show you what care God takes of me, and how, as is always the case, He has given me consolation in double measure to compensate for the annoyance I have received. The very day I wrote to you, I heard from the Pope's Mæstro-di-Camera that His Holiness had most unexpectedly assigned me a pension of two hundred crowns. I had neither asked for it nor thought of such a thing. Knowing this, I went at once to find Father Philip, who, it turned out, had already heard the news; and I told him I was prepared to do exactly as he wished, and either refuse or accept the pension, or even make it over to Messir Antoniano to refund the expenses of the church. I made this offer knowing that the Father had, only a short time ago, asked His Holiness for something wherewith to pay that priest. However, the father would not listen to any of these offers, and bade me accept the pension, and go at once to thank His Holiness; which I did. The Holy Father was very affectionate to me; but of that I had better say no more, lest I should seem to boast. I protest before God, *portio mea sit in terra viventium.*[7] Afterwards, by command of His Holiness, I dined with the Mæstro-di-Camera, and, thinking that he might have suggested the matter, I thanked him; but he declared that he had never mentioned the subject, and believed that His Holiness had done it entirely of his own accord, having been pleased at learning that I had refused the three hundred crowns from Portugal. This is all that occurred then.

---

[7] "Let my portion be in the land of the living." -Editor.

"Afterwards I spoke to Father Tomaso [Bozio], and told him that though the pension was given to me personally, I wished to hold it in common with him to defray his literary expenses. At first he refused, but I was so urgent that at last he consented. I did not make the same offer to Father Antonio [Gallonio], as I knew that he was not in need of it. All that has taken place has caused some little envy on the part of His Holiness's retainers, who say that none of them have received such a large pension. They say the Holy Father has shown me most marked favour. To God be the glory, *nobis confusio faciei.*[8] You see by this the renewal of the usual miracle : as our sufferings in Christ abound, so also do our consolations abound in Him."

To the amazement of Baronius he received the announcement three months later that Clement intended to grant him an additional annuity of two hundred crowns. "When I heard this, I confess I was astounded," he writes to Talpa, "and many difficulties in the way of accepting the pension occurred to me. I wrote at once to Frascati to ask the Mæstro-di-Camera to thank His Holiness, but to tell him at the same time that I stood in no need of further assistance, as what he had already given was quite sufficient for all my wants, and that it was not fitting that I should abound in wealth, nor edifying that one belonging to the Congregation should be thus loaded with annuities. I have had no reply to this letter, but Father Pompeo, when he returned from Frascati, said that the Mæstro-di-Camera had duly conveyed my message, but that His Holiness- had replied: 'It is our wish

---

[8]   "But to us confusion of our face." Baruch 1:15.

that he should have abundance, and more than he needs, so that he may get on the more quickly with the work he has on hand.' To this the Mæstro-di-Camera replied that I had already more than I needed, but then His Holiness said: 'Advance it to him then, and he can spend some of the money on the place at Frascati.' For he has seen our house there and was pleased with it. The Mæstro-di-Camera added that His Holiness had been much pleased at my refusing the five hundred crowns sent by the Bishop of Coimbra. I must tell you in confidence that not only did that Bishop refuse to pay any attention to my letters, but he replied to me with his own hand, and actually sent a policy for the five hundred crowns, which, in spite of his instance, I refused to accept. But I cannot think how His Holiness came to hear of this." Thus to the praise of friends and the adulation of strangers there were added these expressions of enthusiastic appreciation on the part of the Supreme Pontiff, more insidiously dangerous to the humility of Baronius than the grossest flattery.

St. Philip might discontinue one mortification after the other when he saw the perfect spirit in which Cesare received them; but nevertheless he remained anxious to the end. Shortly before he entered into his reward, the Saint called Baronius to him. "Cesare," said he, "know that you have much to be humble about, and especially about your writings, which are not the fruit of your own learning, but solely and manifestly the work of God." "Yea, father," replied Cesare, "I know it well. All that I have written I owe to God and to your prayers." Thrice did the Saint repeat his words, and thrice did he draw from his son the same answer, the same protestation of humility. Having done this, St. Philip was satisfied. He had done what he could on earth to mould the workman of the

Lord; and then he passed away to perfect his work from heaven.

When, in reply to his holy father's anxious questioning, Cesare replied that he owed everything to God, he spoke only what he felt to be the simple truth, and gave utterance to the thought which was ever uppermost in his mind. His sense of dependence upon God and the spontaneity with which he attributed to Him everything that he was, or was able to do, shine out conspicuously on those few occasions when his humble reserve allows us to peep behind the veil. He did not often reveal his inner life on paper, but at rare intervals in his correspondence with Father Talpa he broke out into spontaneous confidences, which go far towards supplying the general lack of details about his interior state and show how, all throughout his laborious, distracting and absorbed life, the one thought of the presence of God and his own total dependence upon Him reigned supreme. "I believe," he writes on one occasion, that "my work is directed by the hand of God rather than by my brain. I have experienced this more than once. *Ipsi gloria in sæcula.*"[9] "As for what you say in praise of my work," he says again, "I know for certain that everything I write is a visible and sensible gift of God. Sometimes, when I begin to write a difficult part, God suggests to me words and ideas which I had not thought of before. His be the honour and glory, if so be He deign to help me. I beg you all to join with me in trying to thank Him better, and pray that I may have light to see the manifest truth, and cast myself into the abyss of my own nothingness."

---

[9]   "To Him glory forever." -Editor.

116

So reticent was Baronius on paper about his own interior experiences, and so loth was he to write about himself, that though his devotion to our Blessed Lady was so great that—mindful of his mother's dedication of him—he looked on himself as her special property, he rarely alluded on paper to this great devotion. Each volume of his Annals was, however, placed explicitly under her protection in what he calls "his usual peroration;" and he habitually printed a monogram composed of the letters C.S.M. in his books and on his papers, explaining it as signifying *Cesare servus Mariæ.* "I receive everything through the intercession of the Blessed Virgin," he wrote to Talpa in a fit of rare confidence on this subject. "She protects me and my affairs, and especially watches over every word I write. She directs my pen, and does not suffer me to remain long in affliction."

Through all his labours, researches, correspondence and interviews Baronius had a rare gift of keeping himself in the presence of God. The thought of God was that to which he returned as his home and rest the moment the immense strain of exterior work was removed. Nor indeed did he wait for the strain to be removed, for through it, and because of it, he lived sensibly before God. On those rare occasions when exterior distractions threatened to disturb his peace, he checked and bridled himself by such words as these: "*Contine te domi, Cæsare; siste domi,*—keep at home, Cesare; stay at home," and, thus self-rebuked, he cast from him all disturbance of mind. Without this rest in the presence of God he could not have lived under the pressure of his work. He never sat down to write without invoking the Holy Ghost, and placing himself under the protection of our Lady; and even while he wrote he uttered aloud favourite ejaculations, mostly from the

117

Psalms. The words most constantly on his lips were: "O Israel, how great is the house of God, and how immense is the place of His possessions!" Something in these words supplied a want of his soul, and, by the thought contained in them of the majesty of God, lifted him out of the monotonies and dust of life; and whether he lay awake in his bed at night, or whether he were poring over manuscripts and unearthing the facts of centuries, these words sprang spontaneously to his lips. He used, moreover, to write down bits of Scripture and short prayers on the fragments and parings of parchment which he cut from his sheets, and lay them on the table before his eyes. Such passages as these from the Psalms are still existing on these scraps: "He hath set my feet upon a rock and directed my steps." "Thou art my portion in the land of the living." "O Lord, my portion, I have said I will keep Thy law. He hath exalted me upon a rock, and now He hath lifted up my head above mine enemies." It is to be remarked that the same common note of exultation runs through all these ejaculatory prayers by which Baronius sanctified his work. It was in truth given to him—whenever the will of God allowed him time to lift up his heart, and leisure to rest his thoughts in Him—to feel unmixed joy, comfort and elation.

He placed his great work in an especial manner under the protection of St. Peter the Prince of the Apostles, as Vicar of Christ. His one object in writing the Annals—its keynote, in fact, manifest on every page—was the exaltation of the Holy See, and the demonstration of the primacy of St. Peter and his successors from the time when our Lord made him chief Pastor of His Church. Every document Baronius studied, every manuscript he unearthed, elucidated this great truth to himself, and his object was to impart his acquired knowledge to the world. So undisguised was this intention that the enemies of the Church writhed under his words, and pronounced that his book ought to be called the Annals of the papal power rather than those of the Church. His devotion to the Holy See was one with and inseparable from his devotion to the Prince of the Apostles, and he fought all his life for its liberties. For this object he braved public opinion most fearlessly, and sacrificed his worldly prospects in its defence. How little he could disconnect St. Peter and his successors in his own mind is illustrated by the opening words of his dedication of the first volume of the Annals to Sixtus V. "To you, Holy Father," he says, "do I dedicate these first fruits of my labours, to you the Vicar of Christ and the successor of the chief of the Apostles. It is as if I dedicated it to St. Peter himself, and through him to Christ."

He gloried in anything and everything which marked him as belonging to and depending on the Holy See. At that time the German and Swiss heretics had begun to give Catholics the now well-known name of Papists. Baronius accepted the name and adopted it with exultation, saying that no name could be more glorious for a Catholic to be known by, and that he would like it to be inscribed as an epitaph on his tomb. It reminded him of the ancient though equally glorious nickname of "Romans," bestowed by the Arians on Catholics.

Every day of his life for thirty years, however busy he might be, and totally regardless of heat or cold, rain or wind, Baronius made a visit to St. Peter's. Having first given an alms to the beggars who crowded the steps, so as to secure their prayers, he went to the bronze statue of St. Peter, as well known to those who visit Rome now as it

119

was to him. Kissing the foot and placing his head under it, he would utter the ejaculation *Pax et obedientia*; and then, having thus offered himself and his work, he made this act of faith, "I believe in one holy Catholic and Apostolic Church." It was Baronius who in this way introduced the devout custom, now so widespread, of kissing the foot of this image of St. Peter; and his imitators were so many that even in his lifetime the bronze foot began to be worn away. Then, going to the confession of the Apostles, he threw himself on his face before their tomb and prayed for the needs of the Church with such emotion that when he rose to his feet his eyes were red with weeping. As he left the Basilica, he paused before the Navicella—Giotto's fresco of St. Peter walking on the water—which met his eyes in the portico, and offered up this prayer before it: "Lord, who didst deliver Peter from the waters, save me from the waters of sin;" and after this, with strength renewed, he returned to his room and took up his daily burden.

Pope Sixtus V

King Henry IV of France

CHAPTER XI
Henry IV

O N the 30th of January, 1592, after three brief pontificates extending together over only two years, Cardinal Aldobrandini, the devoted friend of the Oratory, and a penitent for many years of St. Philip, was elected Pope under the name of Clement VIII It may be said that with his accession to the chair of Peter peace and tranquillity of mind took their departure from the life of Baronius and that from that moment the hidden life which he loved so well, and which he contrived to lead in spite of the turmoil of his correspondence with the outer world, was at an end. For four years, since the publication of the first volume of the Annals, he had striven against the publicity and universal notice which it had drawn on him. It had been a struggle, but so far it had been successful and, thanks to his energy of will, he had thrice escaped being made a bishop. Even before his name had become famous by the publication of either Martyrology or Annals, Gregory XIII had fixed on him for the See of Sora, being probably moved thereto by the machinations of Cesare's kinsfolk. Later, Sixtus V wished to appoint him to the See of Teano, and Gregory XIV to that of Sinegaglia. To both these Pontiffs Baronius pleaded, and successfully, that if he were raised to the episcopate he could no longer continue the work of the Annals; and, fortunately for him and for the world, his great work was too near the hearts of both Popes to allow them to turn a deaf ear to such an appeal.

From henceforth, however, Baronius's struggle against publicity was to be hopeless, and each year, as it came round, dragged him further from his seclusion. St. Philip, who was now seventy-seven years of age, felt no longer equal to holding the office of confessor to Clement after he was raised to the papacy, and suggested Baronius as a substitute for himself. The Saint knew that this connection with the papal court would be most antipathetic to Cesare, but he had the interests of the Church too much at heart to deny to the Pontiff an adviser so well calculated to help him in the great work for God which he was to effect in his pontificate. It has been, moreover, suggested as an additional motive for his action that, foreseeing Clement's designs for the promotion of Baronius, he considered that the choice of him as confessor would anyhow act as a check on his being raised to the episcopate.

Baronius did not accept the office without a protest, and once more alleged the incompatibility of such a position with the progress of the Annals, but the Pontiff exhibited in this case that pertinacity and strength of purpose which on every occasion proved too strong for Cesare's powers of resistance. He, however, admitted the force of Baronius's argument so far that he contented himself with asking his presence for one hour every evening, and left him perfectly free for the rest of the day. For some reason Clement changed this arrangement later, and demanded his attendance in the morning as well, though he did so apologetically. "The fatigue of going every morning to the Quirinal is coming to an end," Baronius wrote to Talpa, "and I find that the arrangement is intended to last for only a short time. His Holiness does not employ words of command towards me, but pursues a method which has more force, for he prays me, with the greatest humility, to remain at Monte Cavallo, and not forsake him. He also (I blush to record his words) asked my pardon for putting me to inconvenience. So you see how I am situated. For ten days he has been laid up with his usual gout, but he still wishes me to go to him every morning, for if he cannot stand to say Mass, he desires to receive Communion."

It is recorded in the life of St. Philip how Clement, after a vain attempt to induce the Saint to receive a Cardinal's hat, lost no time in promoting his companions. First Bordini was made bishop, and then the Pope's choice fell on one still dearer to St. Philip, and through him he commanded Tarugi to leave Naples and come to Rome. The Saint knew well enough what such a summons portended, and probably communicated his fears to Cesare. With the latter, however, the desire to see Tarugi, and the delight at the prospect of once more dwelling under the same roof with him got the better of the forebodings conjured up by his recall to Rome. "As to the coming here of Father Francesco Maria," he wrote to Talpa, "it seems to me that it amounts to a command from His Holiness so that if he could without injury to his health come soon, I think it would be pleasing to God. I do not see how His Holiness could force him to accept the episcopate, and if he has any higher dignity in store for him, absence will not save him. If he were to come at once it would give edification for every one knows that His Holiness has sent for him. However, I want to have him here, so, perhaps, I do not speak dispassionately. May God's will be done in all things." Tarugi did come to Rome, and, in spite of Baronius's optimism and his own resistance and diplomacy, he was raised to the archiepiscopal See of Avignon. Cesare had yet to learn the strength of Clement's will.

For some years before Cardinal Aldobrandini was made Pope, Europe had been agitated by the question of Henry of Navarre's right of succession to the throne of France. It is a matter of history how a Catholic league was formed in that country to exclude him, on the score of his being a Huguenot, from any right to the crown. When Henry III was assassinated in 1589, the approximate danger of a Protestant claimant to the throne became a reality, and the burning question which had moved the Christian world reached its climax. So strong was the detestation aroused by the thought of a heretic sovereign being seated on the throne of St. Louis, that the Catholic party joined hands with Spain, the hereditary enemy of their country, as a means to avert the disaster. Philip II was not one to waste this opportunity, and, in defiance of the Salic law, which limited the succession of the crown of France to the male line, he claimed it for his daughter Isabel, by right of her mother, who had been sister to the late King.

This question troubled the last years of Sixtus V, in whose breast the hope of Henry of Navarre's conversion as a settlement of the affair fought with his fierce horror of the thought of a heretic on the throne of France. He hoped against hope for Henry's conversion, declaring that he would be willing to go on his knees before him to gain it and this hope made him strong against the persuasions and semi-threats of Spain. On his granting an interview to Henry's envoy, the Duke de Luxembourg, the Spanish ambassador, Olivarez, carried his expostulations so near the verge of insolence that the fiery old Pontiff dismissed him summarily from his presence, saying that no prince had power to dictate to the Pope. Yet Sixtus wavered, and when death overtook him he was still in the dilemma whether his fear of quenching the smoking flax ought to make him turn a deaf ear to the haughty demands of a secular power which claimed to be the uncompromising champion of Catholicism.

No like resistance did Philip of Spain meet with from Sixtus's three successors, Urban VII, Gregory XIV, and Innocent IX. Through Cardinals devoted to his interests and pliable to his will, the Spanish monarch practically controlled their election. In each case he named seven candidates, declaring that he would accept no Pope unless chosen from those seven; and in each case one of his nominees was elected, who, by predisposition, threw the whole weight of his influence against Henry. Gregory XIV, a most holy man, who had led an ascetic life far from the world, espoused the cause of the League and Spain as though it were a crusade, emptied the coffers of St. Angelo of the gold so carefully collected by Sixtus V during his pontificate, subsidized the Parisians in their resistance of Henry, and equipped an army which he sent into France under the command of his nephew, Ercole Sfrondrato. But Gregory lived for only a year after his election, and his successor, Innocent IX, died in a few weeks; so that in less than two years after the death of Sixtus V a fourth conclave was assembled, which Philip of Spain sought to control in the same way as those which had preceded it. This time the object of his interference was frustrated, for, though the name of Cardinal Aldobrandini had, for the sake of appearances, been added to the list of those of more decided Spanish sympathies which was presented for selection to the Cardinals, it was destined that in him, when he ascended the Chair of Peter, Philip should find a Pontiff whom he was unable to mould to his will.

In spite of his firmness of character Clement's position was very difficult. Even had he felt sure that his recognition of Henry would be for the good of Christendom, he found himself, whether he would or not, pledged to the cause of Spain and of the League. His legate was in Paris, avowedly devoted to the interests of Philip and the papal troops were in France opposing the army of Henry. It was impossible for the new Pontiff to recall either of these, and, as it were, unsay what had been said by his predecessors. It is true that Henry now, partly by policy, and, we may venture to say, greatly by conviction, expressed his readiness to be reconciled to the Church. But, unfortunately, he had once before submitted, in order to save his life after the massacre of St. Bartholomew, and had subsequently returned to his heresy and Spain was not slow to point out with insistance to Clement that it was impossible for him to give absolution to a relapsed heretic. All this had weight with the Pope, but if he hesitated, as he did, for three years to restore Henry publicly to the communion of the faithful, it was not from fear of Spain, "whose domineering ways," as he said, "were becoming oppressive to the papacy," but because, however great might be his conviction of the advantage to Christendom of Henry's reconciliation, he could not bring himself to believe in the king's sincerity. He confided to the Venetian ambassador his conviction that Henry never would be sincere, but would remain *hereticus relapsus*[10] to the end.

---

[10] "A relapsed heretic."

Nor did time alter his opinion, though Fleury steadily professed his allegiance to the Catholic Church, and, pending the public recognition which he hoped to obtain from the Holy See, was in 1593 reconciled by the Archbishop of Bourges, conditionally on his future absolution by the Supreme Pontiff, this proviso being necessitated by the nature of his case, as that of a lapsed heretic. In spite of this proof of Henry's honesty of purpose Clement still hesitated, and protested anew to those who pleaded the cause of the King of Navarre that he would not believe in his sincerity unless an angel from heaven came and whispered it in his ear.

No angelic messenger was sent to clear up the Pope's doubts but there was a saint at his very door who acted the part of mediator. Humanly speaking, the peace and balance of Europe would not have been restored when they were, had not St. Philip been in Rome, with his great disciple at hand, not only to be his mouthpiece, but to throw the whole weight of his own influence over Clement into the balance in favour of Henry. St. Philip's far-seeing sympathies were entirely with the French King, and he made no secret about it. As for Baronius, his conviction of the justice of Henry's cause, based on and confirmed by the judgment of the Saint, was invincible. He was possessed of an almost romantic attachment to and belief in the King of Navarre and a story was current that when he was shown Henry's portrait he kissed it enthusiastically. It must be admitted that one strong motive of his partizanship was detestation of the interference of Spain—a detestation which would have been directed with equal strength against France, had she been the culprit, as she had too often been of old, and had sought to domineer over the papacy. Baronius had but recently lived through the four conclaves, and it was no secret how Philip II had tried, and in three cases successfully, to influence the elections. So strong was Cesare in his convictions as to which was the right course for Clement to pursue, that when St. Philip was dissuaded by such members of the Sacred College as Cardinal Borromeo and Cardinal Cusano from speaking his mind to the Pope, Baronius, with holy liberty towards even the Saint, implored him, and effectually, not to listen to the words of men, but to speak as his conscience bade him.

Never through all his life could Baronius, whether wisely or unwisely, look at anything in the light of expediency, but only and solely in the light of principle. He, for his part, had no misgivings as to Henry's sincerity. He believed in his protestations of fidelity to the Church, and felt that not only was the salvation of the king's soul at stake, but also the peace and balance of power in Europe. Therefore he strained every nerve to accomplish the desired end. He redoubled his penances, as was his wont in times of public emergency, and fearlessly sought to move the Pope's will. Bernabei, in his life of Baronius, says that he cast himself at the Pontiff's feet, and pleaded the cause of Henry simply and solely as a case of conscience, without a thought for anything save the interests of religion, the welfare of the Church and the salvation of souls. The part he was playing was well known to the partizans of Spain, and he received ominous warnings that his life might be in danger if he persisted in trying to influence the Pope. Cesare, however, was not a man to be moved by threats; and to those who sought to intimidate him he boldly replied that he would be only too happy to give his life for the glory of God, the peace of the Church and the salvation of souls. His desire for martyrdom was a reality, and the menaces received made him stronger than ever in his partizanship.

He did not confine himself to the use of persuasion. Turning to account his vast knowledge of historical precedents, he drew up on paper all the reasons in favour of Henry's reconciliation; and this document had considerable influence in Rome. Paruti, the Venetian ambassador, says in his despatches to his government: "Men think that the Pope is very much influenced by Padre Baronius, author of the famous Ecclesiastical Annals, who is at present confessor to His Holiness. He has drawn up a statement addressed to His Holiness which I have contrived to see. His chief object is to prove that the King of France should be admitted to confession and reconciled to the Church on his profession of repentance. He concludes his statement by citing many instances from history and extracts from the decrees of Councils, demonstrating by precedent that if the King be willing to confess his errors it would be unlawful to refuse him absolution. Although the decrees against relapsed heretics are most severe, still he shows that it is in the power of the Pope to restrain and limit their application. In answer to the objection made that the King is insincere in his professions of contrition, the writer says that all arguments must be based on the assumption that he is speaking the truth, for that God alone can read the thoughts of the heart. Opinion generally is in favour of Padre Baronius's arguments; but the Spaniards are very active on the opposite side; and their theologians pursue the Cardinals, armed with fresh objections and knotty points. Solemn processions have been made throughout the city to implore the Divine grace for a favourable decision of the question."

While Baronius thus threw his energies into the cause of the King, St. Philip worked through him, and one day—it must have been during the last weeks of his life—he sent a message by Cesare to the Pope, telling him that if he would absolve Henry, he would himself undertake to answer to God for it. Some years afterwards, on an anniversary of his blessed father's death, Baronius alluded to this incident from the Oratory pulpit. Among those present in the church was Cardinal Duperron, Cesare's confidant and Henry's adviser during the whole transaction. Baronius appealed to him from the pulpit to bear testimony to the truth of his statement, and Duperron, rising to his feet and raising his berretta, said that he was but too willing to confirm it.

Still, however, Clement hesitated; and it was given to Baronius to bring him to a decision. In the strength of his convictions he boldly declared that he would no longer hold towards him the position of confessor if he delayed to grant absolution to the King. This uncompromising boldness staggered the Pope; and he turned with renewed fervour to prayer for guidance in this great decision. Paruti, the Venetian ambassador, relates that on the feast of our Lady's Nativity, nine days before he took the final step, Clement went barefoot in the early morning from the Quirinal to St. John Lateran. There, having visited the five privileged altars, he said Mass, and then went up the Scala Santa on his knees. From thence he went to Santa Maria Maggiore, where he prayed with great fervour. Having administered Holy Communion to his household, he preached to them and exhorted them to pray to God to guide him in this matter of the King of France, protesting that in everything he had done about it he had had in view only the glory of God, the good of religion and the salvation of souls. He wished that his tongue might shrivel up if he spoke anything but the truth.

On September 17, 1595, nearly four months after St. Philip had entered into his glory—where without doubt he was working for the welfare of Christendom as he had been unable to do on earth—Clement, casting aside all fear of either offending Spain or giving scandal to over-zealous Catholics, conferred solemn absolution on Henry, represented by Cardinal Duperron and Cardinal Ossat; nor did he ever repent of his decision. Duperron, when free to do so, went to Paris to give Henry a full account of the memorable scene in Rome, and wrote an account to Baronius of what took place: "On the 19th of this month, His Majesty, in the presence and at the hands of the legate, ratified all that we had promised in his name before the Pope, and explicitly added a declaration of adherence to all that the Bull contains. He did this so joyfully that all present were delighted. When he was given the roll to sign, some one suggested that he should have a table brought on which to rest it. 'No, no,' he replied in a loud voice, 'my hand will not tremble when I sign; for I am taking no false oath!' I tell you this, knowing how pleased you will be on account of your affection for His Majesty and for France."

We can trace in this letter marks of the close friendship which existed between Duperron and Baronius, a friendship which owed its origin partly to the deep interest which both took in the affair of Henry's absolution, and partly to the similarity of their tastes, and the literary efforts directed by both against the modern enemies of the Church. With Henry IV himself, Baronius kept up a casual correspondence; and the letters of the King clearly show the gratitude which he felt towards

Cesare, and contain in so many words the acknowledgment that he was indebted to his intervention with the Pope for the happy turn taken by his affairs. He frequently begged him to continue his good offices in the same direction, and offered in return to give him anything and do anything for him in his power—offers which, as stated above, were invariably declined by the great son of St. Philip. On one occasion Baronius sent a protege of his, named Taboul, to Paris with a letter of introduction to the King, and Henry regarded the implied request for patronage as a personal favour to himself, and could not do enough to befriend the man.

What pleased Baronius far more than all the King's protestations of affection towards himself were his repeated assertions of loyalty to the Holy See, and his expressed desire to tread in the steps of St. Louis and the worthier among his ancestors.

The historian dedicated the ninth volume of his Annals to the King of France, and in a letter drew his attention to the noble Christian deeds of Charlemagne and others, and implored him never to degenerate from their example. "Mon cousin," the King wrote back, "I have received with thanks the beautiful volume of the Ecclesiastical Annals. By describing therein the piety and devotion of the Kings of France, my predecessors, and the courage with which they worked for God and His Church, you testify to the affection which you bear me and my kingdom. You have indeed proved your affection in other ways, as has been related to me by the Count de Sillery, my ambassador. I wish, therefore, to thank you and assure you that your good will towards me is precious in my eyes, as coming from one whom I greatly venerate both on account of his exemplary life and because of his great learning, which fills the Church of God with admiration. I assure you that I will take to heart your good advice, and bear it in mind so as to excite and strengthen within me the desire and intention with which God has inspired me to imitate the virtues and zeal of my ancestors; for I am by inheritance the most Christian King, and the eldest son of the Church. I wish to prove myself worthy of the many favours I have received from the goodness of God, and to devote myself and my strength for the glory, liberty and exaltation of the See of our Holy Father the Pope and the Sacred College of Cardinals. And should the occasion ever arise when I could be of service to yourself, or to any one whom you may commend to me, you will see the proof of my good will towards you." Henry never lost an opportunity of extolling Baronius to others and when he died insisted on attending in person the Requiem Mass offered up in Paris for the repose of his soul.

CHAPTER XII
Disturbances Within and Without

I F Henry of France was aware of and duly grateful for the share taken by Baronius in the successful issue of the momentous affair recorded in the last chapter, Philip of Spain was by no means oblivious to the part played by him in thwarting his plans. His resentment against the great historian dated back some years before the absolution of Henry for, previous to his connection with either papal court or politics, while he was still leading an undisturbed life at the Oratory, Cesare had expressed his disapproval of the arrogant claims of Spain with a freedom which had offended her king.

The third volume of the Annals, written, though not published, during the pontificate of Gregory XIV, had been, by the advice of St. Philip, dedicated to the King of Spain. Baronius knew instinctively the disfavour with which he was regarded by the latter, and looked on the dedication of the book to him as a very tentative measure. "I took the King's preface to the Duke of Sessa," he wrote to Talpa in 1591, "and he, after keeping it for eight or ten days, pronounced it excellent, and could suggest nothing either to add or omit. His theologian, a most learned man, told me that he, too, had read it and highly approved of it. Deo gratias that these perilous waters have been so safely navigated. The Duke asked me to send the King not only the third volume but also the first and second. This will be very expensive." However, notwithstanding the politeness on the part of his representatives, Philip never even thanked Baronius for the dedication of the volume. At the time Cesare said nothing about it, and it was only in 1597, six years afterwards, that this act of discourtesy transpired in a letter, in which he urged the Naples fathers, in their own interests, to mention their connection with him as little as possible in their dealings with the viceregal court. "For," he adds, "I must tell you that I received neither written answer nor verbal message of thanks from the King for the third volume. Nor was any notice taken of a letter which I wrote to him, such as is customary for Cardinals when raised to the purple to write to all the sovereigns. I can smile at this, nay, even rejoice, *propter magnam justitiam ista pati.*"[11]

Ere long the Spanish authorities showed their displeasure with Baronius in a way which was more tangible and injurious than the empty rudeness of leaving his dedication unacknowledged. After he had been connected with Clement VIII for about two years, when the question of Henry's absolution was becoming very burning, the news fell on Baronius like a thunderbolt that the Ecclesiastical Annals had been put on the Index by the Spanish Inquisition.

"Rome is talking of nothing but this censure that has been passed in Spain on the Annals," he wrote to Talpa on the 29th of June, 1594. "Several people have spoken to me about it. Now that it is a public matter, I will reveal to you a secret which I have told no one. A certain unmarried woman of Terna has been my penitent for many years. She is the simplest of creatures, totally devoid of idle curiosity, and has received from God a wonderful gift of

---

[11] "I have suffered these things on account of great justice." -Editor.

138

foretelling future events. One morning in the confessional this person gave me what purported to be a message from the Madonna, namely, that I was to prepare myself for a great trial; and she earnestly repeated her words. I wished to know what kind of trial it was to be, whether sickness, calumny, or what other kind. She replied without binding me to secrecy that the trial would not be sickness, nor would it be calumny against myself, but against the Annals; and that I was to be subjected to a very severe trial on their account. I thought no more about her words, for I could not conceive from what quarter such an attack could come, seeing that the book had met with general approval. However, on the very same day, in the morning of which what I have told you occurred, Father Germanico, with whom I am very intimate, came to my room and told me sub sigillo this affair about the Inquisition. I was stupefied, all the more as this woman knows nothing about my writings in particular; and the fact that she told me what she did so very opportunely, on the very day that I heard the news, has made me think that she was suffering under no delusion, but rather acting by divine monition. I should have told you that after she had spoken she added the injunction to stand firm and fear nothing, because the Madonna would help me, and told her that I should triumph in the end. This is what took place, but let it be *sub secreto*:

"I cannot take any steps in the matter till I know about it both more circumstantially and more certainly. I have, however, done this much. Seeing that the matter had got wind in Rome, I took the opportunity to talk about it, half jestingly, to Cardinal Borromeo, the Prefect of the Congregation of the Index, and also to Cardinal Cusano. They have both offered to help me, and bid me fear nothing. His Holiness has so often expressed his approbation of the Annals that I feel sure he will protect them. I have fear of only one thing, which is that the Cardinal of Toledo may gain his ear. I have found His Eminence so full of contradictions that I have even asked myself whether all this may not be his doing. However, I will not affirm this, lest I should be judging rashly. I have heard that the Spanish Inquisitors put books on their Index *ad libitum,* just as it pleases them, without assigning any reason; and this custom is universally found fault with. I have the greatest faith that the Madonna will defend my cause. As soon as I receive authentic information, I shall go to His Holiness and point out to him that the Spanish Inquisition has done this solely because I stand up for the liberties of the Church. I am confirmed in this opinion by what took place in the last year of the pontificate of Pope Sixtus. A book written by one John of Roas was published in Spain. It was directed against the liberties of the Church, and was approved by the Council, dedicated to the King, and signed by one of the Inquisitors; but it has been lately placed on the Index here in Rome on account of the blasphemies it contains. You can see from this what sort of spirit is prevalent among the Spanish Inquisitors; and these being the facts, I think that His Holiness will protect and defend my book. I say to those who speak to me on the subject that there is not really any different opinion about the book held in Spain from what there is elsewhere; all the more as the Master of the Sacred Palaces, who has read all I have written, is a Spaniard and a most learned and scrupulous man.

"But God tempers the bitter by the sweet. A book was sent to Rome written by a learned Fleming, who in a long disquisition about all historians, whether Christian or pagan, arrives at the conclusion that I hold the first place among writers of ecclesiastical history, and speaks most honourably of me. I think His Holiness has seen this book; or at any rate he has heard it spoken of. To God be all the glory. Let us go on praying, and leave other people alone."

This affair, the expression of petty spite against one who had the courage to speak the unpalatable truth, died a natural death, and left the reputation of the Annals absolutely untouched; but it all tended to prove to Baronius that his days of hidden life were over, and that, in spite of himself, he must mix himself up in politics. Against his will he had to take sides; and, while one great power lavished affection on him, he incurred the dislike and vindictiveness of another; and both these results of his fearless fidelity to principle were equally distasteful to him. Nor were the disturbing influences of public affairs all that ruffled the surface of his life; for the course that events took in the Oratory, simultaneously with these exterior agitations, troubled him even more than they did.

For the last three years of his life at the Vallicella, Baronius was Superior of the Congregation. In 1593 St. Philip made up his mind to resign that office, so as to spend his short remaining span of life relieved from the burden. When he laid this determination before the fathers and asked their consent, they one and all refused it. How could any of them, his early companions, imagine life in the Congregation without St. Philip as their father? He then entreated them to accept his resignation; but even for his sake they could not bring themselves to make the sacrifice. Seeing that all he could say was useless, the Saint, still firm in his purpose, had recourse to Cardinal Borromeo and Cardinal Cusano, and asked their help in overcoming the loving obstinacy of his sons. In these two, less interested than the fathers, he found warm supporters. On July 7, 1593, they addressed the assembled Congregation, and told them that their Father Philip entreated them to yield to his wish to spend his remaining days in peace and quiet. "He will not," they went on to say, "cease to be your loving father and help you before God. His desire is that you should choose in his stead Father Cesare, the senior in the Congregation, and the eldest of his spiritual sons. The Holy Father agrees that Father Philip should resign, and that Father Cesare be chosen in his place."

There was a dead silence when the Cardinals ceased speaking. The fathers knew that they would have to yield, and Baronius at last lifted up his voice. He said that further resistance was useless, and they must give Father Philip this last proof of their love. But on one thing he insisted as a right, namely that he himself should not be made superior in the informal way proposed; and he claimed that the election should be carried out according to the constitutions of the Congregation. There was reason in this request; and as St. Philip did not press for an immediate release from his duties, the two Cardinals consented to whatever delay was necessary. The election had to be made by the two houses of Rome and Naples, for they formed but one Congregation, and were under one common superior. So an exact account of what had taken place was sent to Naples, and the election deferred until letters, or some of the fathers in person, could arrive in Rome. It was on July 23 that the election took place, with the result that Baronius was unanimously chosen by both houses; and St. Philip said that he should now die in peace as he left the government of the Congregation to Cesare.

As to the latter, when the fathers went up to kiss his hand as their new superior, he sent them to kiss first the hand of the Saint. Then he embraced all the fathers, exclaiming, "We are brothers—brothers!" He could think of no better words by which to show that as long as their Father Philip was in their midst there could be no further distinctions. For nearly two years Baronius had his holy father by his side, and he never arrived at any decision without taking counsel of the Saint, as whose mere mouthpiece and instrument he regarded himself.

There are but few details recorded of the manner in which Baronius filled the office of superior; but such few as exist are distinctive and characteristic. His long years of study, even though he had never been exempted from the various community duties, had caused him to live to a certain extent alongside rather than in the midst of the rest of the Congregation. Now, on being elected superior, the first thing he did was to study the rule in the crude form in which it then existed, and give his mind over to it as a special study. The part that his vow of humility played in his life, and the long and carefully acquired habit of obeying rather than commanding, made him somewhat over-diffident in his new office; and he made it his practice to govern by example more than by precept. He was never known to direct any members of the Congregation to do anything which he was not first ready to do himself. A young father, for instance, begged, on the plea of his time being taken up by his studies, to be excused from reading the notices before the sermon. Baronius did not, it is true, grant the request, but ignoring, with rare humility, how more than fully occupied he was himself, undertook when necessary to fill the young father's place. "Do not let this trouble you," he said. "At any time that it is really inconvenient to you to read the notices, tell me freely, and I will do it for you." True to his vow of humility, and governed by the modesty inherent in all really great minds, Baronius was never forward in offering an opinion or tenacious in holding it. He was so genuinely desirous that the right thing and that alone should be done, that he was unusually ready to admit the force of any argument brought against his own conclusions; and, without the shadow of a thought of self, generously admitted any error of judgment on his own part. Two faults in government, however, are recorded of him. His own truthfulness was so transparently pure that he could never bring himself to believe that any one uttered an untruth or even an exaggeration. There were busybodies in the Congregation who made mischief by putting the conduct of individuals before him in a wrong light. Baronius never stopped to examine the truth of these accusations, but believed them and acted on them, and often, therefore, corrected without cause. He was, moreover, hasty of temper, which, though he had brought it under wonderful control by dint of long combat, made him at times over-severe. He was, however, always ready to make humble and generous amends for any act of impatience, and not only craved the offender's pardon, but did everything in his power to remove any sting which might remain. Often did he lie flat on his face in the church, imploring God's pardon for his hastiness.

None of these disturbances either from without or within affected his application to his great work. He published the fifth and sixth volumes of the Annals during the first two years of his tenure of the office of superior, and this in spite of a stringent rule which he imposed on himself of never permitting his literary work to interfere with his duties in that capacity. He always obeyed a summons which called him from his work, as if it were the voice of God.

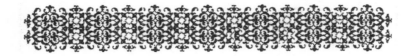

CHAPTER XIII
The Hanging Sword

MUCH as the events described in the last chapters may have marred the tranquillity of Baronius's life, they were not the principal agents in the disturbance of his peace of mind. During these years he was the victim of a constant dumb, and sometimes acute, dread of the dignities which the Pope might have in store for him. Nor were his fears groundless. Clement had openly declared his intention of proving his love for the Oratory by the promotion of the sons of St. Philip. It was only some unknown words, whispered by him into the Pontiff's ear, which saved the Saint himself from the dreaded purple, and not all St. Philip's expostulations and entreaties were able to save Tarugi and Bordini from being torn from the Oratory to be made bishops. Well might Baronius and well might his holy father tremble lest his turn should come next. For a time he found comfort in the manner in which Clement loaded him with one pension after the other, with the sole object of enabling him to make progress with the Annals. If the Pope had the completion of the work so much at heart, it was scarcely likely that he would put wilful obstructions in its way. The hopes raised by this aspect of the case were, however, doomed to be shattered; and it was scarcely a year after Clement's elevation to the papacy, and only two months after he had compelled Baronius to accept a second pension, that grave rumours were spread abroad throughout Rome as to the Pope's intentions towards him.

"I must tell you in confidence of certain plans for me of which His Holiness privately informed Cardinal Paravicino," Cesare wrote to Talpa in December 1592. "I am too bashful to describe more fully what these plans are. I had in consequence formed a project, which I confided to Father Giulio, of hiding myself in our house at Frascati; but I gave up the idea as it occurred to me that I should be compelled to return here on account of the Annals. Then I asked myself whether it would be advisable to hide myself in Rome for a few days, but came to the conclusion that neither of these plans would avail to avert the danger. The best thing I can do is to unite with some spiritual people whom I know intimately, and offer up fervent prayers that God may remove this thought from the mind of His Holiness. God has so loaded me with His favour that the conferring of any worldly honours would detract from rather than increase my dignity.

I have also to consider the peril attached to that kind of thing, as well as the impediments which it would put in the way of my writing the Annals, to say nothing of the scandal which would be taken, and a multitude of other valid objections which suggest themselves to me, all of which tend to show me that it would be better for me to remain as I am than go up higher. I have great faith in Sister Orsola, to whom I give you leave to communicate all I have written but speak of it to no one else. Ask her to obtain from the holy Mother of God that I may be permitted to remain as I am. Forgive me for troubling you with all these things, which fill me with confusion but I wish to leave nothing undone which could help me, should the blow fall."

Just ten years before Baronius wrote thus to his friend, Sister Orsola Benincasa, to whom he refers, had come to Rome with, as she affirmed, a message from heaven to Gregory XIII, by which he was urged to proceed more vigorously with the reformation of the Church. The Pope had delivered to St. Philip the commission to test and try her, and prove whether the spirit which governed her was the Spirit of God. Baronius must, undoubtedly, have witnessed many of the Saint's crucial trials of this servant of God, in which, maybe, his holy father had employed him as his instrument. Be this as it may, the result of his experiences was that he trusted in Orsola's prayers as in those of a saint.

There is but little doubt that elevation to the purple was the danger alluded to in the letter last quoted. On that occasion the peril passed away, but less than two years after, in 1594, it was renewed. This time the Pope made St. Philip the confidant of his designs on his son, and the Saint, in his turn, confided his forebodings to Baronius; and the latter poured out his woes to Talpa in language which shows how intensely his repugnance to the dreaded dignity had increased during the last two years. He wrote thus:

"I must tell you a secret of the same nature as that which I confided to you on a former occasion; and I tell you in order that you may help me by your prayers and by obtaining those of others. *Ne nos inducas intentationem.*[12] A few days ago Father Philip called me to him privately and told me that he had had an interview with the Pope, who informed him that he had a serious intention to make

---

[12] "Lead us not into temptation." -Editor.

me etc., etc., etc., as he had once before told him he would. On that occasion the father had withstood him, so this time His Holiness put it before him in the form of a resolution. Hearing this, I threw myself at the father's feet and prayed him to prevent it if it were possible. I gave him leave to say anything he chose to His Holiness as to my incapacity, my ignorance, and such like deficiencies, if he thought it likely to make the Pope change his mind. Nor would I get off my knees until the Father had promised to do this. I do not know what he has done, or what has been the result. I moreover begged him, if His Holiness were quite resolved to promote some of us, to suggest Monsignor of Avignon [Tarugi]. This is exactly what took place. I must tell you that I have heard the same report from other quarters; but I do not attach much importance to that sort of rumour. I tell you this in confidence, and I pray God that I may die rather than offend Him even venially. You know better than I do the state of the Congregation, and you know the trouble I have to keep things going even as they are. I am nearly fifty-six years of age; my hair is quite white, and it seems to me that death cannot be far off, for I am completely worn out by my labours. So this is not the time to dissipate my mind with matters for which I have no aptitude. Rather is it time to retire within myself and weep for my sins, *antequam vadam et non revertar.*[13] I know, also, the envies and detractions to which I should be exposed. I ask your help and counsel."

Two months later he wrote again: "Acting on your advice, I have once more protested to Father Philip and

---

[13] "Before I shall go and not return." -Editor.

told him that I will hold him accountable at the Day of Judgment if he does not put every possible impediment in the way of this affair. I know not what he will do, for he answered me ambiguously. But I hope in God, and I beg you of your charity to pray to Him to give me grace to wait and prepare for death."

Once more the storm blew over. Perhaps the Pope put aside all present intention of making Baronius a Cardinal, or of in any way removing him from the Oratory, entirely in condescension to St. Philip's wishes, and to avoid giving him pain. Nevertheless, the Saint probably knew that all intervention would be ultimately in vain, and that, sooner or later, the dreaded blow had to fall on Cesare. This was, no doubt, why he responded ambiguously to the latter's entreaties. Indeed, in an era when Popes had placed themselves at the head of the revival of Catholic literature it scarcely required the prescience of a saint to foretell that a man like Baronius would be raised to the purple.

For years St. Philip had had what may be called a presentiment that both Baronius and Tarugi would be Cardinals. On one occasion General Aldobrandini, a nephew of Clement, not yet Pope, expressed his surprise at finding two Cardinals' coats of arms in the Saint's room. "What!" replied St. Philip, concealing, as was his wont, the inspirations of God under the veil of a jest "and do you not know that after my death two of the Congregation are to be Cardinals?" Often, no doubt for the purpose of teasing him, he would place a red beretta on Cesare's head and as far back as twenty years before his death, ere Baronius was known to the world, he spoke of him as a future Cardinal. On the strength of this prediction Father Neri, of the Society of Jesus, asked the Saint if he thought Cesare would ever be Pope; and St. Philip's prompt reply was,

151

"Cardinal, yes; but Pope, no!" In this prediction, most completely verified, the Saint was guided neither by natural reason, nor by the probability of things for once Baronius was raised to the purple, there seemed every likelihood of his further elevation. As will be seen later, at both conclaves held after Clement's death and during his own lifetime, his election was more than a probability, and was, humanly speaking, averted only by the desperate efforts to which his humility drove him.

Terribly scared as he was for a time by the current rumours of his elevation, Baronius's low estimation both of himself and of the position he held in public opinion enabled him to forget his fears as soon as their immediate cause was, for the time, removed. However, his alarm increased tenfold when, early in 1595, the Pope insisted on his accompanying the papal court on its annual holiday expedition. This was the first occasion that such constraint had been put on him, and he took the Pope's persistence as the very worst of omens. "I am not, as the saying is, bound by one leg," he wrote to Talpa on April 14 in that year, "but I have a cord placed round my neck, and I am led whither I would not go. I can unite my voice with those who said: *Cervicibus minabamur nostris, et lassis non dabatur requies.*[14] The Holy Father, knowing through the *Mæstro-di-Camera* that I usually go in the spring to Frascati for a little holiday, has begged me to go with him instead this year as far as Nettuno and other places, which will keep us away till Ascension Day. If the weather permit, he means to start on Monday. See to what I have

---

[14] "We were impelled by our necks, and while weary, no rest was given us." Lamentations of Jeremiah, 5:5. -Editor.

come in my old age; for to have to follow the court is a proceeding most antipathetic to both inclination and vocation. I am, in truth, filled with bitterness and sadness; and more than the trouble of the actual moment I dread the future. I see no means of escape, though the mighty hand of God is strong, and able to do all things. I pray Him that if it be for His honour, and if there be no other way out of it, I may be set free by death. Far rather would I die than have to pass my old age at the court, which would imperil my salvation to no slight degree. I hope that you too will pray in this spirit. My trouble increases, for 'I am become a stranger unto my brethren, and an alien unto my mother's children.' Pray to God that He may deliver me from the devil who walketh at noonday, who changes himself into an angel of light, and who, under pretence of benefiting me, would rob me of the better part."

Before leaving this more hidden portion of Cesare's life to follow him along those rougher paths trodden by him after the dreaded blow had actually fallen, it is well to try and catch what few glimpses are afforded us of his inner life while he was still in the Congregation, and seek to penetrate the occupation of his thoughts apart from the Annals, so far as his close application to them, enforced by his holy father, allowed him leisure of mind. There were times when over-work brought a cloud of despondency over his usually bright spirit, and created a doubt within him as to whether he were serving God in the way really intended, and whether, instead of consuming his life, pen in hand, he ought to be spending it for God in some other way. We know that he wished to go to Milan; and over and over again he would have given much to be at Naples. Doubtless he thought that in either of those places he

153

would have found to hand more direct work for souls than it was given him to do in Rome.

One of those to whom he at times opened his heart and showed himself as he was, was de Marquais, Abbot of St. Martin's. From a letter written to him by the latter we can gather that Baronius had, in a fit of despondency, confided to his friend his misgivings as to the real value of the Annals, and his fears lest the absorptions and distractions of his life as a historian should make him neglect the care of his own soul. "Do not be cast down," wrote the Abbot in reply. "Eat the bread of life and drink of eternal wisdom; and so will you more easily reach the Mount of God. You have not got to live for yourself alone, but for the Church of God and the good of your fellow men. Acquit yourself manfully, and your heart will be comforted, and God will sustain you. Truly it belongs to our mortality to be filled with fear when we look forward to the day of our judgment; but perceiving as we do so many earnests of our eternal happiness, and experiencing as we do the work of the Spirit of God within us, why should we be anxious and tormented of soul? Be of good heart, my Cesare, and think of nothing but of persevering until you have completed your work, which is so pleasing to the Church, and which will live for ever. When it is finished, then by all means devote yourself solely to the thoughts of eternal life; and I feel confident that at the last day the just Judge will give to you, who have worn yourself out by your labours for Him, a crown of justice."

Bodily fatigue had much, if not everything, to do with these fits of discouragement. After the completion of his first volume Baronius completely broke down, and in October 1588 St. Philip sent him to Monte Cassino for rest and recreation. He had constantly hoped to spend at

Naples any holiday granted to him, but he wrote to Talpa from Monte Cassino that he was too worn out to attempt the journey there. After this break-down he took an annual holiday at Frascati every spring, in the house belonging to the Congregation; and while there he put away all thought of anything but God alone, and in Him found the rest he needed. A tablet in the church at Frascati, inscribed to "Cesare Baronius who used to come here for retirement while engaged on the Annals," connects his name with the place; but more living was the memory which lingered there of how he employed his days of repose. Those who had known him handed down the tradition of how he used to wander about the woods, lifting up his heart to God by holy ejaculations, and how he would at times cast himself flat on the sward praying aloud, and at others throw his arms round the trunks of the trees, embracing them in the fervour of his love.

It was rarely that Baronius confided to paper any descriptions of his interior trials, and still less frequently did he indulge in anything like self-pity. But here and there in his correspondence we come across a few words which reveal the secret of the increasing fatigue with which he laboured, which sanctified his soul while it slowly consumed his life. In 1592, before his work had reached its climax and before he was carrying it on under the crushing difficulties which afterwards beset it, he thus wrote to Father Bencio of the Society of Jesus, who, in writing to him, had apologized for troubling so busy a man. "Your letter found me, I will not say burdened, but simply prostrated by work. But believe me when I tell you that although, as you but too rightly fear, I be weighed down and oppressed; your words proved a solace to me and served the purpose of David's harp, the sweet sounds of which drove the evil spirit out of the hearts of men, and restored them to a better mind. As regards your solicitude about my health, I know that my hold on life is precarious, and is prolonged solely by the prayers of my brethren."

It was not only the actual labour of his researches, correspondence and compiling which was wearing out the life of Baronius. Could he have approached his work light-heartedly it would not have thus consumed his strength: The contrary was the case for the sense of the responsibility of an ecclesiastical historian lay heavily on him, and at times he was almost scrupulous in his fears lest he should not be doing the work as perfectly as he might. To him the profession of a writer on divine things was a sacred office which must be approached with pure heart and clean hands. The similitude of such a writer to Bezaleel, the workman of the Tabernacle, often occurs in the pages penned by Baronius and he enlarges on the idea in his dedication to Clement VIII of the sixth volume of the Annals—the last completed and published in St. Philip's lifetime. "No man," he says, "however distinguished in intellect or excellent in virtue, is sufficient of himself to handle sacred things. This is clearly demonstrated in Scripture by the example of that artificer who, though employed on only the mechanical structure of the place wherein God was to be worshipped, was declared by Moses to be thereby specially united to divine things. The Lord has filled Bezaleel with the Spirit of God,' said he, with wisdom and understanding and knowledge and all learning, and to work in gold, silver and brass, and in engraving stones and in carpenter's work. Whatever can be devised artificially He hath given in his hand.' Yet Moses adds that even this work, so well done by aid of the Holy Spirit, was not to be used for God until it had been blessed. If then he who handled only the materials intended for the future service of God had to be himself given to God, how much more is expected of him on whom falls the burden of expounding those things which belong to the truth of the Church. Without doubt he should be ever filled with the Spirit of truth, so that he may complete his work standing firm in the truth."

Docile as was Baronius to the will of God, which destined him to spend his life in His service in a manner uncongenial to his nature, his aspirations remained uncurbed, and he was often possessed by a generous desire for martyrdom—a longing to prove his faith by his blood rather than his pen—which broke out at times in fervid words. "I have said, and I always will say, O Lord," he writes in his Annals, " behold, I come, ready, if Thy grace permitted it, to testify to the truth of Thy Church with my blood rather than with my pen; for no voice is more powerful than the voice of blood, which, being shed, cries out from earth and reaches unto heaven."

It may be said that Baronius lived in an atmosphere of martyrdom, as indeed do all even to this day who tread the sacred soil of Rome watered by the blood of the soldiers of Christ. All things combined to make the sense of this especially vivid to the mind of Baronius. St. Philip's long hours in the catacombs before he began his apostolate could not have been without an effect on the minds of his sons and disciples. Since that time, and contemporary with the commencement of the Annals, the catacombs had been opened out, their treasures revealed, and their relics and inscriptions examined. "Rome was astounded," writes Baronius, "to find in its midst, beneath its very suburbs, concealed cities once dwelt in by Christians in the times of persecution, and still full of the tombs of the martyrs." His own researches had familiarised him with those early heroic ages, and while he wrote he lived over again the lives of those who had suffered for the faith. Nor, in his day, was martyrdom or the occasion of it a mere historic fact, belonging to past ages or connected with remote parts of the world, as it is now with us. In the lifetime of Baronius, Catholics were actually shedding their blood for the cause of the Church in England, in Poland, in Germany and in the Netherlands. Those with whom he corresponded dwelt on hallowed ground, and their words filled him with a holy envy. In answer to the Bishop of Roermond, who had described to him the sufferings at the hands of heretical persecutors experienced by Catholics in the Netherlands, he thus poured forth his soul in burning words: "What can I say of myself? I sigh and groan in my desire to weep with you, and with you shed my blood. Woe to me, who stand idle and useless in these times of cruel assaults! It oppresses my soul that while others are being ennobled by a glorious apostolate in the Indies, and while the crown of martyrdom is being won by soldiers of Christ fighting in the ranks of the Church, I, a miserable sinner, weighed down by my burden, am like to that servant who could not dig and was ashamed to beg. Would that I could say with him: 'I know what I will do!'"

CHAPTER XIV
The Year of St. Philip's Death

ALL through this portion of Baronius's life, with its fears, its passing fits of despondency and its hesitancy as to the will of God, his holy father was with him, "guarding him by his vigilance and governing him by his counsel." Indeed, looking at Cesare's life during those years in the light of what we now know it to have been, we cannot even imagine it without that constant aid, too sacred to be made known to others, secret and silent as the voice of conscience or the whisper of guardian angel, withheld like them from the gaze of man, although, without their hidden prompting, each one's soul would be void. But the days were coming when St. Philip was to be taken from him; though like the other fathers Baronius was slow to understand that he must leave them ere long. Such a thought was only fit to be cast behind him before it was even framed; and yet at times it insisted on making itself heard.

"I feel for you," he wrote to Talpa in December, 1592, "for I too am troubled with the same thought as you. It is only lately that it has seemed true that we have to lose our blessed father." These words were written when the Saint was recovering, from that severe illness during which the Congregation thought from moment to moment that his soul would take its flight, and after which he insisted on giving up the office of superior. Yet when the end came it took them all by surprise. The end did come, as we all know, on May 26, 1595. On the night of the 25th he knew the time was at hand and told his sons so in words which they could not or would not understand; and then he sent them to their rest. But Father Gallonio heard him moving in his room, and hastening to him found him dying. It was Cesare who commended his soul to God and sped it on its way to heaven; so too when the Saint, sitting on his bed, uttered no word, it was he who cried out: "Father, and are you leaving us without even a word?" And then their father opened his eyes once more, smiled and raised his hand a little—and then left them.

Baronius had small doubt that his holy father had passed to the vision of God; but it was an index to his simplicity of soul and loyalty to the Church, whose voice he would not forestall, that he had a solemn requiem Mass celebrated for the repose of St. Philip's soul; and public prayers were said for him at the Oratory, while outside in the city, men were already proclaiming him to be a saint. However, in the solitude of his own room Cesare could no longer act a part, nor could he coerce his will to say a *De profundis* for him whose intercession he felt impelled to ask. He turned in his dilemma to God and earnestly besought Him for guidance; and having prayed he, full of faith, opened his breviary at random, and his eye lighting on the words of the seventy-ninth Psalm, *Respice de cælo*, etc., he accepted them as an answer to his petition for light. Hesitating no longer, he took up his pen and turned the words he had read into that prayer so familiar to all the clients of St. Philip, but which, however familiar, no one who attempts to tell the life of Baronius could leave unrecorded.

"Look down from heaven, holy Father, from the loftiness of that mountain to the lowliness of this valley, from that harbour of quietness and tranquillity to this calamitous sea. And now that the darkness of this world hinders no more those benignant eyes of thine from looking clearly into all things, look down and visit, O most diligent keeper, that vineyard which thy right hand hath planted with so much labour, anxiety and peril. To thee then we fly; from thee we seek for aid. To thee we give our whole selves unreservedly; thee we adopt for our patron and defender. Undertake the cause of our salvation, protect thy clients; to thee we appeal as our leader. Rule this army fighting against the assaults of the devil. To thee, kindest of rulers, we give up the rudder of our lives. Steer this little ship of thine, and, placed as thou art on high, keep us off the rocks of evil desires, that, with thee for our pilot and our guide, we may safely come to the haven of eternal happiness. Amen."

On the day of the Saint's death Baronius commissioned Father Pateri to write and announce the news to the Naples fathers perchance his heart was too full to let him write himself. But the day after he supplied the omission, and in his letter there is a ring of orphanhood which no one can fail to perceive, combined with a tone of valiant effort to grapple with the almost impossible task of facing life and coping alone with the exigencies of the Congregation. "Yesterday," he writes, "I sent you by a special messenger the news of the happy death of our blessed father Philip, who is now in heaven interceding for us. Now I add a few words for your consolation, to tell you that we here are all united, steadfast, and settled in great peace. We are all resolved to persevere in the same spirit of union and charity in which our blessed father conceived us, begat us, and brought us up. The advice which those who wish us well have given us is to follow in the footprints left by our blessed father

161

and we believe that you also will continue in the same mind, proceeding from the same source. We are sending you the chapter which our blessed father left us as his last testament in the days of his convalescence from his last illness but one, to be the foundation of the whole Congregation. It has been examined by us and approved in repeated Congregations without one dissentient vote. Nor do we doubt that you, as his sons and heirs, will accept that which the holy and blessed testator committed to us as his last codicil. I have no time to write more, being beset by the numerous visitors who come to condole with us. His Holiness offers to confirm our Constitutions if we can gather them together; so, if you remember anything, please let us know. The blessed father told me especially to write and tell you to pray fervently for the needs of France and Hungary. Do so, and commend the same intention to Sister Orsola."

St. Philip was dead. He who for well-nigh forty years had guarded Cesare by his vigilance and governed him by his counsel had passed to heaven, and left him, in the words of one of his own favourite similes, rudderless on the great depths of the ocean. At no point of his life had he been more in need of help; and this his holy father knew but too well, betraying his anxiety of mind by the thrice repeated question which he put to him shortly before his death. What was to happen to Cesare now? With his "stern exactor" no longer by his side, with his vow of obedience to him a dead letter, what was there left to act as spur or bit? The work which he had undertaken unwillingly, and solely at the call of obedience, was now a delight to him, and the labour which had at first been so irksome had brought its own reward, and was a matter of such keen absorption that his chief contrariety lay in his inability to devote more time to it. He was, more over, fifty-seven years of age. All remnants of youth had fled, and with it those aspirations after more active work for souls, by the mortification of which his sedentary labours had been sanctified. What then, humanly speaking, was to save Baronius now from the selfishness and crotchets of advancing years? What was to prevent his becoming a mere book-worm, with the holiness of his work forgotten in the natural passion for study?

Cesare knew his necessities, and the perils likely to beset his path; but a remedy was ready to his hand. In the solitude of his room, in the first hours of his bereavement, he had lifted up his voice to his holy father and implored his protection; and we can with confidence assert that from that moment to his last hour he led his life under the shadow of St. Philip's guidance. When, three years afterwards, he manifested his soul to the world in the dedication of the eighth volume of the Annals, he was but putting on to paper that which had been the voiceless cry of his heart from the moment his holy father left him. "Now from heaven where thou dwellest, give me still stronger aid, and let thy perfect and consummate charity succour me still more; . . . so that, still holding the reins of my life, thou mayest guide what remains of my old age that it stumble not." Such was Cesare's appeal to his holy father, and truly it was not sent up in vain.

At the distance of three hundred years we can see the helping hand held out to Baronius; and the workings of grace are so manifest that it would be impossible to mistake them. But few things in his life are more striking than his inability to recognise the help as such when it was sent to him in answer to his supplications. While safeguards against surrounding perils and means for the

163

sanctification of his state were being showered on him, he ceaselessly cried to God to remove them as so many impediments to his salvation, so many dangers under which his soul might succumb.

Cesare's soul had raised itself heavenward by his obedience and suppleness to the touch of the Saint. The blessed days of obedience to him whom he loved were no more, but God with scant delay supplied the want, and placed his neck under a yoke not of his own seeking, submission to which destroyed what relics of self remained. The interruptions of those living in the world have been likened in their effect to the call of the bell in a religious house; and truly such summons was not to be lacking during the remainder of Cesare's life, which was to abound in relentless interruptions and distractions of the most antipathetic kind, to which those contrived by the ingenuity of his blessed father were as nothing. The writing of the Annals was obviously the work which he was called to do for God; but so torn in twain was he by his life of wearying and ignoble distractions, by the imperative calls of senseless etiquette and social amenities, whereby no soul was apparently benefited, that he made but poor progress with his work; and in spite of the aid of secretaries and servants, whom he had never employed before, he found it more difficult to produce a volume in every two years than he had found it previously to produce the same in half the time.

It was probably solely on account of his affection for St. Philip that Clement listened to his remonstrances and took no further steps during his lifetime about the promotion of Baronius. After the Saint's death, however, he lost but little time before conferring on him a dignity destined to lead almost immediately to the cardinalate.

Baronius was, however, possessed of such a happy gift of dismissing anxiety that in spite of previous panics, and in spite of the continued mutterings of Roman gossip, he threw himself into his double duty of superior of the Congregation and annalist without even a latent misgiving as to the Pope's intentions. He had no care except concerning the completion of his seventh volume, already overdue by some months, and destined, as it turned out, not to be published for more than a year after his holy father's death.

Thus, when the blow fell—gentle as it was at first—it took him quite by surprise, and well-nigh crushed him by its suddenness.

There exist few autobiographical narratives more graphic than that contained in a letter written by Baronius to Talpa on December 3, 1595, describing the manner in which the dignity of apostolic protonotary was forced on him. The account would lose if not given in its entirety: "I scarcely venture for very shame to take up my pen to write to you," he begins; "for I have tidings for you which, while they cause me confusion, will fill you and the fathers and brothers with pain. Behold the lightning; but now the thunder has to follow!"

"On Monday evening, November 20," the narrative continues, "His Holiness, having made his confession as usual, seated himself, contrary to his custom, in his chair of state, as if about to perform some pontifical action. Then he began thus: Father Cesare, we desire a favour of you, namely, that you will not refuse us that which, being desirous of your services, we are about to ask of you.' Thus he went on, speaking in these words and others equally modest and humble. I, having a presentiment of evil, interrupted him and would not wait for him to finish.

'Blessed Father,' said I, 'Your Holiness fills me with fear by such an *exordium* (preface). Who does not know that I would always serve you without being thus entreated? His Holiness then went on to say that he wished to confer on me the title of protonotary, which he considered suitable to the profession of the writer of the Annals; and that, as there was now a vacancy among those dignitaries, he wished to give it to me. I replied warmly that the Annals had been received with favour in all parts without my bearing such a title, so that there was no necessity to confer it. If, however, His Holiness were determined to make me protonotary, let him consider it sufficient to confer on me a merely nominal dignity, as he had done in the case of Galesino. The title, I persisted, with no obligation to wear prelatical robes, would be sufficient. He must not for one moment think that I could accept any dignity which would necessitate my dressing as a prelate: such a thing would confer no honour on me, but would cause shame and scandal. I told him that several ecclesiastical dignitaries had come from Germany and other parts to visit me, and having found me in a threadbare and shabby cassock had told others that they had been filled with more admiration by this than they were by the Annals themselves, as they had pictured me to themselves as being surrounded by servants, magnificently dressed and scarcely approachable. This and much besides did I say to His Holiness; till he, perceiving such opposition on my part, fulminated the terrible decree that I must submit by holy obedience."

Even then I was not silent, and complained at his issuing such a command without even giving me time to think; and I told him that it was not customary to act in such a manner by any one. I quoted the case of the

Cardinal of Avignor, to whose protests he had listened more than once, whom he had summoned to his presence several times, and whom not until he had done so had he commanded by holy obedience to submit. And I besought him to give me a little time to think and pray. But he replied that it was enough. He had been thinking the matter over for some time, and had offered up many prayers, and said Mass for this intention, and had made up is mind. When I repeated my supplication he did not even listen, but repeated his command by holy obedience. This had such an extraordinary effect on me that it took away my power of speech; so that when I tried once more to defend myself, I stammered and my voice trembled, and I was unable to express my ideas. Seeing my distress of mind, His Holiness laughed, and renewed his command in the same terms. But even then I tried to defend myself, and seeing that he would not listen to arguments I had recourse to entreaty; but neither was this of any avail. However, seeing that he could not force my consent, His Holiness changed his tactics somewhat, and rang the bell; and behold there entered the Mæstro-di-Camera and Mgr. Diego, carrying with them a bundle of purple prelatical robes. His Holiness, rising from his seat, ordered that I should be bereft of my habit, and that when I was robed I should be taken to the next room, where he would await me, and would give me the rochet pontifically. All this took place in his study where he had been to Confession.

"When the Pope had left the room the two gentlemen set to work to remove my cloak by force, which I with equal force tried to fasten round me. This contest went on for some time, for I declared that I could not endure the shame of returning in a different garb to the house, which I had left as a simple priest. From the violence of my

167

emotion the perspiration poured from me so as to saturate my shirt. Perceiving at last that I could not fight against two, I threw myself on the ground and besought them to entreat His Holiness for at least one day's respite; and I declared that I would return next day and do as he wished. I promised not to take flight. These gentlemen had compassion on me, and one of them went to place my petition before His Holiness. He came back into the room and reproached me; and, though he consented to the delay, he said that he did so unwillingly and was much annoyed. I was not to think, said he, that I should escape, for he had quite made up his mind. He then dismissed me and I left his presence not a little sorrowful—so much so that the change in my countenance caused surprise to all the attendants.

"Father Germanico had that evening accompanied me to the palace; and when the *Mæstra-di-Camera* left the room I took him aside and told him what had taken place, begging him to bear witness to the fathers how resolute the Pope had been about this matter. I must tell you that His Holiness, seeing how upset I was, and wishing to pacify me, told me that he did not wish me to leave the Congregation, nor change in any way my present mode of life; and that he desired me to continue to preach and hear confessions at the Oratory as before. And when I complained how unfitting it would be for me to have a retinue of servants, he said he would be satisfied if I kept two. When, furthermore, I told him how great was my repugnance to wearing purple robes, he gave orders that though they must be shaped like those of a prelate they might be made of black material. I could not persuade him to dispense me from being dressed as a prelate whenever I went outside the house, for he said that to do otherwise would give cause for complaint to the whole body of protonotaries. At first he exempted me from attending the chapel but as an afterthought excluded certain solemn days from this exemption.

"I returned home late, and without saying a word to any one I went to the Father's tomb and prayed him instantly to help me in this hour of need, even as he had when living helped me ofttimes in my necessity. Then I called a congregation of the fathers, and related to them the whole tragedy; and they were greatly dismayed and affected by the unforeseen misfortune. We discussed what could be done, and it was resolved that next morning two of the fathers should go on behalf of the Congregation and beseech His Holiness to take the needs of the house into consideration. Cardinal Cusano was requested to approach His Holiness with the same petition; and he offered to obtain the intervention of both Cardinal Paleotto and the Cardinal of Florence. But none of these arrangements could be carried out, for early next morning Mgr. Diego arrived, bringing the purple robes with him, and bearing a command to me from His Holiness to put them on at once. Mgr. Panfilio and the Abate Maffa came with him into the sacristy, together with several other gentlemen; and these, acting in concert, unclothed me with violence and robed me against my will. *Convertat Deus monstra in bonum.*[15]

"I declare that I was covered with confusion, and the more my honours increase so much the more shame do I feel. During these last few days several Cardinals have been to visit me, and others have sent their gentlemen to call on me. At home I wear my habit, and have an

---

[15] "May God convert the monsters into good."

169

ordinary room, though the fathers would like to give me an additional one. This, however, I refused to have. As to the servants I have added only one and he lives outside; the other is my secretary. Every morning I am in my confessional for at least an hour as before; and I also preach as usual in the Oratory. In short, here at home no one could guess from anything I do that I am a prelate. I have forbidden the fathers to call me Monsignor, but Father, as before. In the afternoon when I go out, but only to the palace, I wear my black prelatical robes. But it has happened that others who have the same dignity as I, have complained of this, seeing that a purple robe is ordained for use; and the Pope, having heard of this, told me most modestly that it would be well to avoid singularity.

"I forgot to tell you that when I argued so warmly with His Holiness, he told me that I ought to be very grateful that he did not take me away altogether from the Oratory, and that I should remember how he had acted by Monsignor of Avignon, and had better rest satisfied. But even then I could not be silent, and protested that I had far rather he sent me to the Indies or to England to work for the glory of God than make me go about Rome in prelate's robes. Whereupon he replied that I deserved to be punished for such resistance to holy obedience; and I retorted that it would be better to commit me at once to prison in the Torre di Nona than to send me back to the Oratory in such a guise. In short I perceived that, were it not that he held me in some respect as his confessor, he would have spoken more angrily; for indeed I gave him no slight occasion for displeasure by my overbold speech and lack of reverence.

"Behold, my father, what has occurred! *Periit fuga a me.*[16] As you love me pity me. Console the fathers, and may they forgive me for being a cause of sorrow to them. Even as matters stand now I am afflicted, and the fear of worse to come aggravates my affliction. I think it would not be unbecoming were you, in the name of the whole Congregation, to write to His Holiness under cover to the Mæstro-di-Camera, earnestly beseeching him to be satisfied with what he has done without going any further and placing before him the needs of the Congregation. There is much more about which I could write to you, but I am as one stunned."

Thus violently was this dignity thrust on him—a dignity hateful to him in itself, and more hateful because of the certainty in his mind that it was the forerunner of further promotion which would altogether sever him from the house of St. Philip. It is necessary to bear this presentiment in mind to understand the deep depression which took hold of him and the way in which he spoke and acted as if his life were over for without it, in spite of his antipathy to its robes and pomps, his present dignity might have sat lightly on him, entailing as it did no substantial change in his life.

---

[16] "Flight hath failed me." Ps. 141 (142): 5.

St. Philip appears to Baronius in a dream.

CHAPTER XV
The Blow Falls

T HE knife was in Cesare's heart, and the line taken by his friends aggravated the wound, for congratulations on what had occurred poured in from all parts from those who admired him and his works. The very answering of these letters from his friends was painful, for he was torn in two between his wish not to seem or be ungrateful and the pain, to say nothing of the humiliation, of receiving felicitations on what was the cause of keen suffering to himself. This internal conflict can be perceived in his answer to the Bishop of Ratisbonne, who had added a further sting to his congratulations by pointing out that such an accession of rank as his could not fail to lead to the Sacred College. "Your letter was pleasing to me," Baronius writes, "in that it proves that you do not cease to bear me in your mind and heart. As for me, however, I feel as if I were bound by fetters of gold, far heavier than were they made of iron; and, what is worse, I cannot glory in them as St. Paul gloried in his chains. You must know that this purple scorches a man who is advancing in years, nay more, knocking already at the gates of death. High honours are bitter to such a one; and all he desires is to be left quiet. He loves solitude, in which he may unite himself by contemplation to the things of God. I know that your prognostications are inspired by the affection you bear me; nevertheless, they are abhorrent to me and have filled me with sadness."

The flattering terms adopted by some of his correspondents hurt him still more keenly than their congratulations and predictions. Even Abbot Rescius, who was a real and appreciative friend, and whose affection for Baronius was based on a true knowledge of him as well as on his admiration for the Annals, even he could not refrain from honeyed words, and styled him in his letter another Moses, Jeremias, Esdras, Basil, and Gregory. Baronius's reply was couched in very plain language, and reveals the profound contempt in which he held himself. "When I read your letter describing me in such sublime language," he wrote, "those words of St. Gregory Nazianzen, 'Love causes deception,' occurred to my mind. This has certainly been the case with you, Rescius, for the great affection you bear me has evidently magnified me in your eyes; whereas, if you judged me rightly, you would see in me nothing but a despicable and miserable creature. As I behold myself more closely, I cannot listen without displeasure to the praises of my friends. I groan in the bitterness of my heart when I read such words as yours, and they pierce me as though they were so many javelins. Then I say to myself 'Cesare, those who call you blessed deceive you, do not believe them; rather believe yourself. He who lives inside a house can see how full its corners are of dirt and rubbish. You can see your poverty from within, and should be filled by the bitterness of gall and wormwood on account of the multitude of your sins.' Those who are outside, seeing the threshold adorned with wreaths, jump at once to the conclusion that one who is wealthy dwells within; but do not you, a prudent man, judge thus by appearances, for if you questioned the inhabitants of that house you would learn that within there are things to be found as evil as those of the Augean stables."[17]

Thus did Baronius write to his friends in the outside world, allowing his bitterness of soul to be perceived without purposely manifesting it. But to his brethren in the Congregation he wrote unreservedly. To Father John Ancina, B. Juvenal's brother, he who, in earlier and happier days was charged by St. Philip to sweep out surreptitiously the over-burdened historian's room, Baronius wrote as follows: "Remember me in your prayers, and beseech God either to deliver me from this burden, or else to remove me from the land of the living. If He will grant me neither of these petitions, may He strengthen me with a perfect spirit."

Still more unreservedly did he write to Father Juvenal: "I did not answer you sooner, because I was overcome by a most profound sadness by this new and unexpected calamity which has overtaken me, which the longer it lasts adds more and more to my shame and confusion. Would that He who makes the light to shine out of darkness would deliver me! I rejoice exceedingly to hear that you have taken time to reconsider your intention. The fathers here rejoice likewise, and do not cease to pray for you. O, happy are you who can take time to think; and miserable am I who, being thrown into the toils, have no fraction of time to myself; on which account I could weep,

---

[17] From mythology, the *Augean stables* were in the fifth labor of Hercules, in which he had to clean vast stables with where many cattle resided as well as defecated in a single day, though they had not been cleaned in over 30 years. Classical references like this were common and needed no explaining in Baronius' time, as well as the times of the author. -Editor.

and shall weep for eternity. Farewell. Have pity for me as you would for a man condemned to the gallows."

This letter was written under peculiar circumstances, and refers to B. Juvenal's renunciation of a purpose to leave the Oratory, about which it is necessary to say a few words. The whole family of St. Philip had been filled with sorrow and consternation by the effect produced on Ancina by the loss of their common father, from which they were all alike suffering. The hatred of the world caused by the death of him to whom he owed his vocation, and whom he loved so dearly, made Juvenal think for a time that God was calling him to leave the Oratory for a more severe life. This proposed defection was a fresh blow to his friends and companions, whose one idea in life just then was to carry out their Father's designs as faithfully as they could. Moreover, the Congregation was suffering under the loss of several of its most valuable members. Bordini and Tarugi had been taken from it, and the sword was hanging over the head of Baronius. All knew that their desertion was not of their own doing; but that one of St. Philip's sons—especially Juvenal—should, as soon as his back was turned, desire to cast off his habit, filled them with dismay.

It was with a mixture of grief and indignation that Baronius, the superior of the joint Congregation, wrote to Juvenal. "What have you done? May God forgive you. When I read your letter I trembled as if I had been overthrown by a thunderbolt. Are you so forgetful of yourself and of your brethren as to contemplate an action which would stamp you with the brand of fickleness and us with that of cruelty? You long for quiet? So be it; who denies it to you? How many corners are there in our houses, here, or at Naples, or at San Severino, where you

176

might seek it? Our Father did not leave you the example of deserting your post, and thinking only of yourself. On the contrary; even when he was eighty years of age he never lived for himself, but always for the good of others, by night as well as by day, even to his last hour. We ought to imitate him, beloved brother. Let it be our rest to live in many labours as behoves apostolic men. Let it be our highest glory to be able to say, 'I have laboured more than any.' And forget not that a grown tree cannot be transplanted into other soil without injury to itself. . . I conjure you to write to me again and restore peace to my soul, lest, stunned as I am already, I be overcome by excess of grief." Tarugi also wrote, and, after a struggle with the temptation, Juvenal renounced his purpose, and wrote to Baronius to tell him that he had done so. In the interval Cesare had been crushed by what had befallen himself, and was preoccupied by his misfortune. Thus, while welcoming the news, he poured out his own trouble to his friend in the letter quoted above.

During this period of fret and despondency Baronius was still holding the office of superior. He had hoped to be released from it at latest in the summer of 1596, when his three years' tenure would be completed; but after St. Philip's death he was re-elected, and confirmed in the office for another three years. He wrote to the Naples fathers saying that no one could describe how much he quailed under the thought of governing the house for three more years, especially now when he felt unusually incapable of bearing the burden. He implored the help of God, and protested that he was not fit to be a lay-brother in the Congregation, far less to be placed at the head of a community of which he was the most unworthy member. Little did he think when he thus cried out to be relieved of his burden that his release was to be effected by means with which he would have willingly dispensed.

Baronius lived through the first months of 1596 with the sword hanging almost sensibly over his head; yet, curiously enough, as it did not fall at once, he forgot that it was there. Partly by temperament, partly from the daily absorption of his work, as he strained every nerve to get his seventh volume through the press, he ceased to believe in the reality of the danger. "It made me laugh to read your letter," he wrote to Ancina, who could not so easily dismiss anxiety, "and to see that you fear that for which there is no cause whatever for alarm. May God deliver me from all other evils; as for this one I am quite safe. Do not so easily persuade yourself that asses can fly, even if they do wear trappings." Though, however, Baronius thus lightly dismissed his fears of any further elevation, he took some precautions, and begged Cardinal Paravicino to use his diplomacy, and if the Pope were really bent on promoting one of the Congregation to the purple, to direct his attention adroitly to Tarugi who, being already Archbishop of Avignon, would not be much injured by further elevation. "My counsel pleased the Cardinal," he wrote to Talpa. "May God see fit to carry it out. We must pray, for the heart of the king is in the hands of God."

Thus things went on till the time came round for Baronius's annual holiday at Frascati. There, in the month of May, St. Philip appeared to him by night in a dream or vision, and warned him to take heed to his salvation, as God willed something of him. This monition filled him with alarm, which was increased when he found on his return to Rome that the city was alive with fresh rumours as to his promotion at the approaching Consistory. Cesare could no longer ignore the imminence of the danger, and

178

in a panic consulted the fathers of both houses as to whether he would do well to seek safety in flight. One and all voted against such a step, and Father Talpa's answer, framed with his habitual practical common-sense, embodies the advice which was given by all. There was, in the first place, he wrote, nothing but rumour to act by, and if the Pope had no intention of making him a Cardinal, such an action on his part would be open to misconstruction, and attributed to eccentricity. Flight, moreover, could be no final remedy, for though it might avert the danger on this occasion it would only defer it. Were he to disappear altogether, it would give rise to scandal and misconception, to the injury not only of himself but of the Congregation as well. As to the Annals, it would be their destruction. The only thing to be done was to divert the Pope's mind from his purpose, and to obtain for this end the intervention of influential persons.

"I write thus before the event," Talpa continues. "It remains for me to counsel you should what we fear become an accomplished fact. The question is whether you ought to accept or refuse the dignity should it be offered to you by your superior. Before giving an answer, let us face the whole matter. We must presume that in all appointments the Pope has in view solely his duty, as Pontiff, and the satisfying of his conscience. And we must likewise presume that you are considering only what is expedient for you in your state of life, and that you wish to act according to your conscience, and judge how your salvation, which you must on no account imperil, would be affected by your decision. Both St. Gregory and St. Thomas say that one who is offered an elevated position should refuse it absolutely, and should persist in his refusal short of obstinacy, which is the vice opposed to

179

obedience; and that even this limit may be passed if there are involved neither disobedience nor opposition to the expressed and precise wish of a superior. In face of such obedience a man must humble himself with fear and trembling as did Moses; but he is bound to refuse explicitly unless an equally explicit obedience binds him.

"This doctrine is sufficient for general cases, but in your case there is another aspect to be considered, namely the injury which your elevation would entail on the Congregation. This aspect requires even closer study than the other, for in one case only the individual is affected, and in the other a body which includes the individual; and in this instance it is not a mere member, but its head which is concerned, the removal of which would stop the circulation through the whole body.

"You ask me to give you my sincere opinion, so I say that, supposing your interests as an individual were alone at stake, I, knowing you as I do, should not hesitate in my advice. I say that notwithstanding the efforts you have made to avert the blow, you should put your neck under the yoke at the mere call of your superior, without waiting for an express obedience. But, on the other hand, my regard for the interests of the Congregation forbids me to counsel anything short of absolute refusal within the limits of obedience. As regards this threatened loss to the Congregation, I trust that the Pope, once the circumstances are placed before him, will desist at once from his purpose, and will consider our irreparable injury rather than his own pious desire to provide the Church with strong pillars. Seeing that he is so rich in subjects, surely he will not need to rob the Congregation of its one ewe-lamb for his banquet. We must also take into our consideration the effect as a precedent on the actual and future fathers of the Congregation. All this being the case, I can but exhort you to be full of courage, and leave behind you an example of steadfastness such as was exhibited by the holy Eliezar."

Thus prepared, Baronius sought refuge in prayer, fasting and penances, hoping to avert the calamity, and vowed that he would make a pilgrimage, barefoot, to the seven churches if God would vouchsafe to grant his prayer for deliverance. His soul was full of a bitterness which manifested itself when any one dared to allude to what might be before him. Thus when one day some gentlemen, profiting by the rumours of his approaching elevation, requested him to take them into his service when he should be a Cardinal, his only response was to throw himself on his knees and pray to God aloud to remove the burden from him, and let him die rather than compel him to bear it.

As the decisive day drew near, authentic rumours reached the Oratory that Baronius's machinations had met with success, and that it was nearly certain that Tarugi would be raised to the purple. On the evening of June 9, the very day before the Consistory, Cesare returned from his usual visit to the palace full of joy and elation, and told the fathers that the Pope had openly declared his intention of promoting none of his relations, nor any members of his household, of whom Baronius considered himself one and that this exclusion removed all fear from his breast. His confidence increased when, during recreation after supper, Cardinal Sforza came in, bearing a message to the fathers from the Pope to the effect that it was his intention to give a Cardinal's hat next day to Tarugi. "Blessed be God and His holy Mother," cried Baronius, "the danger is past!" And so indeed it seemed. But even before Sforza had

181

taken his leave, Clement's nephew, Cardinal Pietro Aldobrandini, arrived, conveying a command to Baronius to remain at home next morning pending a summons to the palace to be himself made a Cardinal. Baronius turned pale and staggered as he stood, and all he could say was: "I thank you sincerely for bringing the message; but it is impossible for me to accept the dignity."

The Pope had put off going to bed till Cardinal Aldobrandini's return, and was anxiously awaiting Baronius's answer. He had not forgotten the scene that had taken place on a previous occasion, and he knew that a hard struggle awaited him now. When Aldobrandini repeated Cesare's words, Clement exclaimed: "I am not going to listen to anything. He will go on making excuses to the hour of the Consistory!" The Pope's mind was indeed made up, but his courage failed him at the prospect of the fight which lay before him; so he bade his nephew remain that night at the palace, in order to intercept Baronius should he try to approach him; nor would he retire to rest till he had given strict orders that Cesare was on no account to be allowed to go near him.

To return to the Oratory. As soon as Cardinal Aldobrandini had turned his back, Baronius, in spite of the lateness of the hour, called a Congregation. Having put everything before the fathers, he again suggested flight. But they unanimously declared that such a thing was simply out of the question, as no one so well known as he could conceal himself for long. It was finally settled that the only course to pursue was for him, accompanied by Father Fideli and Father Pateri, to obtain an audience with the Pope at a very early hour, which was possible for him, as, being a member of the papal court, he could demand access to the Pontiff's bed-chamber.

Cardinal Aldobrandini was still in bed when Baronius arrived at the palace, and there Cesare besieged him, declaring that he would not stir from the place until he had had an interview with the Pope. However, Cardinal Pietro was obdurate, being, indeed, afraid of his uncle's wrath; but when Cesare fell on his knees and besought him, his heart melted, and, regardless of Clement's express prohibition, took him to his room. When in the Pontiff's presence, Baronius threw himself on his knees before him, and asked permission to speak; which being granted, he poured forth words anxiously thought out in the weary hours of the terrible and sleepless night through which he had just passed.

"Do not, I implore you, Holy Father, crush me with this burden," he said, "for I am advancing in years; and, as I told you on a previous occasion, it has always been my intention, confirmed by vows, to end my days leading a hidden life in the Congregation. You know the pain you have already caused me by compelling me to clothe myself in these purple robes and, indeed, my pain increases every day. But now that you propose to snatch me altogether from the life I have hitherto led, I feel the burden too great to be borne. O where should I find strength to take up or even endure such a dignity? So unfitted am I for it, and so unworthy to be exalted that my fall will be great indeed, and my soul exposed to damnation. And even if this dignity be thrust upon me, it is impossible for you to ignore that the wisest and holiest of men have cast off such burdens and have fled to distant places and buried themselves in obscurity. And how about heretics? Will they not vilely insinuate that I wrote the Annals only to obtain honours? I know, Holy Father, that you wish to add authority to my writings by increasing my dignity; but the only result will be to give the enemy no slight occasion to accuse me of ambition. Even Catholics, who know how in my writings and sermons I have inveighed against the worldliness of seeking ecclesiastical preferment, if they see me not only Protonotary, but—which God avert—a Cardinal, what will they think? I know also, Holy Father, that you wish the Annals to be completed; but how can I work on them in the midst of the obstructions of strange duties? Do not, I implore you, Holy Father, snatch me from the haven in which I am, even from the bosom of my Mother, the Congregation, and expose me to the waves of a life of distractions, floating on which even the most skilful make shipwreck."

"No, no, Cesare," replied the Pope quickly. "We are not going to let you leave these walls except as a Cardinal. You must bend your will, for we have not decided thus without much thought and prayer." Clement would have fain avoided an interview with Baronius, and evidently shrank from the sight of the pain he was inflicting; but he had firmly made up his mind to listen to neither pleading nor petition, and was ready with an answer to every one of Cesare's arguments. "Have no fear for your salvation," said he, "as if sanctity could not exist in a high position. Our chief reason for conferring such a dignity on you is to show that it is quite compatible with holiness of life. The hand of the Lord is not shortened, and with the burden He will give you strength to support it. Let heretics rail as they will; let them censure and calumniate you as much as they choose; do you prepare your mind for the post. Pay no attention to what the world says; for a well armed man need not lightly fear attack. Truth always makes itself known at last, and it will become manifest to all men that this dignity was not of your own seeking. We know your inclination towards solitude and a retired life, but remember that none of us are placed in this world for our own sakes, but for the common good of all, and that very often our tastes have to be thwarted and disregarded. As for the Annals, we will take care that other business shall not interfere too much with your continuance of them. Therefore, submit yourself, and accept our will in everything."

Then, having said these decisive words, the Pope turned to Cardinal Aldobrandini and bade him take Baronius to his apartment and instruct him in his various duties. But Cesare could not and would not accept the verdict as final, and with loud lamentations passionately implored the Pope for the love of our Blessed Lord not to inflict such suffering on him. Then Clement, growing angry, and resolved to put an end to the scene, replied "Now, Cesare, you are indeed more obstinate then is becoming. You should submit yourself more calmly to our decision. Therefore, by our apostolic authority we now command you to submit under pain of excommunication," Cesare reeled under the effect of these words, as if he had been struck a heavy blow, and, painfully keeping back the words which rushed to his lips, he burst into tears. Then Cardinal Aldobrandini, taking him by the hand, led him like a helpless child from the room.

185

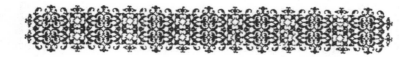

CHAPTER XVI
Its Immediate Effects

A FTER the Consistory, and when Baronius's fate was sealed, he was taken to the apartments which the Pope had ordered to be prepared for him, adjoining the Vatican library, and near Clement's own suite—a proximity which proved to be a fruitful source of interruption to his work. There Cesare shut himself up alone, and no man knows all that passed between his soul and God. Two things alone we know. During those hours of solitude he solemnly renewed his vow of poverty as far as it was compatible with the state to which he had been called; and he made another vow, faithfully kept under difficulties which will be related further on, not only never to aspire to the papacy, but to do all in his power to prevent his election to the See of Peter, and, with this object in view, never to curry favour with men of influence, nor let human respect keep him silent when he felt impelled to speak in the cause of truth.

The elevation of Baronius to the Sacred College necessitated the election of a new superior of the Congregation. The choice of the fathers fell on Father Angelo Velli, who, as soon as the election was over, went to obtain the Pope's blessing, and on his way visited Baronius to tell him what had transpired. At once Cesare knelt down and kissed his hand. Some present remonstrated, and tried to raise him from his knees; but, turning to them, he protested that as a priest of the Congregation to which he belonged, he was only doing what befitted him. Poor Father Velli, filled with confusion by this public scene, fell also on his knees, and tried to give the new Cardinal the honour that was due to him.

This little incident is but typical of the affectionate relations which Cesare kept up to the end with the Fathers of the Roman Oratory. His greatest solace was to go to them and act as if nothing had occurred to sever him from the Congregation. He said Mass when he could at the Vallicella, and gave Communion. He often preached in the church and sang Vespers in the choir on Sundays and festivals. He frequently dined with the fathers, not as a guest but as a member of the Congregation, refused all distinctions, and even joyfully took his turn in waiting. His greatest treasure, as he called it, was the key of his former room at the Oratory which he carried about him. The room was kept vacant for him, and, when he could, he went there for rest and refreshment.

Tarugi, severed as ruthlessly from the house of St. Philip as Baronius, likewise visited the fathers frequently and took part in the Community life though in this, as in still weightier matters, the differences in the temperament of the two Cardinals was manifest. Francesco Maria, who ever watched over Cesare in a semi-paternal manner, had misgivings lest, in his great love for the Congregation, he would entertain for individual fathers such particular friendships as might be contrary to the spirit of St. Philip. On one occasion, when both were supping at the Oratory, Tarugi, seeing Baronius take one of the fathers aside in the recreation room to speak privately with him, publicly rebuked him, and reminded him that this was contrary to the injunctions of their holy father.

It was Baronius's desire to assist the Congregation by every means in his power. He never denied himself to any

188

of the fathers, and wished them to consider themselves entitled to approach him at all hours. If one of them visited him at the Vatican and seemed to hesitate to interrupt him, he at once threw down his pen. "I pray you father," he would exclaim, "not to treat me thus. Act towards me as you would towards the porter of the house."

But do what he would, a little stiffness grew up between him and the Roman Congregation, which was dispelled only by his last illness and death. It is evident from words he let drop in his confidential letters to Talpa that the fathers forgot their former brother and companion in the Cardinal of the papal household, and feared by confiding in him to introduce the thin edge of the wedge of meddling from outside in their affairs. "I have spoken to Father Angelo about the business of San Severino," Baronius wrote to his friend a few years after his elevation, "but I know by experience that my recommendations have but little weight with them, and they think it better to give no excuse for interference from outside in the affairs of the Congregation. So do not be surprised if nothing comes of my request." "I am sorry for your annoyance," he wrote again, "and I am also sorry that I am not in a position to help you, for it is not the way of the fathers here to confide in me. So I can work only *ab extra*, and do not quite see what more I can do for you."

Thus it was still to Naples that he turned for sympathy in his labours and weariness. However, the fathers there were also inclined, from the strangeness of the position, to be a little ceremonious with Baronius when he was first made Cardinal; but a few words of friendly remonstrance on his part put matters straight between them. "The boxes you have sent me have arrived safely," he wrote to Talpa but a very short time after his elevation. "I am ashamed to think that the poor should give in this manner to the rich—for such the world esteems me to be—and I thank you much. I pray you in the future to be more free towards me, for it is not necessary for us to cultivate friendship by ceremonies and compliments for I love you all as my brothers and masters." It was not only the ceremony which the Naples fathers observed towards him which pained Baronius. He perceived that their respect for his position made them less candid in their criticisms of his writings, on which he had depended from the beginning. "As to my book you praise it too much," he writes to Talpa. "Now I am a Cardinal, I fear you are not such severe censors and correctors as you were before, and as I would like you to be still. I do wish you would not spare me, for you ought to be my faithful friends and not flatterers. Now, more than ever, what I write requires to be sifted and distilled."

His remonstrances were effectual, for we can find no further traces of ceremony in the familiar correspondence which he continued to keep up with Talpa, though, owing to the increasing pressure of business in his life, letters did not pass between them with the same frequency as in former days. Father Juvenal, also, wrote as unrestrainedly as ever, and freely mingled salutary admonitions in his correspondence. "I read your letter with delight," Baronius wrote in answer to Ancina's congratulations on his promotion. "It was all the more pleasing to me because it was sprinkled with the salt of good advice, which made your words very savoury to me. Continue to write to me in the same way that you have begun, and to the plentiful admonitory condiment add some prayers for me before the throne of God."

Few letters passed between Cesare and Juvenal without a friendly passage of arms. Baronius wrote to him about his troubles as brother would write to brother, but even in the midst of his confidences he could not restrain from teasing his correspondent on account of his readiness in administering fraternal correction. In one of his first letters after his elevation, having poured out to his friend the bitterness of his spirit, he continued thus: "It is better to go to the house of mourning than to the house of feasting. What means this house of mourning? It means that you will hear ere long that Cardinal Baronius has departed this life. I know you will philosophise sublimely and say with the wise man, 'Laughter I counted error, and to mirth I said, why art thou vainly deceived?' And verily you will add that all things are vanity, and that 'better is the day of death than the day of birth,' for on the latter we are born into danger, and on the other snatched from it. See then how much better it is to go to the house of mourning if it can turn a man into a philosopher in a moment of time. Think thus of me, my brother, and pray to God for me. Farewell, and be ever my corrector by your salutary advice."

Happy would it have been for Baronius if all his friends had in like manner made wholesome admonitions the theme of their letters of congratulation. Perhaps the most painful result of the blow which had fallen on him were the adulatory addresses which poured in from all parts, the key-note of all the congratulations being the amount of good which would accrue to the Church by his being a member of the Sacred College. Such words hurt his humility, to which, and to the vow which bound him to it, he clung as to his sheet-anchor in the storm. His hatred of praise, which was so strong in him naturally as

191

to induce St. Philip to mortify him through it, was kindled into a flame by the words addressed to him. "When I read my praises sung in such documents," he wrote to Talpa in acknowledging some laudatory verses forwarded to him from Naples, "I seem to see a serpent which makes my flesh shudder, and I wish people would spare me."

The adulation he received and the terms in which it was couched were indeed such as to make any modest man wince. For instance, the learned Nicolas Serrarius went so far in his felicitations as to paraphrase thus the prophecy of Isaias: "Give ear O ye islands, and hearken ye people from afar. The Lord hath called Cesare from the Vallicella, from his narrow cell He hath been mindful of his name.

"He hath made his mouth like a sharp sword, and in the shadow of His hand He hath protected him, and hath made him as a chosen arrow." All the flattering addresses may not have been as fulsome as the above; but the following from the pen of the Bishop of Ravella is a fair specimen of the honeyed words which he was asked to swallow. "No longer are you hidden under a bushel, but, set high on a candlestick, you give light to all who are in the house of God. You no longer dwell in a corner, providing for the salvation of a mere handful of men, but are set upon the great platform of the Church, to be made manifest to and consulted by all men. No longer are you sailing in Peter's bark as one of a multitude, but, standing on the poop by the side of the captain, with him you work for the common good."

Such words as these, to use his own expression, pierced Baronius like a javelin, and, where courtesy permitted, he repudiated them in plain language. To Abbot Rescius, who had thanked God and the Pope in one breath for the service done to the Church by Cesare's elevation, he replied thus bluntly "The sorrow I experience at the dignity conferred on me is quite in proportion with the joy it seems to cause my friends. I ought not to allow these congratulations to displease me, seeing that they are tokens of the affection which my friends bear me; nevertheless you must permit me to deplore this aggravation of the many dangers which threaten my salvation. Knowing as I do by experience the greatness of my burden, my friends owe it to me not to be less prompt with their charity than they are with their politeness. Let them offer up fervent prayers to obtain divine grace for me, so that, in spite of my unworthiness and reluctance, this trial which God has imposed on me may be turned into an occasion of merit, and may conduce to His glory. This is what I expect of the charity of all my friends, and of you in particular."

Not less plainly did he write to Bonciario, a learned professor of Perugia. "Though nothing in all my life has been harder for me to bear than this on which you see fit to congratulate me, I will try to accept your politeness with affection, and see in it a token of your goodwill towards me. But you will do me a much greater service if you will pray for me, and obtain help for me to bear this burden, with which you are so pleased. Entangled as I am in cares and troubles it would be a consolation to think that you were turning your powers to good account in that direction." It must, indeed, have been galling to receive congratulations on what at that time was causing him exquisite suffering. It is almost pathetic to see the struggle that went on at times within him between his annoyance and his gratitude when such felicitations came from those whose opinion he valued too much to fling it back at them. There is a fund of depression lying under his simple reply to Cardinal Frederic Borromeo, in which he says that, seeing him so happy about what had occurred, it seemed as if he ought to try to be happy also.

Some of the letters he received struck a more sympathetic chord. Such an one was written by Baronius's appreciative friend the Abbot of St. Martin's, who, after devoting some lines to compliments and congratulations which he considered necessary, revealed the real object of his letter by pouring out his fears lest the Annals should be injured by the change in their author's fortunes. "Would that the subject of your congratulations had never entered into my life," Baronius wrote in reply. "You would have better cause to wish me joy were I lying in prison in defence of my faith, momentarily awaiting the arrival of the executioner, as we know to be the case with many men in this century. For what are these purple adornments, these insignia without government, this purple without empire, what are they but martyrdom? They have been imposed on me, and have to be endured, but do not congratulate me on them. But you may rejoice about one thing. The dignity conferred on me has not taken me from the Annals, which the Pope himself urges me to go on with. The seventh volume is now ready and the index completed. The eighth is in my mind and, God willing, will be published by the end of next year. Farewell, and aid me by your prayers to her whom you love, the holy Mother of God. This letter, though so short, being written with my own hand, is a token of my affection for you."

The fear lest the Annals should suffer had been a great aggravation of Baronius's dread of the cardinalate, and it was a real relief to him to find that Clement had spoken

194

sincerely when he gave the assurance that every facility should be afforded for their completion. In the dedication to the Pope of the seventh volume, published after his elevation, he thanks Clement fervently for his consideration, and gratefully enumerates the facilities afforded by him for the continuance of his work. "Among the multitude of benefits which I have received from Your Holiness," he says, "I count it not the least that you have provided for the continuation of the Annals, and that though you raised them with me in dignity you did not with me remove them from the Congregation. Furthermore, when you called me to the Sacred College, you did not withdraw the allowance you had previously made to facilitate their progress, but you have, on the contrary, promoted the work and showed your desire for its completion. In order that I may devote myself more assiduously to my labours connected with them, you have endeavoured to relieve me of such business as would interfere with my work on them, and have desired that the greater part of my day should be kept free from interruptions, and entirely devoted to the Annals."

In spite of the comparative facilities afforded him, and in spite of the Pope's manifest goodwill, the occurrences of the last two years had interfered gravely with his work. The year 1594 had seen the publication of the sixth volume; but it was not till the end of 1596 that it was followed by another. This delay disturbed Baronius's orderly mind, and in apologizing for it in his dedicatory letter to Clement, he lays the blame partly on the importance of the subject matter, but chiefly on the Pope's action towards himself. "I am not without a fitting excuse for the tardy appearance of this volume," he writes, "for—and I speak but the truth—the burden of the honours and dignities which it has pleased Your Holiness to lay on me so unexpectedly and undeservedly, have, partly by their nature and partly by my want of custom, had an impeding effect on me, similar to that of long and flowing garments placed on one running his course swiftly with loins girt. First you made me protonotary, the trappings of which dignity, being totally unsuited to our Institute, were impediments rather than coverings, a burden rather than an honour. When to these you added the loose and flowing robes of the august purple, my course, hampered by the constraints of the new life, was still more retarded. Indeed, it was with me as it was with David when he could not walk clad in the king's armour, being, as he said, not accustomed to it."

Baronius was not satisfied with clearing his reputation of the charge of dilatoriness through the medium of this dedication, the spread of which would be as world-wide as that of the volume which it prefaced; but he resolved to utilize the same means of publicity for a further purpose. He seized the opportunity to give tongue to the sense of soreness under which he was labouring, and to let the whole world in general, and the Pope in particular, know how hardly he thought himself treated. By this course he could lodge his protest with the Holy Father, and force him, as it were, to listen, without danger of interruption or the imposition of silence at his hands. After excusing himself for the delay in the publication of the volume he goes on in words, in which his love for the holy Pontiff and feelings of gratitude towards him can be seen struggling almost visibly with his sense of resentment.

"I had resolved, and had confirmed my purpose by repeated vows (of which God is my witness) to remain till death leading the hidden and simple life of our Institute, which I had hitherto so happily led. Bearing ever in mind that they who occupy the first places are exposed to greater condemnation, I wished to keep myself within the safe shelter of private life. . . . When a prudent man contemplates the eminent, sublime, and absolute sanctity of life required in one chosen to be a member of the Sacred College, how can he be otherwise than filled with fear by the consciousness of his own incapacity, and recoil with despondency of soul from the peril presented, and do his utmost to avoid it? Considering all this, I say that you cannot complain, Holy Father, that I seemed reluctant to do your will. My expostulations had been effectual with Your Holiness's predecessors when they also wished to tear me from the haven of a quiet life. When I besought them they dispensed me from these honours. But you, by whom I knew myself to be loved more than by them—you I vainly implored. Though you loved me more, when I craved indulgence you only treated me the more severely—I was as it were torn in pieces by your retainers; your door was shut in my face until by much praying I was admitted to your presence, which would inspire awe to the very angels. To all my supplications I received but one answer, for with a loud voice you threatened me with the terrible sentence of excommunication if I resisted any longer, and did not submit at once. Perhaps I should have still resisted had not this bolt, bursting from the sky and sending forth the blast of everlasting damnation, cast me to the earth."

The realization of the absolute sanctity which, as he told the Pope, was in his opinion required of one in his exalted position, was the noblest side of Baronius's repugnance to his new dignity. At first the feeling of his unworthiness quite overwhelmed him; and it was with

197

unaffected humility that, after reproaching Clement for the manner in which he had thrust him into the Sacred College, he proceeded to express his astonishment how he could have thought of setting him, the least among men, on such a pinnacle. In another letter, addressed to the College of Cardinals, he draws arguments for his consolation from God's frequent choice of weak vessels for His greatest works. Not only did He select untaught fishermen for the most sublime office which it can enter into the heart of man to conceive; but when He willed to call the cultivated Paul to a like office He would not do so until He had first cast him down and made him grovel on the ground. The Scriptural simile from which he drew most consolation was that of the twelve rough, rude stones taken by God's command from the bed of the Jordan, to be set up as a lasting monument, typical of the Church.

CHAPTER XVII
Kicking Against the Goad

BARONIUS' abhorrence of his position was not always thus under his control and subject to the will of God, but often took the form of a blind detestation of the thraldom in which he found himself. Again and again did he privately implore Clement to release him from his burden, but the Pope steadily refused to be moved by his entreaties, and must have dreaded those passionate interviews. It was, however, long before Cesare gave up the hope—amounting at times to confidence—that the time would come when he could cast off the hated purple and end his days in private life. Sometimes, in a fit of uncontrollable irritability against his lot, he would snatch his scarlet cap from his head and fling it to the nearest bystander, with the command to take it to the Pope, so that he might never see it again.

On one occasion, when he was talking with two other Cardinals, intimate friends of his, one of them related how sickly and delicate he had been before his elevation; but that he had been in perfectly good health ever since, which happy result was jokingly attributed by the other Cardinal to the magical properties of the red cap. Baronius hearing these words, could not take them as a mere joke, but, snatching his own skullcap from his head, cried out passionately: "And I, miserable wretch that I am, began to grow old when I put it on, and have been consumed away with sorrow ever since." "It was impossible for Cesare to jest, or allow others to jest on this subject. When conversing one day with Jacopo, Abbot of Crescenzi, a most holy man, whose character and tastes were congenial to his own, he begged this friend to pray that he might at least die relieved of the purple. "Take care," replied the other teasingly "if you refuse to die a Cardinal, you may have to die a Pope." "Wretch that I am!" cried Baronius impetuously, refusing to see the spirit in which his companion spoke. "I have not known a single moment's peace since I was torn from the Congregation! O, will no one hold out any hope that I may some day return to my room at the Vallicella, to die where I passed so many years as a simple priest, and spend the brief remainder of my life in my former state, divested of these trappings?"

His protest to the Pope in his dedication of the seventh volume has been quoted but he could not be satisfied with expressions as guarded as those there used. In his peroration [foreword] to the same volume, for which portion of the work he usually reserved his bursts of eloquence, he proclaims his misery to the whole world. "O why didst Thou bring me forth from the womb," he cries with Job; "why received upon the knees; why suckled at the breasts? For now I should have been asleep and still, and should have rest in my sleep with kings and consuls of the earth who build themselves solitudes.' Such thoughts being mine I do not cease to extol that wise old man Berzellai, who, being invited by the King to live in his palace in quiet, security and magnificence, replied: 'I need not this recompense; I beseech thee let thy servant return and die in my own city and be buried by the sepulchre of my father and mother.' Thus did he rightly prefer the sepulchre of his fathers to the King's court, and valued regal splendour less than the rustic life which he had

hitherto so contentedly led. Happy that man, and much to
be envied! That which he besought was granted to him.
He was not held against his will by the King's command.
He was allowed to return with joy to his own, and finish
his course in peace. As for me, though I be removed with
violence from peace, quiet, and all other good things, there
remains only one thing for which I can pray. Though,
indeed, I be cast down by anxiety, sadness and woe,
though I be full of trouble and thrown into the midst of
perils, let me not be without thy protection, O holy
Mother of God. When, as I climb up the slippery path and
approach the summit, and that dread moment comes
when my eternal salvation hangs in the balance, do thou
give me thine unfailing aid, and hold me up as I totter. Do
thou loose the tangled skein; do thou cut the thread of this
irksome and burdensome life, so that I may not
inadvertently barter away eternal glory for mere vanities."

Baronius's hatred of the cardinalate and all that it
entailed, and his fixed desire to rid himself of it at the first
opportunity, fostered the spirit of holy liberty inherent in
his nature, which so publicly characterized him during the
later years of his life. On one occasion he was censured by
some courtier acquaintances for having urged the Pope to
bestir himself to relieve his starving subjects in a time of
scarcity. They declared that he had no right to worry the
Pontiff about such disagreeable matters, seeing that he
was indebted to him for his elevation to his present rank.
Cesare replied that in acting as he had he was far from
wishing to annoy the Pope, but had been moved solely by
the distress of the people. As for the cardinalate it did not
count as a featherweight with him, as he had received it
reluctantly, and was ready to seize on the first occasion
that presented itself to resign it, and return to his room at

the Oratory, the key of which he always carried about with him. Baronius extended his hatred of his dignity to the colour representative of it, and partly from aversion, though probably also from his love of simplicity, he refused to have his chapel or his furniture draped with purple; except on one occasion, when he converted into bed-hangings a discarded robe, too worn out for even his use.

Cesare was not apt to write or talk about his secret soul; indeed, the manner in which he avoided speaking about himself at all is mentioned as one of his most marked characteristics. Thus, in spite of the misery of mind which we know he went through during the first years after his elevation to the purple, before he bent his will to that of God and found peace in so doing, we can trace no self-revelations even in his intimate letters to Talpa. Occasionally, however, an undercurrent of his melancholy can be discovered running through what formed the ostensible subject of his correspondence. "Go on praying for me," he says in one letter, "for though, thanks be to God, my bodily sickness is cured, that of the soul continues as before, and is much more dangerous." "Added to all my many troubles," he writes again, "this has befallen me. I did not see our Cardinal [Tarugi], who passed through Rome as it were by stealth. This has caused me no small suffering; and my only comfort is that it is all the will of God. I stand holding my cross which, because it is of gold, seems to others not to be heavy, though verily it weighs me down more than if it were made of iron. Help me by your prayers." "Although I have no business about which to write to you," he says in the one and only letter in his whole correspondence which is devoted solely to confidences about his state of mind, "I feel a great desire to write to you, knowing that it will do me good, and hoping that it may move you to pray for me. I beg of you to do so without fail, for now that I am growing old, and see death approaching, I must soon have to appear before the dread tribunal to give an account of myself. The vanity of this life is such that it gives birth to the delusion that we are immortal. May God preserve me from falling into such a state of intellectual darkness. Still I fear, for I am human and frail."

From some of the above quotations, all of which belong to the year 1597, that which succeeded his elevation, it can be seen how much he craved for the company and advice of Tarugi. This comfort had been allowed to him for a short time soon after the eventful Consistory at which both were made Cardinals. After his elevation Tarugi was removed from the See of Avignon to that of Siena, and in the interval before taking up his residence in the latter city, he dwelt for a short time in Rome, and at the Vatican. It is probable that those brief weeks of communication with Tarugi left Baronius all the more disconsolate and lonely, and created a craving for his friend's advice which he had not known before.

"The first favour I asked of the Cardinal of Avignon," Baronius writes to Talpa in November 1596, "was that, seeing we are living under one roof, it would please him to be my spiritual father, and bear my confessions in the place of our Father Philip, of blessed memory. He granted me this favour and I am already in possession of it. He has desired that I should likewise be his confessor; and so we go on. We have agreed that I shall go and find him three times a week for this purpose."

A few weeks later Baronius again alludes to their communication, with fuller particulars. "The Cardinal of

Avignon's rooms are near mine," he says; "so our arrangement of confessing to each other is easily carried out. We usually go out together in the same open coach; so by God's grace our affairs are progressing favourably. His Holiness is well. He gives out that he wishes this Advent to have an Oratorio in the ante-chamber, with discourses about the things of God. This is a step in advance; but let us pray to God that the light may grow into perfect day. Our preaching at the Oratory begins to be objected to by some of the Cardinals. Let us pray that the word of God may grow, and that human prudence may not, as is its wont, injure the cause of God."

The love which Baronius had for Tarugi was very great, and of a peculiar kind, being, as it were, the shadow of his feeling for St. Philip. When he mastered his bitter repugnance to his dignity sufficiently to compel himself to return thanks to the Pope for raising him to it, he joined the name of Tarugi with his own in his expression of thanks; his gratitude on behalf of his friend being more wholehearted than on his own. "Twice, Holy Father," he says, "have you conferred this dignity on me; for you have conferred it also on my second self, a man of one mind with me, namely the Archbishop of Avignon, a truly apostolic man, a model of ancient virtue, with whom it is my glory to have been brought up, knit together by the bonds of charity in one spiritual school. I exult in possessing him as my brother, spiritually begotten of one parent, namely the blessed Philip Neri. His is the first place, not only by right of primogeniture, but far more by reason of his greater merit, for in virtue I do but run, as the proverb says, at his chariot wheels. Though I will not affect equality with him, I will, as far as is permitted me, follow him with my eyes as he arduously strains after the highest virtue; and I will find my solace in placing my steps in the footprints he has left, and thus will I persevere during the short remainder of my life's course, now drawing towards its close."

Both raised to the purple on the same day, both longed equally to lay it aside, though the desire of Tarugi was more chastened than that of his impetuous friend. When they dwelt together in Rome during that too brief time at the end of 1596, they probably talked over this longing of their hearts and discussed the probabilities of its being granted them.

But in spite of Baronius's almost fierce repugnance to his position, and in spite of what we may call his day-dreams of a future release from it, he was careful to do nothing indeliberately, for it was not till he had been a Cardinal for nearly two years that he actually contemplated putting his plans into execution and opened his mind on the subject to his friends. The long smouldering discontent was then fanned into a flame by the approaching expedition to Ferrara, in which he had to accompany the papal court. The prospect of an absence of months from Rome and from his work—months to be spent in an uncongenial and antipathetic atmosphere—was the featherweight which turned the scale, the last intolerable straw added to his burden, which determined him to make an effort to be quit of it.

As usual he made a confidant of Father Talpa. A letter to him, written in March, 1598, gives us all his reasons for his contemplated step, matured by the misery of two years, yet weighed with a fair mind, subject to the will of God and the counsel of those whose opinion he revered. "I thank you not a little for taking such an interest in my affairs," he writes. "Now, I beg you to listen with patience to a matter about which I have for some time been intending to write to you. I have refrained hitherto from doing so, being doubtful from what spirit my desires proceed. What I now say is in secret and told to you in that spirit of confidence that I had with our blessed Father Philip. I place myself at your feet and make known to you a weighty thought, which I have driven from me several times as though it were a temptation. But, beholding not only its persistency, but that it increases in strength every day, I have grown to think that after all it may be from God.

"From the moment that I was made Cardinal I felt an antipathy to the dignity, which caused me indescribable mental suffering. The only thought that sustained me was the hope that some day I might free myself from the burden and peril by renouncing the dignity; and I have kept on waiting for a fitting opportunity. What has held me and still holds me back is the fear of leading men to say that I am actuated by displeasure at not receiving from the Holy Father that income which befits my station, and which others, even regulars, receive from him. This fear has acted as a powerful curb which keeps me from arriving at a decision. Another thing which holds me back is the knowledge that I should cause great displeasure to His Holiness, who, moreover, might put the same interpretation on it, and think that I was acting under the influence of vexation. These two considerations have hitherto restrained me. I add a third which is not less potent. I should fear to make a great commotion without being after all able to carry out my intention, and thus make everyone talk about me under false pretences and without gaining my object.

206

"Such is my condition, which, as you can judge, is full of bitterness. To remain as I am is intolerable; and yet, I do not see my way to liberty. On this account I am compelling myself to discuss the matter with you. I do not want you to answer, or even to arrive at a decision, in a hurry. I want you to form an opinion matured by much prayer, and to divest your mind of all thoughts of sense. O, would that such happiness could be mine as to leave Rome for ever, and make my noviciate over again in your blessed house at Naples! Then death, which cannot be very far off, would not overtake me unprepared. You know how important it is to spend one's last days well, and devote the short remaining time to preparing one's soul for eternity. Advise me as a true friend, not as a man who judges according to the flesh, but according to the spirit. I have not as yet confided these thoughts to anyone but you, though I may have alluded to my desire in a half jesting way, understood as such by those who heard me. It is impossible at times to restrain a half word or hint, for out of the abundance of the heart the mouth speaketh; as might be the case with one in prison, who talks of the means by which he hopes to make his escape.

"I will add but one word more. The rule given about deciding a vocation is whether or no you find peace in it. Following this rule it seems easy for me to decide that my present state is not my vocation, for I have never, never, never, never found peace or quiet of mind in it. Ponder carefully over all that I have written, and when you have well examined and considered every point, then give me your opinion, but in the utmost confidence."

About the same time Baronius sent to Tarugi a letter very similar to the above and the reply, written not only by one whom he venerated in an especial manner, but by

207

a fellow sufferer, decided the question and settled the future, for we hear no more of his vain struggles, like those of a caged bird, to escape from his gilded thraldom. Tarugi's letter is too full of importance to Cesare's whole career not to be reproduced at length.

"God's mercy has permitted us to live for many years the same life, in the same Congregation, under the same holy father, nourished and brought up by him in the holy fear of God. It has, moreover, pleased Him that we should be of one spirit, and our hearts closely united by the indissoluble bond of charity. Hence I have always been of one mind with you, and shall try to be so in this present instance, the thought of which holds me detached from and superior to all mere worldly affections, and makes me think that we may be able at some future time to accomplish what we desire. Meanwhile, let us rest, knocking all the while at the door of divine compassion by continual and submissive prayer, beseeching God, if it be His will and for His glory, to facilitate that project which is in our mind, and open to us some means by which we may carry it out. And let us pray Him, if our purpose does not please Him, to put obstacles in the way, and enable us to wait and see what time brings forth, without any precipitation on our part. Let us mature our resolution by keeping it to ourselves before God, and not making it known to anyone, even for the purpose of seeking counsel. For, though there is no doubt that the thing is good in itself, it remains to be seen whether God wills it, and if so, at what time and in what manner He would have it carried out. We are not in a position to take so difficult a step rashly, even though it may look to us easy and safe. Were we simple priests so much reflection might not be necessary; but those whom God has set in high places, to which they did not mount of their own will or by their own inclination, must trust entirely to Him for guidance. Eternal loss need not be feared where the danger has not been sought out, and when we walk under constraint; and if we do not in every case act as rightly as we would wish, still we do so in part, and avoid many things which should be avoided.

"And supposing that God does not will this retirement on our part; shall we go against His will? Neither of us wished for our present position. God holds the hearts of kings in His hands and turns them which way He pleases. And if—as is possible—this be our vocation, how can we, having once accepted it, put it lightly aside? How do we know what God wills to do with His creatures? *An non licet mihi quæ volo facere?*[18] Did not Moses choose the easier way when he refused to go before Pharaoh, and bid him set the people of Israel free? So was it with Jeremias when he declined to go forth and preach, excusing himself because he was a child. Yet God willed that both one and the other should yield to Him. St. Gregory, in spite of his lamentations, in spite of his recalling his beloved cell to mind with sighs and tears, could not bring himself to throw down the burden imposed upon him. Neither was it permitted to St. Francis to retire into solitude, but he was constrained to go forth into the world, and devote himself to preaching and the conversion of sinners.

"There is one on earth who has imposed this dignity on us. For the sake of conscience and of gratitude we must not do a thing which could not fail to displease him, and which would certainly not redound to his honour. A step,

---

[18] "Or am I not allowed to do what I wish?" Editor.

so singular, so rarely taken, and one which many would condemn, ought not to be taken without long heart-searchings and much prayer. If we survive the Holy Father (who, however, is more likely to outlive us), a way out of our difficulty might very probably be opened to us. It seems to me that our surest way of being able to keep at anchor and ride out the storm is to keep hope alive within us, praying the while to God to grant us this grace, and waiting patiently for that time to come. I will take no steps without first communicating with you; and do you, I pray, act in like manner by me."

Truly, his holy father St. Philip was not forgetful of Cesare and his sanctification when he moved Francesco Maria to write to him such words of strength and wisdom—words which were like the blessed light of dawn after a night of darkness—bringing with them calm after the storm, and restoring peace to his soul. To follow Cesare through those two years succeeding his elevation, to behold him kicking against the goad and beating himself to pieces against the inevitable, is like watching a man in deadly peril, yet unmindful of his danger, hovering with uncertain movements on the brink of a precipice, though held back from destruction by some unseen hand. We tremble as we see how near this holy son of St. Philip was to making shipwreck of his life and marring his great soul by petulance at his irksome dignity, and resentment at having it thrust upon him against his will, in spite of a resistance which undoubtedly bordered on what was unlawful. The way in which he was saved from himself shows us, as nothing else could, what he would have been without the grace of God, and, by lifting the veil off things unseen, reveals to us his holy father's hand giving him that still stronger aid for which he prayed, holding the

210

reins of his life, guiding his footsteps over the hindrances and obstacles which beset his advancing years, and holding him up that he should not stumble.

When St. Philip appeared to Cesare before his elevation, he warned him not to escape a threatened danger, but to prepare himself for something God willed of him. The true import of these words was making itself clear to his mind, and his letters to Tarugi and Talpa are the last that we hear of his passionate longing to cast off the hated dignity. The battle between God's will and his was over, though the suffering it entailed ended only with his life. A letter, which he wrote to Talpa not long after the crisis which has been related, shows that the conviction had at length forced itself on his mind that it was God's will that he should remain where he was. Hitherto he had been unable to allude to his dignity without a sense of tragedy, and had been intolerant of any attempt to jest about it; [start here] now, however, he could write almost playfully about certain mortifications entailed by his position. "Though," he says, "my preface has pleased all those who have read it, nevertheless even Cardinals must sometimes mortify themselves, and go the way of others unless they wish to be contentious. I am, however, in a state of discouragement, and want your prayers greatly that I may not be overcome by melancholy. Believe me if I did not know that it would offend God, I would at once go back to the Oratory, resume my habit, and return to my former state. I trust that the company of the Cardinal of Avignon may solace me; but do you pray that God may deliver me from pusillanimity and disquietude of spirit."

The Cardinal's Hat of Cesare Baronius.
Santa Maria in Vallicella, Rome.

CHAPTER XVIII
The Expedition to Ferrara

T HE year 1598, the earlier months of which were so blessed to Baronius by restoring peace to his mind, was throughout its whole course one of great importance to him; although the circumstances into which he was thrown were such as to seem at first sight calculated to impede the main object of his life. For eight months he was kept away from Rome, the only time on record of any prolonged absence from the city of his adoption. During these months he was following the fortunes of the Pope in camp and at court, uprooted from his ordinary mode of life, torn from libraries and archives, books and manuscripts, and plunged into the atmosphere and pomps of a semi-military pageant and progress through the State of Ferrara.

Ferrara was a papal fief which had been held for generations by the House of Este. Duke Alfonso, the last of his line, who was now holding it, was slowly and surely dying. At his death, since he had no heir to succeed him, the State would in all equity revert to its suzerain the Pope; and such a claim had been prospectively brought forward and maintained by Sixtus V and his successors. Alfonso, hoping to evade the exigencies of the claim, had, during the last months of his life, appointed Cesare d'Este, a distant kinsman, to succeed him; and no sooner had he breathed his last than this young man was proclaimed Duke with much pomp. His reign was short, and has to do with the biography of Baronius only as far as it influenced the events which succeeded his usurpation. After due and unheeded warning Clement VIII pronounced sentence of excommunication against the intruder; and Henry IV of France, who was looking out for an opportunity to prove his loyalty to the Holy See, espoused the cause of the Pope. This combination of spiritual and secular arms proved too strong for resistance. Venice and other Italian States, which had supported young Cesare, withdrew, and he, finding himself alone, relinquished all claim to the Duchy on January 12, 1598.

The prospect of war, and the prompt measures taken by Clement VIII to raise a papal army when Don Cesare had usurped the throne of Ferrara, filled the heart of Baronius with sadness. He shrank from the prospect of blood being shed in defence of the rights of the Church, and yet he could not endure that these should be trampled on. "May God make known to you the trouble I am in at the turn affairs have taken in Ferrara," he wrote to Talpa on November 8, 1597. "I am in a dilemma. Either I must advocate giving up Church property, or else I must advocate war in order to recover the State. There lies no middle course between these two extremes. Oh, father, father, why am I a Cardinal, and my miserable soul exposed to such danger. I dare not commit to paper all that is taking place here but if you knew all, you would greatly compassionate me, for nearly all the Cardinals are eager to fight. We must pray God to put obstacles in the way, for we know what horrible evils are entailed by war. I pray God that He may visit His wrath on me, provided only that the peace of the Church be ensured." A fortnight later he wrote again in the same strain, only more emphatically. "I have prayed," he said, "and do pray that my blood may be shed rather than that of any other.

Considering how humane the Holy Father is by nature, it is extraordinary how set his mind is on fighting on this occasion."

War was averted by the means mentioned above, and the bloodshed which Baronius dreaded so much was never called for. While rejoicing at the rapid and bloodless termination of the affair, Cesare, when writing to Talpa, felt bound to make some reparation for the judgment which, in his terror of the evils of war, he had passed on the Pontiff. "I believe," he wrote in January, when the usurpation of the throne of Ferrara was a thing of the past, "that in all this affair the marvels of the omnipotent hand of God have been sensibly manifested. Everyone is astounded at the turn things have taken, and the evidence of the rectitude throughout of the Pontiff's intention. It teaches us not to censure his actions even if they appear imprudent at first sight. Wonderful things have occurred which it would not be permissible to commit to paper."

Thus all danger was apparently over, and Baronius's life was free to resume its ordinary course. But a trial was in store for him in connection with the Ferrara affair, which, while less serious than the bloodshed he had dreaded, was none the less repugnant to himself. Though peace reigned everywhere throughout the papal dominions, and the military descent meditated by the Pope was abandoned, Clement thought it expedient to make a sort of royal visitation throughout the State of Ferrara, which had been removed for so many years from the immediate government of the Holy See. This visitation and sojourn in the Duchy was to occupy many months, and during the time it was to last, the Pope demanded the attendance of Baronius. By comparing notes and dates it is impossible to doubt that the prospect of this prolonged absence from Rome with the papal court—an unlooked for aggravation of all that made his present position most hateful to him—was what brought Cesare's desire to rid himself of his burden to the climax related in the last chapter.

It was no consolation to him that his friend, Father Angelo Velli, who had succeeded him as superior of the Congregation, had a similar martyrdom inflicted on him. Cardinal Aldobrandini, Clement's nephew, on whom had devolved all the negotiations which resulted in peace, had selected Father Velli to accompany him as his chaplain, and had persuaded the Pope to command his acceptance of the post. Baronius, in the interests of the Congregation, pleaded to the best of his ability for his deliverance from such a yoke; but Clement would not listen, and said that, having pledged his word to his nephew, he refused to withdraw it. "Besides," he added, "I desire that this young man, Cardinal Aldobrandini, who has had so much to vex him should have this one consolation." "I tell you this," wrote Baronius to Talpa, after relating these circumstances, "so that you may not complain of my not having prevented it. Indeed, considering the loss to the Congregation, and the poor Father's own displeasure, I am most deeply grieved by what has occurred."

Baronius did his best on his own behalf to be dispensed from accompanying the Pope. "I am more troubled than I can well describe," he wrote to Talpa, when the idea of the expedition was first broached, "and I sorely need your help. ... This expedition to Ferrara must interrupt my work. On this plea I asked leave to remain behind; but I heard through the *Mæstro-di-Camera* that my doing so had grieved His Holiness. So by his advice, and that of the Cardinal of San Giorgio, I have offered to go under any circumstances, and this the Holy Father has accepted with great pleasure. Blessed be God." Still, he went on hoping against hope that something would occur to overthrow the present arrangements "If this expedition is not the will of God," he wrote, "I think that gout may prove to be an impediment." But in this half expressed wish for a return of the poor Pope's infirmity, he was disappointed. The gout did come, but it did not produce the desired effect. "His Holiness has his usual attack of gout," he writes, "which keeps him from starting; but, though the expedition is postponed, he will not fail to go."

Baronius after this resigned himself to the inevitable, and tried to make the best of his uncongenial exile, though there was one circumstance which seriously aggravated his repugnance to leaving Rome. He was on the very verge of bringing out his eighth volume. "By God's goodness," he wrote towards the end of 1597, "I have begun to print the volume. God willing, I will send you some sheets next week; and I pray that everything may go on without hindrance." Vain hope! In the spring, when the Ferrara expedition was arranged, and he had given up all thought of remaining behind, Cesare wrote to tell Talpa that he was forced to leave the volume uncompleted, as he could not trust the corrections of the sheets to anyone but himself, as the volume was exceptionally important, as it treated of dogmas of faith, where a single error in a single line would cause the whole book to be a failure. "To my deep regret we set forth next Monday," he wrote again in April, just before the expedition started, "and I must interrupt the printing of the volume. I shall take with me what small books I can, so as not to be without some means of study."

The absence of the papal court was much longer than had entered into Baronius's calculations, and he soon discovered that he had not provided himself with sufficient material for work. "Thanks be to God I am well in health," he wrote after he had been away barely a month, "but I am weary with idleness, not having with me the books necessary for getting on with the ninth volume. We shall not return till October at the earliest and the whole summer will be spent in establishing the government of this city and supplying the Duchy with laws and constitutions. ... My father, every day my taste is offended, and in vain do I sigh for my beloved quiet. Help me for Christ's sake." Little did Cesare imagine that this antipathetic expedition with its pomp and parade, its warlike Cardinals, and forced inaction, was to enable him to work for the lasting glory of his holy father, in a way which under other circumstances it might not have entered into his mind to do.

Through all the storms and contrarieties of the last three years, the thought of St. Philip had been uppermost in his heart; and to him he turned on every emergency. The manner in which, under the influence of the blow of his sudden promotion to the rank of protonotary, Baronius visited the tomb of the Saint and poured out his trouble to him before he sought the aid and counsel of the Congregation, is but typical of the constant recourse he had to his holy father. Often, during the dark days of despondency which succeeded his elevation, and afterwards to the end of his life, he would cast himself on his face before the tomb of the Saint, with these words on his lips: "Father, I have sinned before heaven and in thy sight, and am no more worthy to be called thy son."

218

Unworthiness! Such was Baronius's prevailing thought in the presence of St. Philip. He was oppressed by the sense of having failed to be and do that which his holy father had intended for him. He felt his worldly surroundings, unsought though they were, to be unholy in the eyes of the Saint; and, possibly, his chronic unpunctuality with his allotted task, and the publication of his volumes, no longer annually but months and even years after the appointed time, may have weighed upon his conscience like a crime. It is patent from his own words in his dedication how vividly his little feelings of soreness and smothered sense of injustice in connection with St. Philip dwelt in his memory and such episodes as that passing rebellion about the pension may have assumed awful proportions in his soul, and filled him with a feeling of remorse for his ingratitude in the irrevocable past, which obliterated all recollection of the long years of devoted sonship, and the joy which the Saint took in him.

The third anniversary of his holy father's death came round while Baronius was with the papal court at Ferrara, and his letter to Talpa on the occasion reveals this desponding sense of unworthiness and ingratitude in the past. "It was," he writes, "a great consolation to me to receive the account of how you kept the anniversary of our blessed Father at Naples. Though I am so hard of heart I could not restrain my tears. If David the King called him blessed who buried the reprobate Saul, how much greater blessing will you receive at the hands of God for thus honouring the memory of the sepulcher of a saint! Thus will it be with you.

"As for me I am sad at heart because I did not in his lifetime value this servant of God as I should; for which omission I fear I shall have some day to render a strict

219

account. Help me by your prayers, and intercede for me with the blessed Father, that I may be worthy of mercy. And you, my brothers, keep your eyes open to so great a light, and walk securely in it. May God console you even as you have consoled me."

As before said, his holy father was but rarely out of Cesare's thoughts at any time, but just at this time there was much to make his mind dwell on him more longingly and lovingly than ever. He had been a Cardinal for two years—years, as we know, of turmoil and disquietude of spirit, passed in kicking against the goad, in taking every opportunity to revile and protest against the dignity thrust on him, and refusing all solace save in the hope of casting it off. His heart was too turbulent for thoughts of St. Philip to make their home in it. But that was over now. As soon as Cesare became convinced that it was not God's will that he should throw aside his burden, he bowed his neck under the yoke, renounced his dearest desire and was once more at peace. But while submission restored calm to his soul, it deprived him of the food on which it had sustained itself, and in a certain sense he was like to the house empty, swept and garnished. Could he have then thrown himself into his work more eagerly than ever, perhaps it would have proved his consolation but all such human solace was denied him, and just when he seemed to need occupation most he was taken from Rome, and not only plunged into an antipathetic and public life, but reduced to a state of enforced idleness, foreign to the habits of his whole life. This idleness was most blessed to him, for it centred all his thoughts on heaven and his holy father, from whom his consolation was to come directly.

Added to this, outward circumstances and friendships helped to force his mind back on the past, and endowed

220

the never dying memory of St, Philip with fresh life. In a letter to Talpa, after giving a description of the Pope's triumphal entry into Ferrara, and the loyal welcome he had received, which filled the heart of Baronius with an enthusiasm which even his dislike of pomp and pageant was powerless to quench, he went on to tell him of the surroundings in the midst of which he found himself, after the papal court had taken up its abode in the city. "Though;" said he, "rooms in the palace, adjoining those of His Holiness, have been assigned to me, I have elected to lodge with our Father Angelo, who has received me willingly, and has secured a room for me. There we are together as much as we choose. Father Germanico often visits us, and, our Giuliano being here also, it is almost like being once more at the Vallicella. Father Angelo has started an Oratory which is much frequented, and I am to preach on Tuesday. In fact, all in going on well."

This soothing discussion with his friends of happier days, while on the one hand it delighted Baronius, on the other caused a redoubled longing to be restored to the house of his holy father. Under the influence of this regret he wrote the following letter to Father Consolini, whom St. Philip had loved so tenderly in his later years—a man not much more than half Cesare's age, and at that time master of novices at the Roman Oratory. "I ought to crave pardon for having neither answered your letter nor thanked you for your prayers. Though tardily, I do so now. I beg you to continue to pray for me, in union with your novices, my dear sons, for whom I ask a daily increase of grace. Plant, O my father, new seedlings like unto that great parent tree of which they are without doubt the shoots, and train them up in the way in which you were yourself trained. Rest assured that our blessed

Father still lives, and sees and governs his sons, holding in his hand a scourge for the disobedient. As for me, would that you could count me among your novices, treating me as one of them, and correcting me as you see fit with no respect of persons. Oh that it would please God to renew my youth in old age, and fulfil in me that prophecy: 'Thy youth shall be renewed as the eagle's.'"

It was not only through the medium of his sons that St. Philip drew near to Cesare and refreshed his heart. Twice during that summer at Ferrara did the Saint appear visibly to him, to kindle as well as satisfy Baronius's almost sick yearning for him. The first of these manifestations was connected with an event which filled Cesare with melancholy. Among the friends dearest to all the Congregation, and especially to Baronius, was Cardinal Uusano, the bond between these two being strengthened by their common dignity. While the Pope was at Ferrara, he was employed on an embassage to Venice, during which he kept up a correspondence with Baronius marked by an intimate playfulness characteristic of the terms on which they were. The last words that Cusano ever wrote to his friend were: "Oh, how much I wished for your company on our journey; and now that I am back in my rooms at Milan, I long for you more than ever." Soon after he penned these words he was seized with his last illness, the news of which filled Baronius with anxiety and sadness; all the more that he was at the time living in an atmosphere of gloom, for a contagious illness, suspected of being the plague, had broken out in Ferrara, and friends and acquaintances were dying around him, including his own trusted servant, who, in his own words, "was to him as his right hand."

Each letter that Cesare wrote to Talpa at that time conveyed the latest bulletin received of Cardinal Cusano's state; and at last he wrote as follows: "I have been simply struck down by grief at the death of our dear friend and brother Cardinal Cusano, which I had not expected. It has made me ill. *Mœror desiccat ossa.*"[19] He said the Cardinal's death took him by surprise; yet he had been prepared for it in a way about which, with his usual reverent reserve in all that was connected with St. Philip, he said nothing to his friends. One night, during his anxiety about Cusano's illness, the Saint stood by his bedside and said: "That lamp extinguished." While Cesare looked round to see what lamp he meant, St. Philip repeated the words and disappeared. Baronius was perplexed, and offered up many prayers for an interpretation of this apparition. When the next mail brought the news of Cusano's death, which took place at the very hour when his holy father had visited him, it was given him to understand the meaning of the mysterious words.

Once more did St. Philip show how mindful he was of Cesare in this period of desolation. One day, weary of soul and body, Baronius went into his room at Ferrara to rest awhile and, turning his hourglass, seated himself on a wooden chest. Suddenly the Saint appeared before him, and, as was his wont in life, pressed Baronius's head tenderly between his hands. Cesare stretched out his arms to detain him, but they met with nothing in their embrace, and St. Philip vanished from his eyes, leaving him, however, full of fervent and heavenly joy. A striking thing about both these manifestations is that Baronius was not

---

[19] "Grief dries my bones." -Editor's Note.

in the least surprised by them. He lived habitually in a realization of the supernatural, and took it as a matter of course that he about whom he was always thinking should make his presence known visibly to him.

The upshot of this state of yearning for his holy father, combined with his unwonted leisure of mind, which enabled him to bestow thought on matters not necessarily connected with either his work or the duties of his state, was that out of the fulness of his heart he placed on paper that wonderful apostrophe of St. Philip so well known to us as the dedication of the eighth volume of the Annals, which has added lustre to the name of the Saint as well as to that of his son who so lovingly penned it. Without that compulsory visit to Ferrara, and without the idleness of which Baronius so bitterly complained as a calamity, there are things about St. Philip and secrets of his guidance of souls which we should never have known. In a letter written to Talpa on the feast of the Assumption he made known this intention so blessed to posterity. "In the eighth volume, the printing of which is nearly finished," he says, "it has occurred to me to write a thanksgiving to our holy father in place of the usual dedicatory letter. I have been writing it since I came here, and have now sent it to the Roman fathers, who will send it on to you. Examine it carefully, and, as is your wont, give me your advice about it."

So sure was Baronius of St. Philip's state of glory that he set to work to prove his sanctity immediately after his death. He was one of those who were most urgent with Clement VIII, and persuaded him to open the process of his holy father's claims to be raised to the altars of the Church. Baronius, however, was not to witness the fruit of his labours, for St. Philip was not beatified till eight years, nor canonised till fifteen years, after he had himself gone to his reward. But in the interval, as often happens, the populace tried to forestall the decrees of the Church, and sought to canonize not only St. Philip but other holy servants of God by their public veneration. Lamps were burnt before their tombs, and even votive offerings were hung up. This was more than thirty years before such public cultus, anticipating the Church's decrees, was prohibited by Urban VIII; but, even as it was, these proceedings caused much indignation among some members of the Sacred College, who did their best to persuade the Pope to stop them with a high hand. Such devotion, however, always found a friend in Baronius, who, when consulted on the subject by Clement, ventured to tell him that if he censured the popular demonstrations he would expose himself to great peril.

Cesare displayed zeal for the speedy canonization of St. Charles and St. Ignatius, as well as for that of his own holy father. While the cause of the latter of these two saints was in process, so confident was Baronius of his sanctity and claims to the veneration of the faithful that he boldly proclaimed his conviction by act as well as by word, and, taking a picture of the holy founder of the Society of Jesus, he climbed up, and with his own hand fixed it over his tomb. It was a great joy to him to witness the beatification of St. Aloysius, who had died only in 1592; and there is something almost moving in the great devotion displayed towards this young saint by the holy and learned old man. He frequently visited his shrine, made his virtues the theme of his sermons, and had his life read aloud during meals.

The devotion to certain saints is often an indication of the inner life of their clients; and thus it is well to try and

225

discover who were those to whom Baronius was especially devout. As a rule, as is often the case with those who make the first ages of the Church their study, his chief devotion was for the early saints, martyrs and doctors, in whose company he lived, till they became to him as familiar friends to whom he intuitively turned for help in all emergencies. He looked on it as his bounden duty to revere in his heart and by his actions those saints with whom he was in any way brought into connection. Such were SS. Nereus and Achilleus, the patrons of his titular church, with their fellow-martyr St. Flavia Domitilla; such also were St. Fortunatus and St. Sabinus, patrons of certain abbacies conferred on him. St. Gregory Nazianzen and St. Gregory Thaumaturgus were, however, the saints to whom he had the greatest devotion, St. Peter and St. Paul always excepted. As for his devotion to these holy Apostles it was, as it were, the epitome of his loyal and all-absorbing love of the Church. Their pictures lay on his bed when he was dying, to be venerated by his last glance; and a look at them was his Credo, when he could utter no longer.

FERRARIA.

The Church of Sts. Nereus and Achilleus
The Titular Church of Cardinal Baronius

CHAPTER XIX
Sanctification of His State

AFTER following Baronius through his years of despondency, and seeing him weighed down by his antipathy to his dignity, it remains to be seen how, in spite of his repugnance and the expressions of his detestation of his position, which he poured into the ears of intimate friends and proclaimed to the public in the pages of the Annals, he never omitted to do his best to turn the abhorrent dignity into an instrument of sanctification. An aphorism, laid down by himself, was often on his lips, by which he maintained that "he who mortifies himself gains most merit, and that there is nothing more pleasing to God than to mortify the will." No one can doubt that, once the first book was over, Baronius applied this maxim to the greatest mortification and contrariety to which his will was ever subjected; nay, it is more than probable that he laid it down on the very occasion when his will sought so imperiously to rise in rebellion against the lot decreed for him by Providence.

When, after the eventful Consistory at which he was raised to the purple, Cesare was conducted to his apartments, he was, at his own request, left in solitude. After reviewing his life as it had been arbitrarily made for him, he indulged in no vain regrets, but there and then did his best to sanctify it by renewing the vows by which he had hitherto ruled his life. His whole subsequent career has to be looked at in the light of these vows, especially those of humility and poverty. This last, as will be remembered, he renewed so far as was compatible with his actual position; and so faithfully in fact and in spirit did he keep this modified vow that he accomplished that which most men in his position would have unhesitatingly discarded as an impossible task.

One of the first things that he did, after his elevation compelled him to leave the Oratory, was to have a small wooden cell constructed inside the stately apartments adjoining the Vatican Library which had been assigned to him; and there he passed most of his days in voluntary poverty and simplicity. The furniture of this little room was of the plainest kind, as can be seen by the minute description of it which has been handed down. His bed, which was about sixteen inches wide, and too short for him, consisted of two boards on which was laid one wool mattress. These details are of especial interest in connection with Baronius's habits, and his confidence to a friend towards the end of his life that for thirty years he had not known what it was to satisfy his desire for sleep. Some—nay many—might have complained that it was impossible to sleep sufficiently well on such a bed, but in his case, so much did his body crave for the sleep that he could not or would not allow it, that even cramped up on that narrow plank he would fain have slept longer. Over his bed there was hung an iron crucifix, which was the only object in the little room to which the name of adornment could have been given. In addition to the bed the furniture consisted of two or three lattice-work chairs, shelves of rough, unstained wood which held the books he had in actual use, a prie-Dieu, and a writing table on which stood an earthenware dish and a pottery inkstand which he used all his life. Besides these, mention is made of a brass basin, and a brass candlestick with flint, steel and tinder. Such was the sum total of the contents of that self-made cell.

He was most particular about the poverty of his dress. It was observed that each advance in rank was characterised by a change in his underclothing. When he was made protonotary, he took to wearing shirts of a much coarser material than he had hitherto worn; and when he was made a Cardinal, he made a further exchange, so that his shirts resembled sackcloth rather than linen. He studiously refused to adapt his garments to either heat or cold, and wore the same clothing in winter and summer, and in the former season was conspicuous for the absence of the use of gloves.

Whatever mortification was entailed by these practices could be hidden from the eyes of men but the shabbiness of his outward attire very nearly passes description. His total disregard for appearances and the exigencies of his position in this regard was, in his opinion, the most obvious means of keeping his vow of poverty. During the eleven years that he was Cardinal he wore the same state robes with which the Pope presented him on his promotion and, before his death, so numerous were the occasions on which he had to wear them, that they were threadbare and in rags. As to his ordinary robes, he indefinitely postponed their renewal, declaring that they would last his time, and that, meanwhile, he could give the price of new ones to the poor, and when at last sheer necessity obliged the purchase, he converted the discarded robes into bed-hangings. He was known to every one by his shabby appearance, and the patched state of his shoes became a by-word. When remonstrated with, not by the Pope but by his fellow Cardinals, on his total disregard for appearances, and was begged by them to spend a little

231

more money on his attire, his only reply was: "Know you not that the revenue of a priest is the Precious Blood of Christ?"

Father Juvenal, fearing that the dignity of his friend might lead him to forget his vow of poverty, wrote to warn him against such a possible danger. "You do quite right to caution me," Baronius wrote in reply; "but know all the same that I am very poor. Were I to die now I should have nothing but poverty to bequeath to my heirs. When you come here you will see for yourself, and smile to find rags under my purple robes."

When Cesare renewed his vow of humility, the chief object in his mind was the rejection of any further elevation, but he was equally mindful to apply it to the daily affairs of his life. Outward occasions of humiliation were difficult to find in his position, but where he could not find them he made them. As a rule he refused all personal attendance to his wants on the part of his servants; but there was one among them whom he habitually kept by him when he was preparing to retire for the night. Far from wishing this servant to wait upon him, his only object was to employ him as a means of humiliation, for every evening when they were alone together he used to kneel down before this man and take off his boots, and after he was in bed he made the servant sprinkle him with holy water. But, notwithstanding Baronius's habit of making himself last and least, there was something so dignified about him that no one was known to take a liberty with him; and though he constantly humbled himself before the members of his own household, they held him in the deepest reverence.

He invited corrections, and when made Cardinal he bound the fathers of the Congregation by a promise to administer them on every possible occasion. When an old man he was, or thought he was, subject to temptations against holy purity; and these he manifested to the fathers, and implored them to apply some remedy. He even turned for correction to strangers, and joyfully accepted and acted on the advice of any who were bold enough to take him at his word. There was a certain poor girl, the simplest of creatures, whom he had rescued from a position of danger and provided for. One day she, in her simplicity, told him that his rochet was too smart, and expressed her astonishment that he should let his grooms wear swords. Baronius thanked her for her rebuke, and said that he would at once change what had offended her. He then went on to explain that he had not perceived either of these little pieces of extravagance, and added with a smile that he was as absentminded as St. Bernard, who walked all day by the shores of a lake without finding it out, the difference being that St. Bernard was a saint and he a poor sinner.

Baronius, as a matter of course, suppressed any ostentation in connection with his position as a member of the Sacred College, or his more mundane dignity as belonging to a noble family. When he attended the profession in religion of one of his nieces, he perceived that, in order to do him honour, his family arms had been set up in the church where the ceremony was to take place, but he refused to go inside the building until they had been removed. He had, moreover, a rooted objection to any inscription being placed on the numerous sacred edifices which he restored. This was the more remarkable as being totally opposed to the universal custom of the day of decorating the most insignificant pieces of masonry with the name of him who had erected it. As far as he

233

could he even kept his name out of documents, and was, on one occasion, sorely displeased because it was mentioned in an indulgence which he had obtained for the Naples Oratory, such mention, as he wrote, striking him as boastful and exposing him to the accusation of desiring praise.

The same humility made him dread a reputation for learning; and on that account he was most unwilling to offer, in conversation, any opinion on those subjects with which he was most conversant; still less could he be induced to speak about himself. Even in his letters he cultivated a familiar style devoid of elegancies, in the fond hope that he might be taken for an ignorant and ill-educated man. He rebuked his secretary when he found him inserting polite phrases in letters written in his name, and he recommended the same absence of artificialities to all those over whom he had influence.

Baronius's life was, in the more ordinary sense of the word, a life of mortification, and even up to late old age he practised the severest bodily austerities, though hidden from the eyes of the world. In all times of public need—into the secrets of which his present position introduced him—he wore a hair-shirt and disciplined himself severely, and even practised the same mortifications every time he was called on to attend a papal function.

There is one marked characteristic of Baronius's austerities which is expressive of his habitual and humble desire for a hidden life. Although, as has been said, he practised special penances when the occasion called for them, it was, as a rule, by making use of every opportunity of suffering forced on him by nature, by turning it to the fullest account and offering it to God, that he led a life of heroic though unknown mortification. Such was the case with the short measure of sleep which he allowed himself, which was necessitated primarily by lack of time and pressure of work. So also was it with his habitual stinting of himself in the way of food. He was scourged by a painful and weak digestion, brought on and aggravated by constant mental strain. The result was that, worn out with his vigils and long hours of prayer and study, he could not, for very weariness, touch food when it was placed before him. Though this want of nourishment increased the malady to such a degree as to cause him agonies of pain, and, as was said of him by a contemporary, converted the process of eating into a veritable martyrdom which eventually brought him to the grave, he would never consent to pamper his appetite, or try in that way to mitigate his sufferings, but adhered rigidly to the coarsest and commonest fare. This reached the Pope's ears, and caused him such distress that he took to sending Baronius dishes from his own table; but Cesare, being unable to refuse Clement's little attentions, changed the hour of his dinner, and thus outwitted the Pontiff.

At length he became so ill under this treatment of himself, that his doctor persuaded him, as a matter of conscience, to relax his severity to a certain extent; but that this relaxation did not even border on luxury is shown by the following anecdote. On one occasion, when he was confined to his bed by his ailments, and could swallow nothing, the physician ordered some chicken soup to be prepared for him. When this was told to Baronius, he sent the most peremptory counter-orders to the cook, and having summoned the doctor gave him a severe scolding for daring to suggest such a remedy, the

235

price of which, he said, would afford a meal to two poor families.

The needs of the poor and the duty of almsgiving were always before him, though, from his constant literary work, his attendance on the Pope and all his other multifarious engagements, he was unable to work in any direct way for either the souls or the bodies of his neighbours. Even before he was taken from the Oratory his dealings with the poor was but indirect, and his alms were characterised by an impulsiveness which betokened an absence of regular work among them. During the last few years of his undisturbed life at the Oratory, under the pontificate of Gregory XIV, when a time of scarcity was prevailing, he sold his only valuable possession, a silver reliquary, and, exchanging its price for grain, he took it himself to a baker, whom he begged to distribute bread to the same amount among the poor. After he was made Cardinal, though his works of charity increased, he was even less capable than before of disbursing his alms in person; though he never refused relief when asked, and every Saturday distributed food to widows and poor girls from his own kitchen. He set aside a hundred crowns a month, or, in other words, the whole of the pension which was his right as a poor Cardinal, and made this the minimum sum to be given in alms; nor would he permit his treasurer to keep an account of the money thus spent. To quiet the conscientious scruples of his retainer, aroused by this unmethodical way of doing business, he quoted the words of Scripture: "Let not thy left hand know what thy right hand doeth."

A certain stamp of impetuosity marked all Baronius' acts of charity; and, as has been already stated, he never refused an alms when solicited. His generous nature and belief in his fellow-creatures' veracity made him a ready prey for impostors; but no number of deceptions could make him learn worldly prudence. "Far better is it," said he, "to be deceived by one who asks an alms in the name of Christ, than to run the risk of turning a really poor man away empty." He requested the fathers of the Congregation and various other priests, as well as his doctor, to keep him informed of any cases of special want that they came across, and at once relieved all such with generosity and self-forgetfulness, depriving himself for this purpose of absolute necessaries in the way of clothing and furniture.

He was as impulsive in his actions as in his gifts. When driving in his coach one day, he was begged of by an old man, not only poor, but evidently suffering. Baronius at once alighted, and, placing the sick man in his place in the carriage, bade his coachinan take him to the hospital, while he himself went into a church and said his prayers till the return of the coach. Another equally unconventional act, if not of charity, at least of kindness, was the loan of his own state mule to the nuns of St. Euphemia, to carry bricks for the re-building of their convent.

A large portion of his alms went in aid of poor students, a work which manifestly appealed to his sympathies but the form of charity to which his soul most willingly lent itself was that of providing dowries for poor girls whose virtue was endangered by their poverty. He sought out such cases by every means in his power, and his sense of responsibility in this respect was so great that he said that he feared that any neglect on his part would be visited by eternal punishment. There exists a letter to Talpa which, besides being illustrative of his mode of life, shows how he was ever on the watch for such cases of danger which might be averted by a timely alms. He was at the time for some unspecified reason, living in the palace of Cardinal de' Medici, afterwards Leo XI, to whom the arrangement gave much pleasure. "Use my house just as if it belonged to you," the Cardinal had written to Cesare, while absent on a political mission, "for I bear you such affection that I would like to hold all I have in common with you and, in saying this, I speak but the bare truth."

"While I was staying in the Cardinal of Florence's palace," writes Baronius in the letter in question, "as I was sitting at the window where I usually work, I saw opposite to me, a poor girl subjected to treatment at the hands of certain gentlemen, well known about the court such as made me fearful for her safety. Seeing what sort of doings were going on, God moved me to send a respectable gentleman in my service to find out about the people who lived in that house; and he found there a poor widow of venerable appearance with nine children, three sons and six daughters, the eldest of whom was twenty-five. The children were disorderly by reason of their extreme poverty; and the poor mother declared that she could not control them, and that not a day passed without a visit from some scoundrel bent on no good. She said, all the same, that she would rather kill her daughters than let them offend God by yielding to such temptations. She lamented that she could not control her children. They had no bread and usually went to bed supper-less; and she could not take them to Mass or the sacraments, because they had no clothes. I then sought information from the poor widow's neighbours, and they affirmed that she had spoken nothing but the truth.

"I then sent for the woman herself, accompanied by a friend, and with the help of the same trusty servitor whom I mentioned as having been sent by me to see her, I cross-examined her. She answered me with tears and tokens of suffering, and told me that she had prayed to the Madonna for four years to send some help, and that, finding that none came, she had begun to lose faith and in her despair she had already relaxed her hold over her daughters, and no longer kept the same watchful eye on them as heretofore; and as for them, they declared that they could not any longer go on living without food. I tried to encourage her, and gave her a measure of wheat and a few crowns. Since then I have obtained from His Holiness a promise to give each of the daughters two hundred crowns as a marriage portion and I am making arrangements that husbands be found for them. If only I could have provided them each with a bag of gold, I should have acted towards them the part of St. Nicholas. These are the true facts of the story of which rumours reached you. If there has been any good thing done, it belongs to God alone."

It was not always that he could obtain the co-operation of the Pope in the rescue of such poor girls, and he was often sorely put to it to raise the money necessary to remove them from danger. With all his impulsive generosity he was prudent, in his monetary affairs, keeping a strict account of what he had, and rarely exceeding it in his expenditure. But there were times when, rather than risk the souls of those in whom he was interested, he had to do violence to his methodical nature and borrow money for the marriage portion of poor girls. There was one such whom he knew to be in a position of most imminent danger. He found a man willing to marry her at once, but only on condition of the promise of five hundred crowns, to be paid in the course of the next five months. At that moment Baronius's treasury did not contain one spare coin but, lifting up his heart to God and putting his trust in Him, he closed with the bargain rather than be accessory to the loss of the poor girl's soul. His confidence in God was not unrewarded, though the time allowed him for the payment of the debt was within one day of its expiration before he could put his hand on the necessary sum. But on that very day a wealthy friend, who knew nothing of the straits in which Cesare had placed himself, gave him the exact amount he required, coupled with the request to lay it out on whatever form of charity he pleased.

CHAPTER XX
The Duties of His State

THERE were certain obvious duties of his state into which Baronius threw himself with energy, and which his discontent with his lot never led him to ignore for even one day. In spite of his love for simplicity, and his resolve to carry it with him into his life as a prince of the Church, he found himself, whether he would or no, placed at the head of quite a considerable household of chaplains, secretaries, retainers and domestics, for whose welfare, both spiritual and temporal, he was responsible, and which, in the language of the day, was known as his "family." St. Philip had gone to his reward when Baronius was raised to the purple but, as on every other subject, he had his views of what was fitting for the household of a Cardinal, and had laid down rules for the government of that of Cardinal Frederic Borromeo, with which Cesare may have been familiar. "You should," the Saint had said, "have in your family just the number of attendants which your rank requires, so that you may have enough to employ for all you wish to do for the glory of God and the service of His Church, without calling in aid from outside. ... Try to have in your family persons who combine the love of letters with virtue; for knowledge united to the spiritual life constitutes true and real learning. For all ecclesiastical ministrations you should employ ecclesiastics; in other matters employ seculars, but let these be men who fear God and lead an edifying life, and though they are not ecclesiastics by profession, let them be so by their virtue and conduct."

Cardinal Borromeo, as Archbishop of Milan, had, of course, a much larger household than Baronius, but, all the same, the retinue of the latter must have been considerable. Mention has already been made of his treasurer and of several secretaries. There were, besides these, gentlemen of position, such as Casata and Martino and probably others, whom he was able to send to act in his name and take possession of his various benefices, and handle the revenues. His valets and grooms with swords have been alluded to and it may be inferred that there were others who filled intermediate positions. Of this household he took the greatest care, and their mode of living resembled that of a religious house rather than a Cardinal's court.

Needless to say that Baronius set his retainers a rigidly spotless example, but more than this, he personally looked after the spiritual interests of each individual. He laid down the standard of what he demanded in the way of conduct, and was severe in his correction when anything was done contrary to it and, though public opinion pronounced him to be too rigid, he would never relax the rules he had imposed. If, however, as sometimes happened, he was carried away by hastiness of temper he was most ready to ask the pardon of even the lowest among his servants. Nay more, if his conscience reproached him with treating any one over harshly, or if the individual considered himself injured, he made a point of conferring some benefit on him in reparation. So well known was this habit that one of Baronius's friends lamented that he had never received any injury at his hands, as he would have been sure to have received some valuable compensation.

The result of such a system was admirable, and the household exemplary. "He lives among his people not as a master but as a father," wrote Justin Calvin, of whom more will be told hereafter. "He stands above and excels the others both by virtue and dignity, but in everything else he makes himself their equal. It is not that he is greater so much as better than they. There prevails around him an atmosphere of great calm, habitual silence, and such modesty that the humblest home might take example from the simplicity and tranquillity which reign in the dwelling-place of this prince of the Church." Justin spoke from his own experience, for when he came, a convert and friendless, to Rome, he was warmly received into Cesare's household.

Baronius's rule, as can be seen by this testimony, was strictly paternal. He desired that all his retainers should approach the sacraments once a month, and on that occasion gave them Communion himself. Every evening, moreover, he assembled his attendants in the chapel for night prayers and the recital of the litanies. On Saturday he preached to them, or invited one of the fathers of the Congregation to do so in his place. When he succeeded in obtaining this assistance, his own enjoyment was great, and he sat listening with riveted attention. The account of the delight he took in the fathers' sermons, and the value he attached to every word which fell from their lips, throws a side-light on the ceaseless interruptions which complicated his life. Very few hours of the day passed without his being summoned to wait on the Pope, whose confessor he continued to be after he was made Cardinal, and whose apartments were near his own. It thus

243

frequently happened that while he was listening to the above mentioned sermons he was sent for by Clement. Making a sign to his household not to stir, he would leave his place to do the Pope's behests with all speed, and this done, would quietly return to his seat in the chapel with as little loss of time as possible.

His great anxiety for the souls of his servants did not by any means make him indifferent to their temporal interests. He entered minutely into the affairs of each, and investigated personally whether their salaries sufficed for their needs. If any one of them were sick, he visited him constantly, looked after his soul, and saw that he was provided with special food and proper medicine. The result of these dealings with his servants was that, however much the outside world might censure his exactitude and severity, his retainers themselves loved him as much as they reverenced him.

He dined with his family at a common table, and established the practice of having a passage from Holy Scripture or from some Italian book of devotion read aloud during the meal and then —introducing the custom of the Oratory as far as was possible in such mixed company—he started some subject for discussion, and invited the opinion of every member of his household. Baronius was, however, rarely without a guest at his table, for he usually invited to it those foreign bishops, priests and learned men who came to Rome on purpose to consult him. He, moreover, devoted himself especially to the entertainment of pilgrims to the eternal city and its holy places. It was his habit to receive them in person to his private apartment, kiss their feet with reverence, and supply their wants with his own hands.

Among his most honoured guests was St. Francis of Sales. Though he was much younger than Baronius, the latter held him in extraordinary admiration. "He is an incomparable man," he said of him. "It is almost impossible to detect in him any vestige of that original sin which is the inheritance of all the sons of Adam." It was mainly through his intervention that St. Francis was appointed Bishop-coadjutor of the See of Geneva, to which he succeeded; and while the Saint resided in Switzerland, he corresponded frequently with him, and sent him each volume of the Annals as it was published. The holy Bishop of Geneva reciprocated his affection and admiration, and when he built the church at Thonon, insisted on Baronius being its protector. When business brought St. Francis to Rome, Cesare not only entertained him at table, but persuaded him to accompany him in his drives, so that they might have a better opportunity of conversing on the subjects most near to both their hearts.

Baronius naturally invited his guest to sit by his side, but this St. Francis refused to do, on account of the great reverence in which he held the writer of the Annals; and, seating himself on the ground, he declared that such was his proper place, namely, "at the feet of Gamaliel."

In spite of his manifold occupations, and desire, when possible, to exclude visitors, Baronius was most courteous to those whom he did admit into his presence. Indeed his interaction with his fellow-beings was marked by an habitual courtesy, which can be traced in the wording of his letters, even when written to intimate friends and the same tone characterised his personal interviews with strangers who came from afar to see him, hear him speak, and ask for his patronage. He preferred, however, to show his real kindness by his actions rather than by polite

245

speeches, and devoted much of his precious time to the affairs of his visitors. In this way he put himself entirely at the service of the Bishop of Ravella, though by so doing he was heaping coals of fire on the head of his guest, who had not so long before roused his keenest indignation by the fulsomeness of his complimentary congratulations. But all that was forgotten in his present desire to be of use to a stranger. "You know," he wrote to Talpa on the occasion of the Bishop's visit, "that I like serving people by deed rather than by word so I shall look out for some opportunity of being of real use to him."

The same sincerity which made Baronius honest in his writings, and recklessly bold of speech when conscience prompted him, rendered him scrupulously careful against making empty promises. He was quick to refuse patronage and intervention when solicited, but he could never bring himself to adopt the ways of many polite public men, and raise false hopes with the object of getting rid of the petitioner. It followed from this that some of his many burdens consisted in trying to obtain situations for needy converts, and others to whom he had promised assistance. He never asked the Pope for anything for himself but he was so indefatigable in asking favours for others, that Clement declared himself utterly incapable of keeping pace with his demands.

In spite of the sense of duty which made him thus solicit favours, the office of patron was always repugnant to him. "It is extraordinary," he wrote to Talpa very soon after his elevation, "what a number of competitors there are for every post, however small, and, of course, still more desire the greater places. I have not learnt the art of presuming, or of being importunate, and therefore I fear that I shall be of but little use to those who seek my patronage, for, after I have asked for a thing once, or at most twice, I cannot go on asking. I tell you this by way of excuse, and it might be well if you passed on my words."

Few appreciated solitude more than did Baronius; but he was no selfish recluse, passing through life with closed eyes. It was not only on behalf of those who were in want of employment that he spent his over-taxed energies. Whenever his great mind discovered the existence of another congenial to his own, he spared no pains in obtaining what he considered to be such an one's due, and used his almost unbounded influence over Clement VIII to effect the promotion of distinguished men. "I believe you know about the new Cardinals who have been created," he wrote to Talpa in March, 1599. "All the selections are, as far as possible, strictly ecclesiastical, and none of them depending on princes. I used my influence on behalf of Mgr. Visconti, Mgr. Silvio, and Father Bellarmine; and, by God's grace, was successful in all three cases. But for several reasons this must remain a secret between us." Some people tried to foment a spirit of rivalry between Baronius and Bellarmine, but without success; for they remained fast friends through life, and were full of sympathy with and appreciation of each other's researches. The only journey that we hear of Baronius making for his pleasure was with Bellarmine to Venice, while the papal court was at Ferrara, during his visit being most affectionately received and entertained by the Jesuit fathers. Bellarmine spoke of the writer of the Annals as "the great despiser of the world," sought his advice in everything, and, when he was made Cardinal, formed his household on the model of Baronius's. When Cesare lay dying, Bellarmine went again and again to the Oratory to inquire after him, and was so much overcome while

247

present at the Requiem Mass celebrated for him that he had to leave the church.

Baronius, who acted as a solicitous father towards his household, who opened his heart to the needs of others, and entered into the wants of congenial souls, whatever their nationality, shut his heart against all those who were related to him by blood. With his parents he kept up communication, but both father and mother passed to a better life while he was still in the seclusion of the Oratory, and before he was known to the world as compiler of either Martyrology or Annals. After their death he remained on severely distant terms with all his relatives. He always had a horror of nepotism in high places; and one of the instances cited of the holy liberty that he exercised as the Pope's confessor, is his fervent exhortation to Clement to avoid family partialities, though there is nothing in any of that holy Pontiff's actions to lead us to think that—in spite of his political reliance on his clever nephew, Cardinal Pietro—he was in any way tainted with the favourite error of his predecessors. The reaction against nepotism, so sternly inaugurated by Paul IV in connection with his Caraffa nephews, was still bearing manifest fruit. Detesting as he did the vice in Popes, it was not likely that Baronius should tolerate it in Cardinals; and in order to avoid the least semblance of, or temptation towards, attachment to his relatives, he kept them at an almost unnatural distance, and peremptorily forbade any of them to seek him out in Rome. If unavoidable business forced him to an interview with any one of them, he was most forbidding and acid in his manner, and allowed no trace of his habitual courtesy to betray itself.

A distant relative, belonging to the Sicilian branch of the family of Baronius, had asked the Naples fathers for a letter of introduction to the great Cardinal of his name. "I wish," Cesare wrote in reply to a communication to that effect from Talpa, "I wish that, as though it came from yourself, you would undeceive this gentleman, who says he belongs to the house of Baronius, and tell him that his kinship gives him no claim whatever on me, for that even my nearest relatives receive nothing from me beyond the barest subsistence."

The fathers of the Congregation thought that he was a little over-severe in this matter of his kinsmen, and more than once pleaded with him on behalf of certain needy relatives. "I beg you, father," he replied on one such occasion to Father Manni, "not even to talk to me on such a subject. It is most disagreeable to me." And he went on to beg him and each of the fathers individually to refrain from mentioning his relatives to him, as it made him really ill. He had quite made up his mind, he continued, and was acting only on what his mother had exhorted him to do when he was first ordained priest, namely, never to allow his family to prey on him. The bitterest memory of his life was that of having been persuaded by the fathers to transfer to his nephew Ottaviano the income of a small priory, the young man's extreme poverty and good character having induced him to consent. On another occasion, he went on to say, he had thought of building a house at Frascati for some of his kinsfolk who were exposed to dangers and difficulties owing to family feuds at Sora. But a certain holy man, to whom he confided his intention, told him that such a thought savoured of the earth and his conscience was so disturbed by these words that he at once abandoned the idea, and distributed among

249

some religious houses the money he had intended to spend that way.

So afraid was Baronius of giving an excuse to the younger generation of his nephews of boasting of their relationship to him, that he would not even give them advice, or act towards them in public as if he had any claim on their respect. However, the following anecdote shows that sometimes impulse so far got the better of him as to make him forget this self-imposed rule. He had for some reason given the use of his coach to a party of young men, among whom was his nephew, a soldier, who was apt to give himself airs. This young man, looking on himself as the hero of the occasion, seated himself in the carriage in the place of honour. "Sit you there!" exclaimed his uncle indignantly, pointing to the lowest place. "Do you think I am going to allow my relatives to disgrace me!" Another time, one of his nephews, who had been murderously assaulted, sought his uncle's protection for purposes of revenge but Baronius would not admit him to his presence until he had promised to forgive the injury.

Cesare's kinsfolk were careful not to forget that both he and they came of noble family but he himself repudiated all allusion to the fact. His refusal on the occasion of his niece's religious profession to enter the church till the family coats-of-arms had been removed, is but one instance out of many of his dislike to all outward tokens of his nobility. He also disliked any mode of address which savoured of a reminder of his noble birth. Hearing a widowed aunt of his spoken of as "the Lady Marcia," he interrupted the speaker. "What are you about, calling her lady," he exclaimed. "Call her plain Marcia." When certain friends complained that this same aunt had been treated with insult by a grand lady, he was not in the least disturbed, and refused to take any notice of it. All the same, he was in reality attached to his aunt and revered her for her piety, as he testified on a tablet put up to her memory in the chapel of St. Sylvia, adjoining the church of St. Gregory, restored by him.

His attitude of severe reserve towards his family was to a certain extent relaxed as regarded his nieces, all of whom he provided with dowries. In doing so, however, he took the opportunity of repudiating all claims to nobility on their part; and having regard to the actual and almost needy circumstances of these young women more than their noble extraction, he refused to sanction any attempt made by them or their relatives to improve their position. On the strength of her connection with himself, the offer of a rich marriage for one of his nieces was made to him, not long after he was raised to the purple; but he at once and decisively refused it. He had written to Talpa about this offer and its rejection. in terms which his friend considered exaggerated; so he wrote again as follows, to explain the energy of his language in the first letter:

"Perhaps I wrote too strongly about the transaction of my niece's marriage, though it is not my wish that the fact of my being a Cardinal should foster any ambition for honours or riches in the hearts of my relatives. As far as I am concerned, I wish them to remain in the position in which they find themselves, and I will relieve them only when they are in real need. They being poor, it seems to me sufficient if I give each of my nieces a dowry of a thousand crowns, which would enable them without difficulty to contract marriages with some of our citizens of Sora, this being the average amount of the marriage portion of the better class among them. *De reliquo nemo mihi molestus sit, nolo ambulare in magnis neque in*

251

mirabilibus super me.[20] Enough for the moment. If on any future occasion I seem likely to act differently, correct me as a lunatic though I hope I shall not need it."

It seems probable that this niece did not after all marry, and that the question of her marriage dowry was never raised; for, some years later, Baronius, in writing to Talpa, expressed his great joy that all his nieces had embraced the religious life. "I will not keep you in ignorance," he wrote in 1602, "that God has inspired my nieces in such a way that, with great fortitude and in the face of many trials, they have all chosen the religious state. Up to the present moment there are eight of them in various convents in Rome, chosen by them on account of the reputation for holiness possessed by these houses. Three are in Santa Maria Maddalena, which you founded; two are at Santa Maria, one at Santa Susanna, and two at San Giuseppe, a new convent of Blessed Mother Teresa's discalced Carmelites, a house of very close observance. This week two were professed and one clothed. *Magnificate Dominum mecum.*[21] There remain three more who, being under age, are being educated at the above convents; and I have no doubt but what they will follow in the steps of the others. I have treated them all liberally, having given them dowries ranging from a thousand to three hundred crowns, without counting their expenses, such dowries being above what is usual. To meet this expense I have had to borrow, but I hope to pay off the debt soon. Other Cardinals did me the honour of being

---

[20] "Let nobody disturb me concerning the rest, I do not wish to walk among the great nor among those more remarkable than me." -Editor.

[21] "Magnify the Lord with me." Psalm 33:4. -Editor.

present at the spiritual nuptials of my nieces, and I, at their request, preached on the occasion. Thus I repeat, *Magnificate Dominum mecum.*"

With his native home Baronius had but few dealings after the death of his parents, but he did not forget his duties towards it. Sora was the spot chosen for the establishment of a community of Capuchins; and not only did Cesare persuade them to settle there, but by his generosity at the time, and subsequent assistance and moral support, enabled them to remain there. In his connection with this community, chosen by himself for the evangelisation of his country, we can perceive the echo of the ungranted desire of his early manhood to devote himself to the service of God in the habit of St. Francis. No doubt, amid the splendours, cares, and turmoil of the papal court, his thoughts often turned, not with regret but with envy, to that home of holy poverty among his native hills.

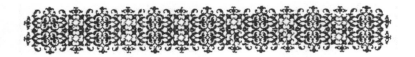

CHAPTER XXI
Benefices

BESIDES such private duties of his state as the supervision of his household and entertaining strangers, there were others of a more public nature into which Baronius threw himself with eagerness. In the performance of these he found, it may be safely said, his only solace during the first year that he was Cardinal, and an interest which, humanly speaking, saved him from melancholy.

When made a member of the Sacred College, Baronius received—it is said at his own particular request—the title of SS. Nereus and Achilleus, though the church had ceased to be titular for uncounted years, and had been allowed to fall into ruins. Cesare had not forgotten the shame and sorrow with which its dilapidated state had filled his heart nearly forty years before, when he stopped before it while making the processional visit to the seven churches. Though on that occasion his desire to restore the church to its pristine glory savoured more of a daydream than an intention, the memory of his desire remained, and impelled him to ask the boon of that heap of ruins as his titular church. He began the restoration as soon as he received the administration of his title, and without waiting to draw any income from it, raised what was necessary on loan. The only part of the church which remained complete was the apse behind the high altar, and its mosaic decorations were in a state of sufficient preservation to serve as a model for the reconstruction of the church in its original style. The work of restoration was one of really absorbing interest to Baronius, both architecturally and archtelogically, and his loving study of early Christian history endowed the dead stones with life, as one by one they were placed in closest possible imitation of the ancient model.

"I have received a brief from His Holiness," he wrote to Talpa in February, 1597, "which gives me permission to remove the bodies of my Saints together with that of their patroness, St. Flavia, all three of which are at present at San Adriano. I am already in possession of their heads, which are now encased in a reliquary of wood, gilt and decorated. I mean to postpone the translation of the relics until the feast of the Saints on May 12. On which day the ceremony will take place with due solemnity. In the church everything has been fitly restored. There is an altar of carved stone, without a frontal. Were it covered with the richest brocade, it would not be as beautiful as it is at present. The stones were given me by the Abbot of St. Paul's. They were formerly part of the confessional, but since the basilica was renovated they were of no use. I also have made a confessional, where the relics will be placed. I have also had a sedia presbitoria made, ambos for the Gospel and Epistle, and engraved candlesticks; and that nothing may be wanting, I have ordered a beautiful paschal-candlestick. I have had the apse painted in antique style, and have had the upper part of the domed arch and the cross finished off with jewels, which looks very well. On one side are five male, and on the other five female martyrs; and under the cornice, above the pontifical throne, is St. Gregory the Pope preaching, and below and around him are the people listening. This has pleased His Holiness very much, and several Cardinals in whose titles

256

St. Gregory delivered homilies wish to imitate it. ... By God's grace every one is satisfied. His Holiness has promised to help me with the expenses. Hitherto I have had no help, so that it has been necessary for me to run into debt, though not for more than can be repaid in a year. Another brief will be issued appointing that the church be served by the fathers of the Vallicella. There are examples of this having been done at San Apollonaris and S. Stefano Rotondo, and some other churches. My title will serve as a halting place when the seven churches are visited, as it is the half-way point of the journey. The fathers are very pleased with it."

It can be seen from this letter how strongly the idea was in Baronius's mind of in some way benefiting the Congregation by his title, and this added a special and personal ingredient to the pleasure he took in the restoration of the old church. "I cannot remember," he says in another letter, "whether I told you of my idea of associating my title with some little hospital, and of buying a vineyard near it to form a sort of endowment for it. By a brief which I shall obtain from His Holiness, this with its trappings will be made over *in perpetuum in pleno dominio*[22] to the fathers of the Vallicella, there being precedents of the kind. My intention in doing this is that the church shall always be able to maintain itself, and not be allowed to fall again into ruin." This last object, namely the preservation of what he had restored with so much trouble and expense, was very near Baronius's heart. His work had been undertaken solely for the glory of God and

---

[22] "Full Dominion forever." This is a Latin legal term meaning the possessor will have complete rights over a piece of property. -Editor.

the honour of his titular saints and when he contemplated it on its completion, he could not but be aware that he had done it well. It was but natural that he should do his best to prevent the undoing of his work and while he did his utmost to protect his title from future penury by the investments about which he informed Talpa, he attempted the more difficult task of bridling the bad taste and vandalism of his successors by leaving the following appeal to posterity engraved on a stone tablet in the church: "Cardinal Priest, my successor, whoever you may be: I beg of you for the glory of God and the honour of His saints to remove nothing, suppress nothing, change nothing, and piously to preserve restored antiquity. Thus may God through the prayers of His martyrs always be your help."

Baronius's joy at the restoration of his titular church was not complete till the relics of its martyr patrons, which had been removed on account of the dilapidated state of the building, were once more placed under the altar. "By God's grace," he wrote after the solemnity of May 12, "the translation was made with great devotion and tranquillity. The Pope had his procession in the morning, and we had ours in the evening. I cannot describe it, as I took no part in it, having, as was decreed by the Master of Ceremonies, to remain in my church to receive the Cardinals, with whom I went to meet the saints when they came in. Praise be to God." Baronius's devotion to the relics of saints was very fervent. In fact, by an effort of vivid, realising faith he beheld in them those actually of whom they were but the sacred remains. Thus when he wrote as above of meeting "the saints" on their entry into the church, he was putting into language the spontaneous thought which was in his heart. This aspect

258

of his devotion came out more strongly still in connection with the gift of some relics which he made to the Naples Oratory. He was able to make the gift, for when the restored church of SS. Nereus and Achilleus was opened, the Pope gave Baronius the right to claim any relics of the two martyrs which were in Rome; and acting on this authority he soon became the possessor of a considerable number. Among other treasures, he discovered a large portion of the martyrs' heads in the church of St. Sebastian, which, with the Pope's permission, he gave to the Naples fathers for their new church.

The letters which he wrote to Father Talpa about this present reveal the profoundness of his veneration for the relics of the saints. "Herewith," he writes, "by special messenger, the two saints are sent to you. I say advisedly 'the saints', i.e., the whole saints, and not even a part of their relics, for such is the expression used by St. Gregory Nazianzen when writing against Julian the Apostate about the virtue and efficacy of martyrs' relics. So then, I repeat, the saints are on their way to you, living in soul and body. Do them fitting honour, be worthy hosts of these denizens of heaven, and pray for me an unworthy sinner; for by sending them away from me I am but expressing my unworthiness and saying, 'Depart from me, for I am a sinful man.' I pray God, who blessed Obed-Edom[23] for receiving the Ark into his house, to multiply blessings on you and those who come after you for receiving into your midst these two arks containing such holy relics."

---

[23] A levite from the family of Korhites who is thought to be a convert to Judaism. See 4 Kings (2 Samuel) 6: 1-12.

A little later Baronius procured for Naples a small relic of St. Flavia Domitilla, whom he associated, and wished his friends to associate with the martyrs SS. Nereus and Achelleus, who were in her service, and in whose company she shed her blood for the faith. "I send you," he wrote, "a small fragment of bone, removed with my own hand from the sacred head of St. Domitilla. Do not think I am sending you too little, for neither quantity nor quality can be measured in such things. Faith, reflecting on the virtue contained in each atom, perceives in it that of the whole body. Behold, now my work with your blessed church is finished. May you comprehend all that charity requires of you in the way of commending me to these saints."

The restoration of his titular church cost Baronius seven thousand crowns more than was covered by the income attached to it. It is a matter of speculation where he procured the means for his many works of restoration as well as for his generous alms, for his income as a Cardinal was exceptionally small. Owing, we may presume, to the delicacy arising from Clement's personal friendship for him, and also to the fact that he allowed him special annuities for the expense entailed by the Annals, the Pope seems not to have given Baronius the usual stipend allowed to Cardinals without revenues, with the exception of an obligatory pension of a hundred crowns a month, which was paid to him. It may be remembered that this omission acted as a powerful check on Cesare's desire to resign the Cardinalate, lest his repugnance to the dignity should be attributed to mercenary motives. The offices he held, even that of Apostolic Librarian conferred on him not long after his elevation, were poorly paid; nevertheless he could not bring himself to ask the Pope for anything. Such delicacy as his was rare, and probably Clement, overwhelmed by the affairs of the Church, and accustomed to be remorselessly solicited for favours, concluded that if Baronius asked for nothing, it was because he wanted nothing; whereas, as a matter of fact, he often found himself in very pinched circumstances.

It is fair to say that the Pope was not wholly unmindful of his needs, for in the course of eight years he conferred on him a number of abbeys, priories and benefices with the object of increasing his income in proportion with his dignity; and it cannot be counted Clement's fault if he forgot to take into consideration the scruples of Baronius's conscience, which forbade him to appropriate a penny of these revenues to his own private expenses. Every fraction drawn from these benefices had, according to Cesare's judgment, to be spent either on the restoration of the sacred buildings attached to them, or, still more, on the care of the souls which depended for spiritual ministrations on these abbeys and priories.

Thus, though the acquisition of the benefices added materially to the interest and responsibilities of Baronius's life, they did not add to his income. It is calculated that in satisfying the claims which he considered his benefices to have on him, he spent the sum of 60,000 crowns.

As an instance of the munificent manner in which he spent his income, it is stated that when the benefice of St. Gregory on the Coalian was bestowed on him, he restored it in the most perfect manner; and each successive year, on the feast of its patron saint, he entertained a number of the poor at the table where St. Gregory had been miraculously supplied with bread. It would be impossible without monotonous repetition to relate all that he did for the restoration and beautifying of the material edifices committed to his keeping. Something, however, remains to be told of the part played in his life by some of the benefices conferred on him; for his devotion to the interests of those which entailed any spiritual responsibilities, and his care for the souls which were in a measure committed to his care, knew no bounds.

The first of the abbeys conferred on him by the Pope was that of St. Fortunatus at Arpaia, near Naples. In this case there was no cure of souls attached to the benefice, but he threw himself into his duties towards the place with his usual devotion, and, as was his wont, made much of the saint with whom he became connected, and placed himself and the interests of the Abbey under his protection. Moreover, he made the life of St. Fortunatus the object of his closest study, and expressed the hope that he might be able to obtain some indulgences for his feast. The greatest advantage of his new acquisition was its proximity to Naples, and the facilities thus afforded of obtaining the help of the fathers in its administration, to which his position in Rome made it impossible for him to attend personally. Moreover, Arpaia being near Naples, the possibility of a visit to the latter place and its Oratory rose before his mind like a vision of hope. "I shall send one of my people to take possession of the Abbey," he wrote to Talpa. "He will look over everything, and I will ask you to help him in any way that is possible. I thank God, for, though I do not wish for the journey, it will give me an opportunity of visiting my dear fathers and brothers at Naples, and afford an excuse for going there."

As with his title, so with every new possession, Baronius's first impulse was to see how he could benefit the Congregation by it, and soon after Arpaia had been

262

given to him, he wrote as follows to Talpa: "I have arranged with the Bishop of Acerra about everything that is necessary for the administration of the abbey. I will tell you what is in my mind. I have, as you know, associated the Vallicella with my titular church in such a way that not only will the fathers be put to no expense, but will be rather the gainers. I have thought of uniting to it also this abbey of Arpaia. A priest must be maintained there to keep the lamp burning and do other necessary things, but what is over shall be spent for the benefit of the Vallicella fathers. I do not think, however, that I ought to do this at once, but must let at least a year elapse first. I am glad that the abbey is small, for if its income were greater the whole thing would be more difficult."

Meanwhile Baronius was not negligent of the material restoration and beautifying of his new acquisition. "I quite approve of the picture of St. Fortunatus which you have chosen for the church," he wrote to Talpa. " I have already begun to commemorate him. Spare no expense where the glory of God and the honour of His saints are at stake. I confess I had rather the Madonna chosen had been a copy of the one belonging to the Congregation, but anything that satisfies you and the Bishop of Acerra satisfies me. . . . Assume full liberty to spend, even if it takes a whole year's income to improve a place which I hope may be some day yours. ... Take charge of everything as if it were your own. These are the orders I have given my servant Casata."

Matters did not go as smoothly with all of Baronius's benefices as they did with Arpaia and soon after taking possession of that abbey he found himself constrained to refuse the gift of another for reasons which he thus describes to Talpa: "His Holiness wished to present me with another abbey in the country of Otranto; but as there is episcopal jurisdiction attached to it, I refused it. In my position I could not visit it, and I would rather be destitute than have the weight of the care of souls on my shoulders. I do not know what is to be done. I have always set myself resolutely against asking for any ecclesiastical benefice, though I thereby incur the blame of many of my friends. However, each one must rest on his own judgment, and the course I have taken seems safer and conducive to a better example."

In another case, somewhat similar to that described in the above letter, Cesare was less fortunate, and was unable to decline the proffered burden; or, rather, he was misled, and surprised into doing the very thing which he declared to his friend that he would never do. "I think I told you that His Holiness insisted on giving me the provostship of Apuglia," he wrote to Talpa from Ferrara in 1598. "He even settled everything without consulting me. I have since discovered something which fills me with consternation, namely, that its real title is St. Sabinus, the See of the Bishop of Canossa, St. Sabinus having been the first Bishop. This is now handed over to me, which makes me tremble, as, unbeknownst to myself, I have been made in a certain sense Bishop of Canossa. On the other hand, it has occurred to me that it may have been permitted by God in order that this extinct bishopric may be restored. I told His Holiness about my intentions, and he is pleased that all this should have come about for the glory of so great a saint. I intend, by adding to the income of the priory, which is in itself about six hundred crowns, to get the See restored and a new Bishop nominated. This done, I shall set myself free, hoping to have pleased God and His saint. I hear that the church is magnificent, very ancient, with beautiful porphyry columns. All this stirs me up to carry out my project."

There were many souls for whose spiritual welfare Baronius became responsible by his new possession. He was powerless to do anything himself to supply the need, and met with no slight difficulty in finding a priest qualified to take charge of the priory. As usual, he appealed for help to the Naples fathers, and put the whole matter into their hands. "Find me a priest," he wrote, "whom I can send with Casata, and who is fitted to look after the spiritual interests of Canossa. I want to find one who will be zealous, and withal good-mannered. I will pay all his expenses, and whatever more is necessary. I have told Casata to pay everything."

The more he heard of his priory, the more weighed on was he by his new responsibilities, and the more urgent was he to supply what was wanted. "I am much displeased," he wrote, "by what Casata tells me of the way souls have been cared for at Canossa. The people are in a state of profoundest ignorance, and the priests who have charge of them are more ignorant than they. The dilapidated condition of the church is but a comparatively small evil, which can be easily rectified. But if you love me help me to provide for the spiritual misery. I want to find a spiritual man as vicar—one who would always live on the spot, and who, being full of Christian zeal, would be a true pastor to these poor sheep, and would preach, admonish, instruct, and do all that is wanted. I have set my mind at rest by resolving not to touch a farthing of the income, but to spend it all for the good of the people and the restoration of the church. I will give everything that is wanted, even if I have to supplement it out of my private means. I would far rather do this than fail in any duty that

265

befits a vigilant pastor. So, my father, minister to the melancholy of which I am the prey, and let me be assured that everything will be done as I should wish. Do not lose time, but start the work before Lent. See to this, knowing that I have it more at heart than anything else in the world; and do not let us waste time in words, but come to deeds at once. I would rather do what is superfluous than fail in the smallest thing that I ought to do."

"There are many timings you have done to please me," he soon after wrote, still more urgently; "but by doing this you will be giving me a pleasure such as you have never given me before. Choose a man who will not seek the things that are his own but the things that are Jesus Christ's. Read in these words my meaning, which I am unable to express adequately, and by carrying it out you will make it possible for me to live without scruple until means can be found to restore the bishopric." In the anxiety of mind caused by his new and weighty responsibility, he even still feared that he had not made his directions to spare no expense sufficiently clear, and was moreover possessed by a misgiving that Casata, in his faithful regard for the interests of his master, might not be as open-handed as was called for by the exigency. Thus he added a hurried postscript to the above letter: "I fear that my agent may be too economical and as, on account of the value of his services to me, I wish to save the vicar of your choice all annoyance, will you arrange about the amount of his stipend? Let him be assured that, in addition to the appointed salary, I shall be sure to recognise his services in a thousand ways. Let him know that he will not have to do with one who does not know how to recompense, or who will do so ungratefully. Arrange all this, so that he may work for souls more joyfully. ... Bid Casata pay for a horse-litter for your journey. I pray you to accept this slight charity."

It is distressing to learn that, in spite of Baronius's generosity and solicitude for the welfare of those for whose spiritual needs he found himself responsible, he did not meet with a reward. In some way or other, Talpa and the other Naples fathers mismanaged this affair of the Canossa vicar; and in the following letter of reproach which he addressed to them Cesare allows us to see the sharp side of his temper: "I do not believe that the good God, who has always taken such care of me even in the smallest matters, would have permitted me to offend Him and my neighbour in this affair of the vicar, concerning which He never let me have the slightest scruple of conscience. Had I been wrong, surely you or some one else would have told me. I hope that some day God will make you all know better, and how much more displeasure your offence causes me than can be covered by the cloak of charity. You will have to render an account of yourself before God and man, though, as for myself, I must always put a kind interpretation on any action of yours, knowing the rightness of your intention. As to Father Juvenal, so far as there has been error, he is the one most to blame, because he had the letter before you, and it was read in the refectory and passed from hand, to hand and it displeases me that he should lay the blame on you. I have given orders that nothing be touched."

What was the blunder committed by the Naples fathers, or what the evil consequences which ensued from it, is not shown in the correspondence. But that its effects were serious and lasting, and that the affair produced a sufficient stiffness between Baronius and his friends to forbid further allusion to the unpleasant subject, is shown by a letter written on January 1, 1600, about six months after the last: "Though," Cesare wrote, "we keep silence about what took place at Canossa through your bad management, nevertheless, as I wish to avoid all appearance of distrust towards you, I will tell you what His Holiness has resolved in the matter. I wished to resign the priory, but he would not have it; and told me that in order that I might feel my conscience quite easy, he would arrange for the appointment of a vicar *in perpetuum, omnibus futuris temporibus*,[24] with a stipend of a hundred crowns. This I have arranged for. As it is so difficult to find any one willing to leave Rome, I will send you the brief, should you hear of any one suitable; and meanwhile I will continue my search here in the hopes of finding the right man. If you come here for the holy year, I will give you some important relics to take back with you. I say this to induce you to come." With this peace-offering the difference between Cesare and the Naples congregation was healed, never again to be reopened. Talpa, however, after holding out repeated hopes of going to Rome for the year of jubilee, never went, aud one more disappointment was added to Baronius's list.

Sufficient has been said of the abbacies and priories given to Cesare, and of the interest and trouble which they brought with them. There were, however, several other benefices, besides those mentioned, conferred on him, including one permanently attached to the office of Librarian, which his sense of justice and the fitness of things made him go out of his way to claim. In a letter to Talpa he put the united income attached to his various

---

[24] "In the future, for all time." -Editor.

268

benefices at four thousand crowns, which cannot by any means have covered what he spent upon them. The only other source of income mentioned, exclusive of the annuities granted to defray the expenses of the Annals, is the monthly allowance of a hundred crowns "given to poor Cardinals who depend on the Pope." This sum, the only one that he was free to spend as he liked, was laid aside by Baronius as the minimum amount to be bestowed in alms.

CHAPTER XXII
Later Communication with Naples

ENOUGH has been said in the last chapter to show that towards the end of his public career, as at its beginning it was to Naples that Cesare turned, there to find the fellowship and sympathy which his human nature demanded. Among the marks of the constant, changeless character of Baronius's friendship with the Naples fathers, it is almost pathetic to find him exposed in his later years to the same kind of trials as pursued him in earlier days, due, as then, to the want of judgment on the part of some of the fathers, and especially Father Camillo, the culprit-in-chief of former times. In fact, these petty annoyances, while they began with the first proof-sheets of the Annals, reached their climax only in 1606, less than a year before Cesare died, and would have no doubt continued in full vigour had not his death cut the knot of this and all his other earthly troubles.

Very soon after the publication of the first volume of the Annals, Baronius was appealed to from various quarters to compile an epitome and publish it with each volume as it appeared. Father Possevino, a learned member of the Society of Jesus, while thanking him for the boon he had conferred on the Catholic world by his history, strongly urged the necessity of an epitome, and offered to do it himself. But Baronius, who to the end was most jealously anxious that the Annals should be touched by none but the fathers of the Congregation, put off accepting an offer which he could not refuse directly, and, meanwhile, urged strongly on Talpa the expediency of getting the work done without delay at the Naples Oratory, so as to prevent outside attempts; with the result that first one and then another tried his hand at it. "I am glad that Father Camillo is seeing to the epitome," Cesare wrote to Father Talpa, "but I pray you to superintend his work, for it is most important that it should be done well. If not, it will be undertaken by some one else." "Father Possevino," he wrote again a little later, " is most urgent in his offers to epitomize the first volume. I have told him that the Naples fathers have already undertaken the work. Therefore exhort Father Camillo to do it well, so as to give no excuse to any other to do it."

However, this matter of the epitome dragged on. The Naples fathers procrastinated, and all their attempts were failures. Baronius, keenly alive to Father Camillo's incompetency, yet unwilling to give offence, let the matter drop, and, in the press of new work, the whole thing went out of his head. Ten years after the question of an epitome had been first mooted, Baronius had a rude awakening. The outside world had not shown the same indifference as he and his friends, and as soon as the copyright of the Annals had expired, the work neglected by the Congregation was freely taken up by a multitude of epitomizers. To add to the injury, Cesare received reproaches for his neglect from the Naples fathers, which drew down on them this vehement rejoinder.

"As to the epitome, the copyright having expired, it is in anybody's power to make one, print one, and do just what he likes. It can indeed be said of us: *Sero sapiunt*

Phryges.[25] Long ago I wrote to you to say that Father Camillo's attempt was much too verbose; and on that account I did not ask him to go on with it. The fact is there ought to have been two or three fathers deputed to look after such an important matter, who should not have let it drop till the work was completed. So long as I possessed the copyright I refused all outside offers on the plea that the Naples fathers were doing the work; but now that it has expired I have no authority, and the thing has been done without my permission. Last year a Jesuit father showed me his epitome, and told me that it had been revised by Cardinal Bellarmine and others of their fathers. I could not refuse it, because I had no power to do so. I have since heard that an epitome has been made in France, and another in Germany, and I cannot forbid them. So, father, I do not see how you can reasonably reproach me. Nor will I, on my side, reproach you for having allowed such an important matter to be neglected. All that has happened has been by the will of God."

Though too late, this letter stirred up the Naples fathers to fresh exertions, and the work was resumed, though far from successfully. "I am in doubt as to the epitome about which you tell me," he wrote to Talpa, in a state of evident conflict between his feelings of gratitude for the trouble taken, too late, by his friends and the conviction that the result of their labours would not serve the purpose required. "You tell me that it will be longer than the one made in Venice, which proves to me how very long it must be. In fact, as far as I can judge, it would

---

[25] "The Phrygians get wise too late." Erasmus, *Adagia*, 1.1.28. By Phrygians Erasmus meant the Trojans. -Editor.

not be an epitome at all, but the Annals themselves
reproduced with everything absolutely necessary
abridged, and everything that looks to you superfluous cut
out. The only effect of such an epitome would be to
extinguish the Annals themselves. I have sanctioned the
work of the Jesuit father, and also that of a learned
Frenchman, who have both made real epitomes (i.e., out of
ten volumes they have made two) which cannot injure the
original. So pray pause and consider, and do not act rashly
in such an important matter. Remember that the object of
an epitome is neither to reproduce the original, nor to
make it contemptible by reducing it. So I beg of you to do
nothing more until the matter has been well thought out
and matured. The one condition which I imposed on both
Jesuit and Frenchman was brevity, and this they have
attended to, or else I should have withdrawn the
permission. I cannot change my opinion, and I wonder
that you, who have always sympathised with the work,
should not see things in the same light."

It never rains but it pours and Baronius, who had at
first complained that no one would undertake the
epitome, now received another attempt to supply the want
from the pen of the Archbishop of Avignon, formerly
Father Bordini of the Congregation. This act of friendship
complicated the case, for in spite of their long years of
intimacy when working together at S. Giovanni, Cesare
did not feel sufficiently at his ease with the Archbishop to
deal as freely with his work as with that of his friends at
Naples. " Besides the epitome you sent me," he wrote to
Talpa in this new dilemma, "I have this week received
several sheets of another, compiled by the Archbishop of
Avignon. I appreciate his labour, for he tells me that he
has contrived to compress three volumes into one, and

274

hopes, by working on one volume at a time, to do the same by the remainder. Now, as it would have been the height of unfriendliness to forbid him to proceed any further, I could do nothing, and have had to let things be. I think it better to let you know my reasons for not refusing his offer, lest you should complain of my having conceded to others what I have denied to you. Do whatever seems good to you, and, with the blessing of God, I will consent to anything."

Baronius, however, repented of thus sacrificing the interests of the Annals to friendship, and recognised that as he had been compelled to accept what served his purpose from outside, it would be mere sentiment to substitute an inferior article only because it came from the desired source. Probably, moreover, the Naples epitome, as—in spite of all protests and prohibitions—he received it sheet by sheet, proved to be more hopelessly bad than he had anticipated; for, in June, 1606, the last year of his life, he wrote somewhat peremptorily to Talpa, putting a final stop to all further attempts. "So as not to keep you any longer in suspense," he said, "I tell you at once that I am not returning your sheets, as the epitome is being made in a way never sanctioned by me, and which transgresses all the laws of compilation. There exist already two epitomes, those of the Jesuit and the Paris doctor, and both of these are unobjectionable and concise and to these a third, with slight alterations, is being added. In order to put a stop to all arguings I shall persuade His Holiness to issue a brief forbidding all further epitomes. Pray do not be offended with me, for I think I am acting in conformity with the will of God."

The trouble about the epitome was not the only vexatious consequence of the expiration of the copyright

275

of the Annals. That it should have been allowed to lapse at all was a cause of bitter complaint to Baronius, for he attributed it to the culpable neglect of Clement VIII, who was so delighted at the prospect of a wider circulation of the book that he overlooked other considerations, and put off renewing the copyright till too late. The Naples fathers, in whose hands Cesare had left all the business transactions connected with the Annals, came in for their share of censure. It was indeed a subject of real indignation to Baronius during the later years of his life to see his Annals pillaged and pirated at will. He was robbed of all power of defending himself, and his entire dependence on the courtesy and sense of honour of those with whom he remonstrated was no slight humiliation. "I must tell you," he wrote, not without bitterness, to the Naples fathers, "that what we ought to have done is being done by others. Lives of the Popes are being extracted by Maiolo, Bishop of Villunara. In Spain, lives of the saints have been extracted, and a compilation has also been taken from the Annals of the traditions of the Church which tell against the German heretics. In fact every one takes from the book what he chooses, I will have Bishop Maiolo spoken to, but I doubt his willingness to sacrifice the result of so much labour and I do not think it can be remedied, though I shall try everything in my power. Seeing this, the result of your negligence, I doubt the efficacy of any measure we can take."

It was his very intimacy and want of reserve which made Baronius thus plain-spoken when any thing turned up to excite his ire against his Naples friends. But such instances are infrequent and though impetuous censures, such as have been quoted, always passed through the hands of Talpa, between him and that father personally there existed no friction. To him Cesare continued to write with his own hand long after necessity drove him to employ a secretary for the rest of his correspondence, and, casting aside the Latin which from long habit had become as easy to him as his own tongue, he poured out his confidences to Talpa in the familiar Italian of his youth. He still gave this friend his full confidence, though, as the strain of life pressed more unbearably on him, the letters he wrote grew fewer in number, till at last there were but two or three written in the twelvemonth. But even then he begged Talpa not to cease his letters, but to write even if he had no communication to make, as "even a simple salutation would be a consolation to him." As a rule, Talpa, the prudent one, was the monitor and counsellor, but sometimes the case was reversed, and Baronius, though in most tender words, administered fraternal correction to his friend. "Accounts have reached us here of your too great austerity and inflexibility," he wrote, when Talpa was at the head of the Naples Congregation. "I believe, all the same, that the report has been spread by those who have been tried. But do not forget that perfection consists in bearing with the infirm and consoling the weak. I will say no more; and I ask you not to reply to this, for you might feel bound to yield the point to a prelate. Let us pray to God for the welfare of the common cause, which is going on as badly as possible. If God does not raise up saints to show forth new, greater, and more manifest signs, we are bound to receive great mortifications."

The Naples fathers, as a body, entirely reciprocated Baronius's affection and were full of solicitude about his health. Probably none knew better than they how terrible was the stress of his work, which was slowly and surely

277

bringing him to the grave. With the new century, when Cesare had entered the seventh decade of his life, Talpa wrote to him to point out that it was now time that he took some care of himself. He at once replied: "I thank you for your good advice to moderate my labours. Such indeed is the counsel which I receive from all who bear me affection; and I have serious thoughts of following it and taking care of myself. But I assure you that it is the things pertaining to my dignity which wear me out, and that my studies are a comparative recreation. Would to God I were permitted to go where I would—go, I mean, where I could enjoy the companionship and sweet conversation of my brothers. However, even to speak of such things is vanity, for there is no possible means of carrying out my desire." It is descriptive of the impossibility Baronius found in sparing himself that, in spite of what he said, his only practical response to his friends' exhortations to husband his remaining strength was to visit the seven churches—a distance of eight miles—four times on foot during the holy year with which the seventeenth century opened.

It was the dream of Baronius's life, impossible though he knew its fulfilment to be, to end his days at Naples or, short of that, to dwell there awhile among his friends. He was constantly on the look-out for an opportunity to pay the desired visit but each time that the chances seemed favourable he was doomed to disappointment, for it was part of the sanctification that was to ensue from his connection with the papal court that his will was constantly thwarted in small things as well as great. He had matured a plan, easy of execution, of visiting Naples by absenting himself from the papal court on its return from Ferrara but at the last moment the Pope dismissed most of his retinue, and elected to travel alone with his nephew and Baronius, so that the plan had to be abandoned. Again, when the benefice of Arpaia was given him, he felt sure that business connected with the abbey would give him the desired opportunity of visiting Naples "privately and secretly." But time after time he had to renounce his project, till the tone of confident hope which had pervaded his letters on the subject changed, and all he could find to say was that he did not "yet quite despair of going to Naples."

There is, however, one letter, written in 1601, which leads us to think that his desire was in a measure granted; for in a formal, ceremonious address to the Naples Congregation collectively, he alludes to what he had evidently seen with his own eyes, and tells them how edified he had been by their zeal for close observance and the modesty with which they carried it out, which led him to believe that the Spirit of God was dwelling in their midst.

It has been sufficiently shown how anxious the Naples fathers were to prove their affection for Baronius by their deeds. They looked after his abbeys and priories for him, and whatever way they may have erred in carrying out his wishes, it arose from mismanagement, and no want of good will. Furthermore, they lavished hospitality on any whom he had occasion to send to Naples, and in this respect sometimes vexed him by outstripping his wishes. Thus when, on one occasion, he had asked them to find a lodging for his factotum Gianbattista Casata, they insisted on putting him up at the Oratory. "I do not wish him to stay with you," Baronius wrote positively; "for I know how burdensome a stranger can be. I must beg you to find him a lodging with some respectable person: that will be quite sufficient." However, in spite of these explicit

279

directions, the fathers insisted on making Casata their guest, which annoyed Baronius considerably. "My orders were," he writes back a little peremptorily, "that he should not go to your house to hassle you, for I know the sort of man he is. *In nomine Domini.* God's will be done." The fathers were more fortunate in the case of another of Baronius's retainers, Paolo Curione, who was out of health, and whom also they received into the Oratory. Cesare wrote to return them the warmest thanks for their hospitality, and told them that Paolo "could never cease talking of their kindness to him."

It was but natural that the Naples fathers should in their turn ask freely for many favours and kindnesses at the hands of Baronius, which he took great pleasure in doing for them; though sometimes what they asked savoured, as we should say now, of jobbery. From a reply to Talpa written in 1601, it is evident that he had been asked to obtain the removal of a certain obnoxious member of the Congregation by getting the Pope to give him some ecclesiastical perferment. "I have asked his Holiness to remove 'such a one' from the Congregation *sub specie honoris,*[26]" he wrote; "but he has given me no answer, nor do I believe that he will; for on another occasion he said that he would never put an additional burden on those who have not given satisfaction in the Congregation, but would rather act on the principle that he who is not faithful in that which is least, etc.'"

Another time, Baronius, at the request of Talpa, asked the Pope for a plenary indulgence for some feast of the new church at Naples, and equally failed in obtaining it.

---

[26] "Under the appearance of honor." -Editor.

"Yesterday evening I asked for the plenary indulgence," he wrote in reply to the request. "I found His Holiness in a new frame of mind (which surprised me), and determined to grant no further plenary indulgences to any place or person whatsoever. I must, in truth, say that I commend him for this decision, for, indeed, the matter of indulgences is much abused. Even in the old days in the Congregation I used to protest against it; and I found others, good and zealous men, who perfectly agreed with me."

Details such as these may be called trivial; but it is by means of them alone that the real man can be known, as, suffering the high strain of his public life to relax, he found repose in an intimate communion with his friends which afforded the one safety-valve without which the high pressure of life would have been impossible, and without which he must have been reduced to an automaton.

So much for this human safety-valve; but the consolation it afforded him was very superficial compared with that which formed the real joy of his over-worked life. It was one of the compensations of God's mercy that He vouchsafed great spiritual consolations to His servant. All day and most of the night Baronius toiled in His service, and never flagged, whether the work were congenial or uncongenial; but when the work was done, and for a few brief moments he was suffured to relax the strain, his soul, like, an arrow, flew straight to God, and the rest he found in Him was rest indeed. In all the weariness of his life, in all the depression raised in his soul by his antipathy to his lot, no symptom of spiritual desolation can be found; and the joy which was the theme of all his works, as he lay on his death-bed, was but the crown and complement of what he had experienced through life.

His gladness when saying Mass was especially great; and when prevented by illness from offering the Holy Sacrifice, he confessed that this earth possessed no greater trial for him. He complained to his friends of being hard of heart and bereft of all power of emotion; yet he often shed tears of devotion while saying his office. It may be said that he never wasted a moment of that rare though precious time when it was permitted him to turn his thoughts directly to God. While driving about in his coach he used to pull down the blinds and give himself over unrestrainedly to the things of the soul, bidding his companion recall him to himself if anything occurred which required his attention. When thus shut into darkness he usually repeated the Holy Name over and over again, or else dwelt lovingly on his favourite interjection, "*Eternitas, eternitas,*" words which were but the epitome of his ceaseless longing for death and the state beyond the grave.

He was always praying and lifting up his heart to God, even in the midst of his occupations; but there were times when an irresistible desire to be alone with Him seized him, and, laying aside his work, he retired into the solitude of his chamber. On these occasions he had to be summoned several times before his attention could be attracted. When, if he did not answer, his servant entered the room, he usually found him prostrate on the ground, motionless in prayer; and at those times the man would withdraw unnoticed, not having the heart to disturb his holy master for the sake of outside calls.

From the hour that Cesare was taken from the Oratory his thoughts turned irresistibly to death. Father Buccio of the Roman Congregation said of him in his funeral oration that "all through his life he was accustomed to meditate on that last hour, so that not only was the impression of death stamped on his heart, but he had its effigy engraved even on the seal with which hee fastened his letters. Whatever he was doing, whether speaking or listening, he was making one long meditation on death and judgment. Thus when death, to which he had so long looked forward, really approached, and found him with strength completely exhausted by his labours and austerities, he calmly awaited it lying on his bed, having no thought but of eternity." It was remarked of Baronius that after he was raised to the purple, he frequently introduced the subject of death into his conversation and into his sermons, as if it were, as was indeed the case, the habitual theme of his thoughts. "Look at Cesare," exclaimed the Cardinal of Verona, "he does nothing but meditate on the grave; and all his delight is in the cross!"

There was scarcely a night that he did not rehearse his last hour and make a special and realistic preparation for death; and after he was in bed, before he allowed himself to go to sleep, he repeated over to himself the Commendation of the departing soul. Verily he spoke but the truth when he said during the last days of his life that death was as a sister to him, with whom he had for years held daily conversation.

These habitual thoughts of death were far from casting a gloom over his life. On the contrary, they added to it an element of joy which it would not have otherwise possessed and if, in spite of overwork, uncongenial surroundings, and suffering health Cesare still possessed a joyous heart, it was because he lived in the presence of death. Eternitas, eternitas, the words which were for ever

283

in his heart and uttered aloud with his lips, whether he were alone or in company, poring over manuscripts and absorbed in his work, or waiting in ante-chambers or driving about in his coach, were but the expression of the exultation of his soul at the thought that time must cease and eternity must come. What was death but a golden portal? And, the wish being father to the thought, he always thought he beheld the shimmer of this gate when in truth it was yet a long way off. When he died, worn out, though only in his sixty-ninth year, his death might be called premature; but he, on the contrary, in his longing for the last passage, considered it unduly tardy, for he had scarcely reached the age of fifty before he spoke of himself wistfully as a very old man, to whom death must come, and, in the order of nature, could not help coming soon.

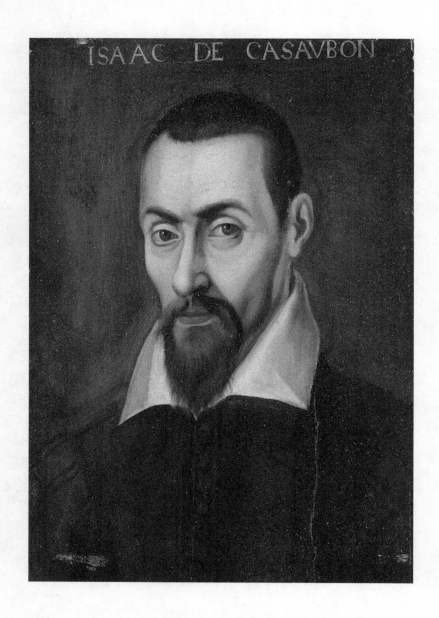
ISAAC DE CASAVBON

CHAPTER XXIII
Protestants and the Annals

T HUS we have followed Baronius through the various minor interests and occupations of his life; we have studied the means by which his state was sanctified, and caught what glimpses are to be had of the compensations, both divine and human, afforded to him by the mercy of God. It is now time to return to the work of his pen, the one absorption of his life, which formed the permanent background to every other occupation.

True son of St. Philip, Baronius, as a priest, had no thought unconnected with the salvation of souls; and the conviction that his sacerdotal ministrations would be minimized, and he himself removed from all apostolic work, was his bitterest pang when he was raised to the purple. He did his best, it is true, to avert such a calamity, and he helped his neighbour when and where he could. He tended the souls of his household like a veritable father and pastor, and sought out and rescued those who were on the verge of a career of sin; but he soon found out that the work for souls which God intended him to do lay in the Annals, and in writing them, he each year found more food for his zeal.

Through his book he got into touch with the whole world and beyond the narrow walls of his self-made cell he lived in the turmoils and troubles of the times, and yearned to apply a remedy to them. The struggle for dominion in Poland between Catholicism and heresy was a matter of living interest to him. The letters which passed between him and the Archbishop of Gnesen were frequent, and in his dedication of his eleventh volume to King Sigismund he reveals the enthusiasm kindled within his soul by the measures taken by that sovereign to revive the faith.

His friendship with St. Francis of Sales kept alive his interest in the state of Calvinism in Switzerland, and to him the Saint turned for sympathy and cooperation. "In writing to you it is unnecessary to explain my difficulties and the needs of this diocese," St. Francis wrote, not long before Baronius's death. "I look upon Geneva as a wretched daughter of Babylon, as a city sucked into the jaws of heresy. As for myself I am as one sent to preach to an apostate people, hard of countenance and hard of heart, and am as a dweller in the abode of fierce scorpions. Wherefore I beseech you to intercede for me with the Holy See, and help me against the workers of iniquity. Do you, with the spirit of the mouth of Christ, with the two-edged sword of the Annals, which you have wielded with such power hitherto, do what you can to procure protection for me, living in the midst of this heretical people."

Baronius, in his zeal for souls, was largely instrumental in founding a college—a branch of the Collegio Helvetico—in the valley of Chiavenna, which was overrun by heresy. At the head of this establishment was a zealous priest named John Paravicino, who, regarding Baronius as his patron, wrote to him detailed accounts of his labours in the Alps, of the apostates whom he had recovered, the heretics whom he had converted, and all that he was doing for the spread and progress of religion in the desolate valleys. His work was so disheartening that it was enough, he said, to kill him and his only

288

consolation was that he had not failed in what Baronius had desired him to do.

We would gladly know from Cesare himself whether he kept up the interest which his holy father St. Philip took in the English College, and the future martyrs—the flores martyrum—who were being trained there. With the envious admiration in which he held those who were shedding their blood for the faith, while he was constrained to sit, as he called it, idle, and carry on the fight with only his pen, it is impossible but what his thoughts often turned to that island of the west, where the very pick of the army of martyrs were laying down their lives for the Church. There can be no doubt of this all the same, it is evident that he regarded the English as a lost people, groping in impenetrable darkness; for when he implored the Pope to send him as a missioner on some forlorn hope, rather than clothe him in the purple robes of a protonotary, he classed the Indies and England together as the *ne plus ultra* of all that was benighted and forsaken.

With Ireland Baronius was in direct communication, for he received several letters from the Bishop of Waterford about the state of religion in the country, and the horrors of persecution. One letter contained a graphic account of the rigour with which the edicts against Catholics were carried out, and how priests were hunted down remorselessly by the soldiery, and, when caught, hung on the spot without trial. Such tales stirred Baronius with enthusiasm, and at the Bishop's request he used his influence to send more missioners, and especially religious, to the aid of the persecuted Irish.

Most people who were anxious for the conversion of individual heretics turned for help to the writer of the Annals. The soul of Casaubon was at that time an object of great solicitude, especially among the more learned Catholics of the century. He hesitated for years between the true faith and Calvinism; and at one time, three years after Cesare's death and just before the assassination of Henry IV, Cardinal Duperron thought he had succeeded in convincing him of the truth. That, however, was Casaubon's last hour of grace, and from that moment he sank deeper and deeper into Calvinism, and was even stirred up by his companions in heresy to write an attack on the Annals five years after their holy author had gone to his reward.

In his earlier and happier days he had a great admiration for both Baronius and the Annals. There is a letter from him to the great historian, written from Paris in 1603, while grace was still struggling in his soul, in which there is a genuine ring of humility towards his correspondent which does him honour. "Certain friends, O illustrious Baronius," he says, "have urged me to bring out an edition of the Augustan historians after Suetonius, and to illustrate their writings by remarks of my own. I had, indeed, but slight acquaintance with the books or manuscripts, but as these gentlemen made the request, I could not refuse, and have done my best to satisfy them. ... As you are too friendly towards me to think anything insignificant, I wished to send you the book at once, and have been diligently seeking an opportunity. But the distance to Rome is so great that occasions for sending are rare, and hitherto I have found none, though, should any occur, I will not fail to avail myself of it. I hope that if you have time to spare in the midst of your severe labours, it may not displease you to amuse your leisure with a subject with which your own writings proclaim you to be acquainted. More than once have I acknowledged my indebtedness to your works and if my arguments and expositions sometimes differ on slight grounds from yours, I do not think that you will find my writings lacking in modesty. Being human, we can all easily make mistakes and be deceived, but may I, by God's grace, never be convicted of resisting the known truth either in this or in any other work of mine."

It was natural that those who were anxious about Casaubon's soul should appeal to Baronius to help them with his conversion. In 1599 he received a letter from the President of the Parliament of Toulouse, the ostensible object of which was to remind him of a former request for his portrait, to be put with the collection of his works—a request which we do not learn that he granted. After enlarging on the reasons for the petition, the President goes on to say, "I have staying with me here the Sieur Casaubon, a personage of great, nay, of rare learning, of very polite manners, and most agreeable conversation. In the hope of bringing him back, by God's help, to the fold of the Catholic, Apostolic and Roman Church, I have persuaded him to write to you, knowing how deeply impressed he is—as indeed he should be—by your writings. So if, under pretext of referring to literary matters, with which in the opinion of learned men he is most conversant, it might please you to try and persuade him and bring him to a knowledge of the truth, and thus hasten the fruition of what I already see in the bud, I know that your words will have great effect on him. For this reason I humbly ask you not to deny this request; and believe me that it would be no small conquest. I will contribute what is necessary in the way of accommodation and hospitality, but all the merit will be yours if you win and bring this great soul to God."

Alas for him, Casaubon refused to be caught in Peter's net; and his memory is connected by most with the attack which his false counsellors persuaded him to make on the Annals. He had been warned for the sake of his own credit not to cast any doubt on the accuracy or veracity of Baronius; and even had he not been thus warned, his own admiration for the great historian's rectitude would have stayed his pen. He threw himself, it is true, readily into the attack, but in the preface to his *Esercitaziones contra Anales*, he could not refrain from paying the following tribute to him against whom he set himself up as an antagonist:

"Who does not know that Cardinal Baronius bestowed such labour on his Ecclesiastical History as to carry off the palm for diligence. He was the first to reduce the acts of the whole Christian Church to chronological order, and this with an exactitude with which he might have harmonised the records of one single city. I do not know whence he unearthed the many facts which were before enshrouded in obscurity. With accurate diligence he made clear the episcopal succession in the principal sees, the origin, progress and extinction of ancient heresies, and the record of the times of the Church, whether tranquil or turbulent. In fact, were it not that he detracted from his merit by his immoderate partizanship for the Church, he would without doubt deserve that all writers both ancient and modern, who have attained to only a portion of his learning, should rise up and lay down their arms before him."

This accusation of "immoderate partizanship" was the usual missile thrown at him by his antagonists when they could not controvert his facts; and with many such it was and always will be the most effective weapon. A whole century after the death of Baronius we find Dr. Cave, in his Historia Literaria, paying the same sort of mixed tribute to him, which is interesting as showing how well known, even after the lapse of a hundred years and in a Protestant country, were the strange circumstances under which the Annals began. "With adamantine courage and superhuman labour," writes Dr. Cave, "did the illustrious author of the Annals compile twelve huge volumes of ecclesiastical history. This manifestly immense work was the result of a preparation lasting thirty years for he did not begin to write until he had related the history of the Church seven times over in the Oratory, each course of lectures lasting five years. The book was written entirely with his own hand without the aid of an amanuensis (as we can readily believe from the life of the author), and was produced in the midst of parochial cares, the hearing of frequent confessions, the delivering of sermons, and all the other necessary business connected with himself and the Congregation, as well as a variety of occupations, of which I need specify only the composition of other literary works. By his great work on ecclesiastical history (from which I confess that I have myself reaped no small benefit), he would have attained far greater renown had he not spent all his labour, ingenuity and erudition in magnifying the papal primacy, dignity and supremacy, exalting it not only above all ecclesiastical, but also above imperial and regal laws; and this edifice he not seldom establishes by apocryphal, suppository and worthless documents. Petrus Pitheus rightly says of this book that it should be named the Annals of the papal power rather than the Annals of the Church. Baronius's sole object in view was to contend against the innovators of his time, namely the Magdeburghers; and to bring forward

293

arguments in favour of the sacred traditions favouring the authority of the Roman Catholic Church."

With such fairness of criticism did Baronius meet from his contemporaries and their immediate successors. It was reserved for enemies of the Church, like Gibbon, to argue against a statement for no reason except that it was made by him. "Baronius," we find written in *The Decline and Fall of the Roman Empire*, "has published the original act [of the gift of the crown of Sicily to Roger Guiscard]. He professes to have copied it from the *Liber Censuum*, a Vatican MS. But the names of Vatican and Cardinal awaken the suspicions of a Protestant and a philosopher."

If Casaubon refused to listen to the voice of grace, there were many other men, probably of equal learning, who were more blessed, and whose conversion through the medium of the Annals was a source of the greatest consolation to Baronius. Among these, the names of Spondano and Scioppio, two of the most erudite men of the time, are especially mentioned. With the conversion of Justin Calvin, a lesser luminary, though a well-known professor of Heidelberg, Baronius took a very active part and the lengthy correspondence between them shows what time and trouble the over-worked historian was ready to bestow on the salvation of one soul. In the absence from his pen of anything that could come under the head of spiritual writings, Cesare's letters to this man are doubly precious, containing as they do many wise counsels relating to the interior state.

Justin Calvin was deeply imbued with the doctrines of his heresiarch namesake. Having, however, been shaken in his religious opinions by a study of the Annals, he entered on a polemical correspondence with their author, and, was finally received into the Church in the beginning of 1601. On hearing the welcome news Baronius at once wrote to him as follows: "I return many thanks to the great and most high God, whose tender mercies, as sings David, are over all His works, for having called you out of darkness into His marvellous light. No benefit, no grace can be greater than this, so see that you cherish it carefully and guard it jealously. Do not indulge in paeans of victory; but rather remember that exhortation of the Apostle to walk circumspectly, not as unwise but as wise, redeeming the time because the days are evil. . . . When the devil has been overthrown, he is apt to rise up with renewed vigour, and assault his former conqueror more violently than ever. Our Lord tells us of the wicked spirit who, having gone out of a man, did not rest, but fetched seven other spirits more wicked than himself, and retook by fraud the soul whence he had been driven. ... Be sure that he will seek you who have escaped him and are now fighting in the ranks of the Church. He may not betray his designs, for he fears lest Saul-converted into Paul by his reconciliation to the Church-should by the fire of divine love deal destruction on the lies by which he is wont to overcome men. You, a soldier of Jesus Christ, beware, and lose not hold on the shield of faith which you have taken up. Be master of yourself, overcome yourself, and take heed that you, who were once in the employ of the prince of darkness, be not ashamed of being enrolled under the banner of Christ your Captain. ... You have, however, no real cause for fear, but only for joy. Rejoice if you are found worthy to suffer anything for the Catholic faith and in defence of the truth. I showed your letter to our Supreme Pastor, who rejoiced to hear the bleating of his one-time lost sheep, who has been found worthy to hear the voice of the Shepherd. He is addressing to you an

Apostolic letter, by which he embraces you as if with extended arms, and by his written words places you on his shoulders rejoicing. In him you will always find a true pastor and father."

Calvin replied to these words by a letter full of fervour and enthusiasm. "I will not disguise from you that I am surrounded by enemies," said he among other things "but he who has ever sounding in his ears, and moving on his lips, those terrible words of St. Jerome, which are like unto a trumpet-blast, 'Whether I eat or drink or whatever I do, I hear a voice crying out to me, 'Arise, ye dead, and come to judgment,'—such a one, I say, easily despises earthly enemies, and rushes dauntlessly into the very teeth of the lion who, as you rightly say, pursues his prey night and day, and seeks to recapture those who have escaped him."

Baronius interested Clement VIII in the new convert, with the result that the Holy Father invited him to come to Rome with his brother, who had likewise abjured heresy. But the journey was delayed for some time by sickness and persecution; and meanwhile the correspondence between Baronius and Justin went on. The latter had lost his profession through his reconciliation to the Church, and put himself and his future at the disposal of him to whom, humanly speaking, he owed his conversion. He had resumed his pen, meaning to wield it in the cause of the truth; but not a line would he publish without Baronius's sanction. "I know you do not want my blood," he wrote; "you want rather faith, piety and constancy. That you may better undertand my dispositions, I beg you to accept the accompanying packet of my Catholic first-fruits, namely my apology for my conversion. For obvious reasons I do not dedicate it to you; but none the less I have written it as a thank-offering

296

to you. When you have read it and weighed it, I shall know better what it is worth. If you disapprove of what I have done, or judge me incapable of this kind of sacred warfare, in God's name give me timely warning, and if I have been over-precipitate, bid me go back into captivity. As for my studies, some urge me to go in for theology, others for jurisprudence; wherefore I beseech you to govern me by your counsel. I am not much versed in theology, but I feel powerfully drawn to the sacerdotal state."

What advice Baronius gave about the great question involved in the last sentence can only be inferred by the future career of Justin Calvin. The generosity with which he gave up everything to obey the call of grace was rewarded, and he was raised to the priesthood, probably before Cesare's death. For when, following that event, he sent a written eulogy of their mutual friend to Father Nicholas Serrarius, he was a Theologian at the Cathedral city of Mayenee. To the other part of the letter quoted above, Baronius answered promptly:

"Your letter gave me part pain, part joy. What you say convinces me of your constancy under adversity; and withal you show your desire to be guided by me in your practices and studies. As regards the persecution to which you are exposed, you are right in your judgment that no evil can overtake you so great but what it can be by good will overcome. As regards the direction of your studies, I believe you could do excellent work in theology by writing an account of the manner in which you received your first impulse towards the Catholic Church."

At last, in September, 1602, Justin Calvin arrived in Rome and was received by Baronius into his own household. The Pope himself gave him the Sacrament of

Confirmation in St. John Lateran, and Justin, having Cesare as his sponsor, cast away the vile name of Calvin, and took instead the name of Baronius. When writing three years later to this friend and second father, he dwelt gratefully on the blessings he had received on the occasion of that memorable visit to Rome. "Having made myself one with you by name," he wrote, "I can be satisfied with nothing I do, and my life is oppressed by the impossibility of returning you adequate thanks. Wherefore, that September day will remain ever sacred in my memory, when, leaving the palace with me and my brother, you led us to the feet of the Sovereign Pontiff, whose kindness to us was so great. When our souls, snatched from heresy, had been strengthened by the rite of Confirmation, you, who stood sponsor to me in this holy sacrament, entered into spiritual relationship with me, and by binding yourself to me thus mystically gave me a pledge of everlasting kinship. You outrivalled the father of the Gospel parable, who, when his son returned to him, stripped him of his rags and placed a ring on his finger. Behold I, a weary wanderer, being received into the family of Holy Church, have cast away the trappings of detestable Calvinism. You not only endowed me with a new name, but so as to express more plainly the love you bear me, blessed and adorned me with your own."

Justin, armed with a letter of introduction to the Bishop, made his home in Mayence, and probably entered at once on his studies for the priesthood. But his one visit to Rome had made such an impression on him that he pined for the Eternal City with a sort of home-sickness. "How often do I think of Rome," he wrote, "redolent with the holy counsels of the fathers, and saturated with the blood of thousands of martyrs. My memory dwells on those morning and evening prayers with the family of Baronius; on the Oratory with its devotions, disciplines, sacred music, and the other hundred ways it has of fomenting piety. All this is engraved on my mind, and so long as I am away from Rome, I feel like a homeless exile. My solace is to try to place my feet in each faintest footprint left by you, and seek to do honour to the name of Baronius by imitating his virtues."

Justin passed from the direct influence of his sponsor, and it is doubtful whether the latter ever again set eyes on him; but Baronius could never forget this man in whose conversion he was instrumental, and kept up a correspondence with him to the end of his life. His love for Justin's soul made him fearful lest he should in anything depart from the way of perfection, and in his solicitude for his sanctity he plied him with counsels which throw a side-light on his own spiritual aspirations. When writing to congratulate him on the return to the Church of a friend of his, the Count Palatine's general, he took the opportunity of bringing home, with delicate touch, the duty incumbent on the recent convert of freely giving what he had freely received. "Did I not already know you to be eager to descend into the arena," he wrote, "to fight the enemies of the Church of God, I might urge on you to help this man in the many ways of which I know you to be capable; and I would pray you to have nothing more at heart than the desire to win souls. But for the reason already given I will refrain from doing so, lest I should seem to doubt your zeal, and lest you might be led to put a wrong interpretation on my words. You know, my *Justus*, what will be the reward of those who instruot others to justice. And if you consider the matter well, I have no doubt but what you will come to the conclusion

299

that the one way to procure an everlasting name is to win to Jesus Christ as large a number of souls as possible. I beg of you to take great care of your health."

Baronius lost no opportunity of bringing home to Justin the full import of matters of doctrine. It was as if he almost doubted the possibility of an ex-Calvinist making a really good Catholic. Yet he was most careful to insinuate his instructions into his correspondence in such a way as not to hurt his friend's feelings by a seeming want of confidence. Writing to him to congratulate him on the accomplishment of a difficult and arduous journey, he goes on to say: "But I am sure you were accompanied and guided by him to whom old Tobias, full of faith, confided his son, who led him in safety, and brought his journey to a successful end. I take for granted that you commend yourself carefully to the saints, and prove yourself grateful to them for the way they have helped you; for we know very well what great power they wield in our interests. By commending ourselves to them we prove our gratitude to them in the only possible way. I am much pleased to learn that you have obtained your doctor's degree, which I trust may turn out for your good and God's glory. I feel confident that the reward is no more than you deserve; do not, I pray you, belie my good opinion of you. The greater your dignity, so much the greater is my solicitude for you; and I have the greatest hopes for your future if you practise that faith and confidence of which I believe you to be capable. But it behoves you to strain every nerve; and may He who by His grace has called you—once His enemy and a rebel—to Himself, reward you, of His great loving-kindness for your labours. May He enlarge the place of your tent, and by many mercies show forth His desire to till you with joy and gladness."

300

The leisure of mind in the midst of his crushing work, which could thus enable Baronius to throw himself into the needs and interests of individuals, cannot fail to fill us with admiration. It proves to what purpose he perseveringly apostrophised himself with the words: *Contine te domi, Cæsar.*[27]

---

[27] "Stay home Caesar." The words of Julius Caesar's wife related in the Latin translation of Plutarch. -Editor.

CHAPTER XXIV
The Last Volumes of the Annals

As time went on, the work of the Annals assumed such proportions that it was all their author could do to cope with it. Adopting a simile from an inundation of the Tiber which devastated Rome in his day, he wrote to Talpa that he was overwhelmed by the work more than by a flood of waters. He was by this time the acknowledged authority on ecclesiastical history, and there was no one who had a knotty point to solve who did not consider that he had the right to appeal to Baronius for an explanation. This increased his correspondence to an almost incalculable degree, and even with the aid of several secretaries he abandoned all attempt to attend to any but the more important letters.

In all that directly affected the Annals he welcomed, nay more, invited letters; and it is almost bewildering to find a whole correspondence devoted to matters which might excusably be called trivial. But as in the beginning so was it to the end, and in spite of the increase of his work, no point of accuracy was a trifle to Baronius; and he bestowed the same faithful care on the minutiae of the twelfth volume as he had bestowed on those of the first, written in the days of his vigour, when he was fresh to the work. An instance of the sort of corrections and suggestions which he asked and was grateful for, may be cited from a letter written to him in 1603 by the Bishop of Novara, who sent him a learned dissertation on the position of an islet of the name of San Giulio, which, as he pointed out, was erroneously described in the Annals as being in Lago Maggiore proper, whereas it really lay in a bay or adjunct of the same, which in former days went by the name of Lago San Giulio. No historical truth was here at stake, but Baronius received the correction with a patience and gratitude which afford a clue to the reputation for accuracy possessed by the Annals.

Nevertheless, all this gave great work, and the writer's brain being charged with such a variety and multiplicity of subjects, it is not to be wondered at that sometimes letters received no answer, or that the business they contained was neglected, to the probable indignation of the senders, who did not make the excuses for their correspondent which they would have made had they known better the actual state of timings. The reproaches he sometimes received, and the apologies they elicited, are a testimony to Cesare's habitual punctuality in such matters. "It is impossible but what you should accuse me of negligence, discourtesy and even stupidity," we find him writing to a Canon of the Sorbonne. "I freely confess that had I not met your messenger, the matter about which you wrote to me would have entirely escaped my memory. However, I am convinced you will accept my excuses. I am simply weighed down by the number of letters which I receive from learned men from all parts; and did I feel it necessary to answer them all, I should have to dismiss all hope of ever finishing the Annals. As a matter of fact, I postpone answering them. I do not struggle, but wait for a moment of leisure, which comes but rarely, and then in such scant measure that it is consumed as soon as it comes. Meanwhile, the matter on which I had fixed my mind escapes me."

This letter was written a few years before his death; but one of the very last that have been preserved, sent to the Patriarch of Aquila at the latter end of December, 1606, shows how he was battling with the overwhelming flood of work up to the very brink of the grave. "To the many and great occupations which are at all times engaging me," he wrote, "I have now, in addition, the printing of the twelfth volume of the Annals, which absorbs my time to such a degree that not only can I attend to nothing else, but I can think of nothing else. For this reason you must not be surprised if the matter connected with the lessons of SS, Hermagora and Fortunatus has been neglected in a way which I would wish to have been obviated, on account of my desire both to pay devotion to these saints and to respond to your kindness. I pray you to excuse me, anyhow, until I have accomplished that which could not be neglected without the greatest inconvenience. I tell you thus freely about my occupations, so that you may the more readily excuse me, and may not attribute my remissness to any lack of desire to be of service to you, but solely to the amount of work I have on my hands. *I will try to do what you want soon. Be sure of my good will.*"

The words in italics are in his own writing, the rarest of events in such letters as the above. For years before his death he seldom wrote a letter with his own hand, though he attended to the substance and composition of each, and ruthlessly cut out any ornamental or flattering phrases put in by his secretary. Baronius found it necessary to employ an amanuensis[28] for his correspondence as soon as he was

---

[28] A sternographer. -Editor.

raised to the purple, and had done the same to a certain extent previously, as he had a secretary in his employment at the time when he was made protonotary. When replying to his friend, the Abbot of St. Martin's, congratulations on his elevation to the Sacred College, he pointed out that the fact of his letter being written with his own hand was a token of special affection—a token which he was not always able to bestow on still dearer friends. "Do not ascribe it to pride that I do not write to you with my own hand," he said to Father Juvenal in a dictated letter sent from Ferrara in 1598. "There is not much leisure to be had at this place."

In direct contrast with his employment of secretaries for his correspondence is the absence of all such in the actual writing of the Annals, every word of which, whether on the rough sheets, or the revisions which embodied the corrections and suggestions of his friends, was done by his own pen. All his biographers, and all those who have in any way borne testimony to the magnitude of his labours, are unanimous in saying that he never employed the aid of a secretary for the Annals.

When contemplating Cesare's many and great occupations, it is necessary to remember that his literary work was not confined to the Annals themselves, even if it was in connection with them that the further use of his pen was called for. Sometimes the publication of a volume necessitated the writing of a complete treatise in answer to the objections brought forward against some of its contents. "The eleventh volume would have been ready for press before this," he wrote to Talpa in February, 1604, "had I not been hindered by writing an answer to a book published by a Benedictine monk who challenges something I had said about the monastic state of St.

Gregory. This has kept me fully employed ever since the beginning of last December; but now I have finished it, and will send you the first part next week. It is to appear under Father Antonio Gallonio's name."

In this case the extra work was in connection with the Annals, but sometimes it was caused by matters quite external to his history. As already seen, Baronius's absorption in his work had no narrowing influence on his sympathies, and he took the liveliest interest in what was going on in the world outside.

If he concerned himself with the political questions of the day, how much more likely was it that he should do so with those which directly affected religion and touched Christian dogma. Loyalty to the Church and devotion to the Holy See were the key-note of his life, and he had no sympathy and scant mercy for any whom he even suspected of being their enemy.

Heresy was simply abhorrent to him, so that in describing it he could scarcely find words or similes strong enough to express his detestation; and in his abhorrence he was quick to see symptoms of the malady in tenets since pronounced by the Church to be at any rate innocuous.

He was much affected by the stir made at the end of the sixteenth century by the propositions of Molina on that vexed question of grace and freewill—dissensions about which had already overspread Europe like a plague during the age in which Baronius lived—while they wrenched souls by thousands from the unity of the Church and threatened to sap the faith of many within the fold, before the Council of Trent cleared the air. The discussion within the Church raised by Molina's book on free will raged hotly for a time, the dispute between the

Dominicans and Jesuits, supported respectively by the secular powers of France and Spain, being a matter of history. Baronius threw himself ardently on the side of the Thomists. To his straight nature, devoid of all concealment and ambiguity, the Church presented itself as being a city verily set on a hill, every doctrine as plain as crystal and as simple as the eternal truths. Therefore anything that he considered to be an attempt to compromise with error or to envelop the crystal truth in sophisms and subtleties was detestable to him. Before the decision of the Church in 1607, which forbade either party to condemn the opinions of the other—which decree Baronius did not live to see—he emphatically declared the propositions of Molina to be quasi-heretical, and wrote an exhaustive treatise on the book, from which he compiled a selection of passages which he considered open to censure.

Writing more familiarly on the subject to the Archbishop of Vienna, who had put himself forward as a supporter of the book, Baronius expressed himself thus trenchantly; " Forgive me if I have been more tardy than is fitting in replying to your letter. I read with delight all that is holy, pure, and orthodox in it but I must protest against that portion, small though it be (which I cannot characterize as such), I mean the portion relating to the controversy about Molina's book. I have read the work, and am disgusted by it, for the author's aim seems to be nothing less than antagonism to St. Augustine (though he does not name him), whom he accuses of negligence, setting himself up in opposition to him as being more vigilant, and more exact in his disputations. Who could put up with his saying such things? The Church of God does not need this sort of commentator, for she, being

308

herself without spot or wrinkle, takes especial delight in purity, sincerity and lucidity. I read and made a note of fifty or more expressions, words and phrases which are, in my opinion, akin, to say the least of it, to Pelagian or semi-Pelagian errors, though he cautiously keeps within the limits of the Catholic faith, or at any rate professes to do so. I think that no one who reads the book without the bias of private affection can deny this. What does the Church want with this Molina book to learn what was said and taught centuries ago by the fathers, councils and decrees? As to our Holy Father Clement, neither in intention, nor by word, nor finally, by decree, has he ever deviated by a nail's breadth from the steps of his predecessors, but he stands firmly by them. It is well known that many holy Pontiffs—Innocent, Sixtus, Celestine, Hormisdas, Felix—have pronounced that in all that pertains to grace and free-will the Roman Church follows St. Augustine. There is, therefore, no need of a fresh opinion; for the matter has been already judged. The cause of Molina's book—what is to be rejected, what altered, what retained—is now *sub judice*. My private verdict, however, is that the Catholic Church has no need of anything wherein there is to be found anything objectionable or needing correction. Warn my friends, the fathers of the Society of Jesus, not to let their credit be imperilled, or questioned, by defence of this book. I love them, God knows, as my fathers; and, to quote the words used by one of them, 'The reproaches of those who reproach thee have fallen upon me.' Farewell; I will say no more."

The exact number of volumes which God would require of him was always a matter of anxious speculation to Baronius. He attached a mystical meaning to the question, which was, moreover, the subject of forewarnings and presentiments. Long before his death he was interiorly convinced that twelve, neither more nor less, was to be the number; for to this effect, as early as 1593, he received through the medium of a vision or dream one of those intimations by which he often guided his life. Just after he had completed his fifth volume, our Lady seemed to stand before him. She held in her hands five barley loaves, which, as he was given to understand, signified his five finished volumes. Then, repeating before his eyes her Divine Son's miracle in the wilderness, she multiplied the loaves, from the remains of which twelve baskets full of fragments were collected.

This vision impressed Baronius with the conviction that it was intended by God that he should write twelve volumes of the Annals; and with this in mind he added the following passage to what he called his "usual peroration to the Madonna:" "To thee, O holy Mother of God, as a thanksgiving for thine intercession and past favours do I offer this fifth volume. ... Do thou present it to God; and look graciously on me, and repay this offering by filling up the full measure of my work. Our Lord fed the multitude which followed Him with five barley loaves taken from the hands of a child, so that there remained over and above twelve baskets of fragments. I may say with Solomon that I too am a child. May I be worthy to receive the gifts of children, and may God multiply by His blessing these volumes which I offer to Him, and by giving them increase, make of them food for the faithful, and weapons by which the enemies of the Church may be put to flight."

In spite of his conviction that God required twelve volumes of him, Baronius made one attempt to stop short of the required number. In 1602, worn out with toil, persuaded that his life was drawing rapidly to its close, and having after two years' labour completed and dedicated his tenth volume to the Emperor Rudolph, he thought of resting from his work. But an interior voice seemed to urge him on imperiously, the manner in which he was constrained to abandon his intention being described by him in the preface to that volume. "Weary with my journey," he wrote, "and having completed one mile, namely the tenth volume, I would have gladly stayed my course. But He who said, 'Whosoever will force thee one mile, go with him another two,' urges me on to a further effort and by those same words vanquishes my resistance, and spurs on my wavering steps." The biographers of Baronius tell us that this interior voice which bade him drag his weary course yet another two miles, rang imperiously in his ears until he brought himself to obey it.

The letter to the Patriarch of Aquila quoted above shows how, in obedience to this interior monitor, Baronius had completed his task, and gone the "two miles" further. At the end of 1606, as he told the Patriarch, the twelfth volume was in the press; but even then his labours were far from finished, for he was correcting the proofs with the same fidelity with which he had revised the first volume eighteen years previously. He had been struggling for nearly three years with this last volume, though he had practically finished it in 1605, at the time of the election to the Holy See of Paul V, but he then came across a mass of additional matter, with which his advancing years and infirmities made it almost impossible to cope. The dedication of this crowning work to Clement's successor was written in June, 1607, barely a

311

week before he was seized with his last illness, and gives an account of the difficulties which beset his path. "In this volume," he says, "are gathered and garnered the fruits of my last labours. I can hold out no hope of any further work. My advancing years and feeble health show me, by no vain presentiment, that the hour for laying aside my earthly tabernacle is at hand. . . . The production of this volume has been slow, and the interval between it and the last longer than on any previous occasion; yet I think that the multiplicity of hindrances by which I have been embarrassed will plead on my behalf for your indulgence. ... First, I have been hampered, neither seldom nor slightly, by my increasing years and the ailments of old age, which is productive of much suffering and many discomforts. Then, when the work was finished and getting ready for publication, a storm arose against the Apostolic See, which, seeing how closely attached I am to its interests, distracted my thoughts from my work. Finally, when, as is my wont, I set myself to write an appendix, the crop of material turned out to be so rich, and the vintage so plentiful, that I had to extend the volume, though, as I venture to hope, neither unpleasantly nor uselessly. Thus it has happened that the volume, nearly completed at the time of your election and promised to you then, has been finished with difficulty only now, two years after that time. ... Encouraged by the benignity of your countenance, which is as that of a father, this, our last infant child, creeps with confidence to your feet, and with what voice it possesses prays you to receive it into your keeping together with its elder brethren, to help them by your strength and defend them by your authority. We commend all twelve to you, but especially this last one which has seen the light, our

Benjamin, begotten in our old age, and borne not without sorrow."

Baronius knew that his work was done; but as of old Noe, though convinced by proof that the earth was dried, would not stir from the Ark till God Himself released him, so Baronius would not stay his hand till God gave him the sign to stop; and when his final summons came it found him pen in hand, and the ink undried on the first pages of a thirteenth volume. He had completed the preface, and when he knew beyond mistake that the hour of death was at band, he called together the fathers of the Congregation, read to them what he had written, and bequeathed to them the task of completing his work. He bade them pay attention before all things to the truth, to enter into the reasons of every assertion, and to sift and digest every fact offered to them from however trustworthy a source. Baronius was most anxious that the great work initiated by St. Philip should be to the end entirely the work of his sons; and he was jealous of all outside interference even of mere epitomizers. His wish has been in the main, though by no means entirely, granted his work was taken up by several writers almost immediately after his death, one and the best of the continuations being from the pen of Spondano, converted to the true faith by means of the Annals. Later, however, in the seventeenth and eighteenth centuries respectively, Fathers Rinaldi and Laderchi, both sons of St. Philip, contributed their share to the continuation of the great work. Several attempts have been made since, but the best among them was due to Father Theiner of the Congregation, who in 1859 published additional volumes which carried the history of the Church down to the year

313

1583; and more recently still Father Calenzio of the Roman Oratory has taken up the work.

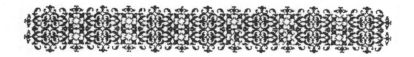

CHAPTER XXV
Holy Liberty

IN his letter to Paul V, quoted in the last chapter, Baronius made allusion to an attack on the Holy See in which he was himself involved, and whereby he was impeded in the completion of the twelfth volume of the Annals. The storm was stirred up by his own liberty of spirit which, when the truth had to be told, forbade him to consider the expediency of times or seasons; and the assault which he this time drew upon himself by his freedom of speech was so fierce that it required all his fortitude to enable him to stand up against it.

Baronius was at no time a respecter of persons, but less than ever did he allow such considerations to influence him when the rights and liberties of the Holy See were at stake. His daily visit to St. Peter's, his daily act of homage as he placed his head under the foot of the Prince of the Apostles were but emblematic of the purpose of his whole life. The freedom of the Church and the unfettered authority of the See of Peter were the interests for which he lived, and were the key-note of his Annals and of every word he wrote. Not only did this spirit underlie his writings, but it was his deliberate intention to make it so apparent that even those who ran might read his meaning. There was not much doubt as to his object in the minds of the enemies of the Church; and, as in the case of Casaubon and Dr. Cave, they writhed under the deductions which he drew from facts which they were unable to disprove. Nor was the annoyance confined to heretics; for many Catholics were exasperated by his arguments.

At the time that Baronius wrote there was a large section in the Church, mainly represented by Spain, the members of which to all intents and purposes set themselves up as being more Catholic than the Pope. This party did its best to prove the error of the Supreme Pontiff's ways in extending mercy to a relapsed heretic like Henry IV; it rebelled against all manifestations of the liberties of the Holy See, and placed the Annals on the Index for upholding them, and this in spite of Rome's approbation of the book. By diplomacy and menace combined, the papal elections were influenced far beyond the sphere of the acknowledged right of veto, with the result that when the Holy See was vacant, a sort of veiled terrorism prompted the votes of the Sacred College, and three times in succession the nominees and close political allies of Spain were chosen. When, however, Clement VIII, thanks to a flaw in the arrangements of the dominant secular power, was raised to the See of Peter, Spain found too late that the Head of Christendom was one who dared to stand alone; and it is not rash to say that one of the chief instruments in the hands of God for asserting the independence of His Vicar was Cesare Baronius.

There is no admissible doubt that it was thanks to him that Clement VIII, in spite of the indignation and opposition of Spain, restored Henry IV to the communion of the Church; nor is there any doubt that Philip II was aware of his intervention, or that the spiteful act of discourtesy of leaving unacknowledged the dedication to him of the third volume of the Annals was nothing but a petty expression of his resentment. The known displeasure of Philip at his predilection for the French king necessitated constant watchfulness on Baronius's part for a misinterpretation of his actions. When, for instance, the force of circumstances, added to the desire of the Holy Father, moved him to dedicate his ninth volume to Henry IV, he had to use every precaution to prevent either the King of Spain or his Viceroy of Naples from taking offence; though by that time, 1600, the reconciliation of the King of France was quite an old story. "I should like to send a copy of the volume to the Viceroy," Cesare wrote to Talpa, "but I refrain from doing so, lest he should take its dedication as an insult. Tell me what you think about it." About a month later, having probably received Talpa's advice and acted on it, he wrote again: "I have sent a copy to the Viceroy, for, when he came to see me here, I promised him that I would do so, and if I failed I should seem to be unfaithful to my word. All the same I have written him a letter with the book, telling him that I had dedicated it to the King of France with the consent of, and even by desire of His Holiness; and I added further words which will, I hope, convince him of my sincerity and the obligation I was under to act as I did."

Even in his earlier years, while leading a private life at the Oratory, Baronius had seen enough to make him detest the meddling of the secular powers with the papal elections, or their interference in any kind of ecclesiastical matters. But later, when his connection with the papal court and his position as a member of the Sacred College let him more closely into the secrets of public affairs, he began at once to make a bold stand on behalf of the liberties of the Church. "Help me by your prayers in these conflicts of mine about ecclesiastical jurisdiction," he wrote to Talpa in 1599. "I spoke on the subject in open consistory with a freedom such as I think God willed me

317

to exercise, but which astonished all the Cardinals. However, what I said gave great satisfaction to His Holiness, even though it did provoke the anger of the Spaniards. But I do not mind, and I never shall care whom I displease nor will I ever conceal the truth through human respect. It would be a great consolation to me were I permitted to lay down my life for the truth."

"I am glad that you approve of the line I have taken in defence of ecclesiastical jurisdiction," Cesare wrote again to Talpa, after he had received his answer to his first letter. "I protest, and ever have protested that I will speak with no respect of persons, whenever the service of God and of His Church is in question. Though all do not follow my example, yet they commend me for acting as I do; and many among the Cardinals have thanked me for speaking freely. Pray for me. It will be no excuse for me to have known and written about the acts of truly apostolic men if I let human respect restrain me from speaking the truth. Would that I could say with St. Paul, 'As long as I am an apostle I will honour my ministry.'"

Baronius, owing to his historical researches, lived so entirely in the atmosphere of the more heroic days of the Church, and in the glorious company of martyrs and doctors, that he did not see things as other men saw them. When severely taken to task by a certain Cardinal for the imprudence of his language, even granted that what he said was true, Cesare answered thus vehemently: "It behoves me to imitate our Lord and Master Jesus Christ, of whom the Gospel says that He taught as one having authority and not as the scribes, which means that He preached with truth and liberty, whereas they, in their adulation of Herod, yielded to that king's taste in everything. Far be it from me, I repeat, to write like the

318

scribes, and not declare the truth freely as did Christ. After Him I turn to the holy fathers of the Church, whose example, in writing, it behoves me to follow. In their maintenance of the truth in the face of those who attacked it, they displayed unbending constancy of soul. They did not make use of cringing, diluted, soft expressions, but, on the contrary, employed a language both grand and strong, mingling with it a sharpness of censure which converted their sentences into so many flashes of lightning. If you look through the Annals you will find scarcely a year in which some such example is not cited.

"By studying the fathers and relating their acts I have by habit adopted their manner of speaking, which should not, in my opinion, be despised, for such speech is bestowed as a gift of the Spirit rather than obtained by human learning. When dealing with heretic or schismatic innovators, or else with princes who corrupt ecclesiastical discipline by their violation of the laws of the Church, or endeavour by their tyranny to reduce her to servitude, I have acquired the habit of writing with the indiscretion which you censure. The words of the prophet, 'Cry, cease not, lift up thy voice like a trumpet, and show my people their wicked doings,' keep resounding in my ears as if from heaven. When Eugenius IV was made Pope, St. Bernard exhorted him to nominate Cardinals who should act as John did towards Herod, Moses towards the Egyptians, Phineas towards fornicators, Elias towards idolaters, Eliseus towards misers, Peter towards liars, Paul towards blasphemers, and, finally, as our Lord Himself acted towards traffickers in the temple. In other words he urged the Pope to choose men armed with zeal against sinners, who should act everywhere and in every way in such a manner as to sweep away the workers of iniquity.

319

Such is the model drawn for us by the Holy Ghost, and if we do not conform ourselves to it we shall be convicted of deformity."

Such words as these were not the outcome of the indignation of the moment, nor called forth by opposition. They were the expression of the ruling principle of Baronius's life; and when he saw history repeating itself in his own day, and beheld princes acting anew the part of Ozias, he trembled at the judgments which they might draw on the earth. "I fear, oh, I fear," he wrote, "that if men persevere in such courses, God the Avenger will arise with an iron rod in His hand, and will, as said Daniel the prophet, break them in pieces like a potter's vessel!" When any attempt was made against the liberties of the Church, Baronius redoubled his austerities, and if a hand were lifted against the Vicar of Christ he made what reparation he could, as though he had seen one strike the Divine Face of our Blessed Lord Himself.

Not content with lifting up his voice himself in the cause of ecclesiastical freedom, Baronius used all his great influence in the Sacred College for the same end, and untiringly exhorted his brother Cardinals to show courage, especially in the matter of liberty of election in conclave whenever they should find themselves called on to choose another Pope. In the eleventh volume of his Annals, written, indeed, while Clement VIII was still alive, but when all men knew that another papal election must, humanly speaking, take place ere long, Baronius seized the opportunity of addressing the Sacred College in words which, while they were made known to the whole world as represented by the readers of the Annals, were protected by their publicity from any attempt to suppress them. "I will not cease to exhort you, my actual and future brother Cardinals," he wrote, "to strive even unto blood against any interference or obstruction on the part of princes in the matter of papal elections. The Roman Church has never suffered more disastrously than she has from this for princes, while they profess to be aiding in the choice of a Pope, are, in fact, playing the part of tyrants and persecutors. What could be more lamentable for the See of Rome than that tyrants and wolves should take part in the election of a new Pontiff? The only object of wolves would be to provide the sheep with a slothful shepherd, so that they might attack the fold with impunity. Never could there be a more fatal thing than to accept a Pontiff at the hands of princes! "

The habitual disfavour in which Baronius was held by the King of Spain and his adherents was brought to a climax by a treatise which he wrote in 1604 about the Sicilian monarchy and its origin, its object being to bring into clearer light the fact that the said kingdom was held by Spain as a fief of the Holy See, conferred in different centuries on Roger Guiscard, Charles of Anjou, and, finally, only a hundred years before, on Ferdinand of Aragon, as successor to whom the actual King of Spain, Philip III, held it. But that monarch, and to a greater degree his father, resented any doubt thrown on his absolute sovereignty over the Two Sicilies, and, basing his pretensions to independence on certain eleventh-century documents which Baronius knew to be worthless, Philip II had imperiously rejected all the overtures and embassages of Pius V and Gregory XIII, the object of which was a just settlement of the papal claims.

When, in compiling his eleventh volume, Baronius came in order of chronology to the record of the foundation of the Sicilian monarchy, he would not shun the duty—nor would Clement suffer him to do so—of sifting the truth to the very bottom, though none knew better than he the dangers of the ground on which he was treading. So buried in darkness and shrouded by myths was the whole subject and the supposed part taken by Urban II, on which Spain based her claims, that he devoted especial and painstaking research to the matter; and so important did he consider it that he ended by writing a separate treatise, which was, however, by desire of the Pope, eventually incorporated in the eleventh volume.

Never did Baronius exhibit greater fearlessness and liberty of spirit than on this occasion, though the storm raised by his treatise overtook him in his old age and filled the last years of his life with trouble and turmoil. He bore the brunt of the tempest alone, though—as it transpired after the death of Clement VIII, which occurred a few months after the publication of the obnoxious volume—whatever he wrote was by command and under the direction of that holy Pontiff. The actual circumstances under which the treatise was written are fully related by Baronius in a letter to Philip III

"It is necessary, O Catholic King," he wrote, "that you should know the part taken in this affair by that wise Pontiff, Clement VIII of holy memory. He knew what efforts had been made by his predecessors, both by letters delivered through their nuncios and by special embassies to the King of Spain, to deliver Sicily from a form of monarchy which was founded in defiance of ecclesiastical laws, and, as was known, based on no treaty. He knew likewise that all negotiations had been made in vain, and had been eluded under various pretexts. Thus he seized willingly on an opportunity which he found offered to him; and when he ascertained that the eleventh volume of the Annals had to treat, by order of chronology, of the acts of Pope Urban II, incorrectly declared to be the author of the same Sicilian monarchy, he urged me by his pontifical authority, nay more, he commanded me, not to treat the matter in question lightly, but to write more at length on the subject and spend more time and labour on it than had been originally intended. He bade me search for documents both ancient and recent, ransack every corner of the Vatican Library, penetrate even into the darkness of the archives of St. Angelo, and search at will through any chests of secret documents which might be there. His intention in this search was that should there exist—which proved not to be the case—any foundation for the Sicilian monarchy, such documents should be brought to light and exposed to the gaze of men. Thus all excuse for denying the claim would be removed, and, as in the case of material excavations, every portion of the foundations might be examined.

"The Pontiff's object was, not to overthrow the badly constructed edifice, but, on the contrary, to prop it up and strengthen it by some contrivance of his paternal affection, so that the Catholic King might preserve the honourable title untouched and without scandal. Such was the purpose of the holy Pope Clement, a purpose worthy of a pontiff, a counsel worthy of the commendation of the wise. As regards the work committed by him to me, I laboured at it with all my strength, taking Christ as my leader and truth as my companion; nor, in spite of my many engagements, did I suffer my thoughts to be turned in any other direction until I had reduced the mass of material to shape. I carried out the Pontiff's desires, and guided myself by his enlightened judgment. I showed him everything I wrote, and he took it and read and re-read it.

While I stood before him expecting some word of approbation of my work, he only sighed and exclaimed sorrowfully, 'I could never have believed that the origin of the claims of the Sicilian monarchy was so illusory!' In order to understand my treatise more fully, he gave faculties to three selected Cardinals to examine it, so that it might be exhaustively discussed and proved before it was passed. When they had finished their censorship, the Pope gave orders that the treatise should be printed, and when he received the sheets he had them read to him once more; and, having again approved the work, he desired that it should be published with the eleventh volume which was then ready."

There is no question that the love of truth and accuracy which governed all Baronius's actions, combined with his eagerness to carry out the expressed wishes of Clement VIII, was the principal motive which prompted the composition of this risky treatise, calculated, as he well knew, not only to irritate Spain, but also to rouse against himself the hostility of the considerable Spanish faction in the Sacred College. As a matter of fact, this last consideration gave wings to his pen; for in the hostility of his brother Cardinals lay the strongest safeguard against his election to the See of Peter, should he survive Clement. He could ignore neither his growing influence in the Sacred College, nor the likelihood of the position he held leading to the papal tiara. That the prevention of this was his ulterior object in writing the treatise is made manifest in one of his confidential letters to Father Talpa. The calm and balanced judgment of that father, which made him the confidant and counsellor of all sorts of men, took alarm at the intention expressed by Cesare of writing an attack on the claims of Spain, for he did not quite trust the discretion of his fiery and impulsive friend. In answer to his cautions Baronius at once wrote the following explanation of both action and motive:

"As to the Tract on the Sicilian Monarchy, you must know that the Spanish claim was the subject of the negotiations of Pius V represented by Cardinal Alessandrino, and of Gregory XIII by means of the nuncio, Facchinetti, who became afterwards Pope Innocent. But neither of these envoys could obtain any satisfaction, for the King would do no more than hold out promises. I have in my possession an account of all that took place, for, as a matter of fact, besides my tract there have been several treatises on the subject written in Spain, though nothing that has been said has produced any effect. Now that the occasion has presented itself for dealing with the subject, it strikes me as right that it should be handled with all possible care and skill, and with that pungency of style which befits a Cardinal of the Holy Church, whose business it is to speak out, and not mutter between his teeth. However, in deference to your opinion I have altered the beginning, and other portions pointed out by you, so that I may not seem to be wanting in the reverence due to His Catholic Majesty. You must know, furthermore, that His Holiness has seen what I have written, and he too thinks it might be somewhat modified before it is printed; and some of the Cardinals are of the same opinion. All this is very agreeable to me, for I hope that if nothing else is gained, it will tend to the salvation of my soul by keeping me in a humble position, and give occasion to the Spaniards to oppose me in the conclave, should I live to take part in it. This is an aspect of the case which is of no small importance in my eyes, but I pray you to keep my reflections to yourself.

325

"I have sent you the treatise so that you may judge for yourself how it is likely to be received in Naples, and all over the kingdom. But I do not send it to you for you to try to dissuade me from its publication, which is being done by the desire of His Holiness. Think well whether it would be advisable that the treatise should be distributed by your friends, as has been done with my other writings. If it might do them any injury, it would be better to get it done by a third party. Let me know about this."

With what indignation the treatise was received in Naples is shown by the fact that the Viceroy, Ponte, condemned to the galleys the bookseller who circulated it. The remonstrances of Clement VIII were totally disregarded, and it remained to his successor, the more severe Paul V, to effect the man's release by pronouncing sentence of excommunication against the offender.

The storm raised against Baronius by the partizans of Spain was even greater than either he or Clement had anticipated; and there can be no doubt that it was due to the ill-feeling engendered in the Sacred College that he was, though barely, successful in warding off his election to the papacy at the conclave held after the death of Leo XI Needless to say that Baronius took no pains to allay the storm, but rather fomented it on every possible occasion by the boldness of his speech. After the death of Clement and before the succeeding conclave, the members of the Sacred College met for discussion at the Palazzo Tolomei. In the course of the proceedings two letters were produced, purporting to have been written by the Viceroy of Naples to Clement VIII, in which Baronius's treatise was severely censured, and he himself recommended to withdraw the pamphlet from circulation. This led to a fiery discussion about the treatise, a large number of the assembled Cardinals protesting that Baronius should have shown more reverence towards the King of Spain, at whose hands he had received many benefits. Others, on the contrary, maintained that Baronius's words in defence of the rights of the Church should stand as they were, and that the secular interference as evinced by the two letters was strongly to be reprehended.

The Cardinals spoke in rotation, and when it came to Cesare's turn to speak, his friend, Cardinal Pamfili, fearing lest he should be carried away by anger, implored him not to commit himself further, but to give his opinion as briefly as possible. As well might he have bidden a torrent to cease to flow for when Baronius rose to his feet his eloquence seemed almost inspired, and filled even his opponents with admiration. Quoting from Scripture, he poured forth fulminations against those who, as he considered it, usurped ecclesiastical functions; and when he finished his discourse by shouting out the words, thrice repeated, "Because the days are evil!" an awe-struck silence fell on the assembly. In this harangue he related to his brother Cardinals the circumstances which led to the tract being written, and added for their information that he had drawn his facts from manuscripts which he was, indeed, allowed to study, but only under a solemn oath not to let them pass out of his hands. After this the dispute waxed so violent that Cardinal de' Medici, afterwards Leo XI, who always acted the part of peacemaker, persuaded the Cardinals to drop the subject altogether, until a successor to Clement had been elected, who would be able, as Pope, to deal with the question.

Baronius had, indeed, written the truth boldly, but with no desire to insult the King of Spain by doing so; and to prove his absence of malicious intention he wrote later a dignified letter to Philip III, part of which has been already quoted, explaining all the circumstances. But he refrained from offering any explanation which could, and, as it turned out, did allay the King's irritation, until the election of Paul V, a man in the prime of life, had secured his own safety from the effects of any revulsion of feeling on the part of the Spanish faction. He even remained silent during the short pontificate of Leo XI, lest his visibly failing health should cause another vacancy in the Holy See, an event which did occur, though sooner than Baronius had anticipated. He explained these reasons for his silence, and impressed upon the King the unaffected joy he had experienced when all danger of being elected Pope was over. "To have gained that dignity," he wrote, "would have been loss to me. I feel my exclusion from the papacy to be no detriment; and I thank those who opposed me, and pray for them with greater gratitude than for those who were in favour of my election. All that is past; and now there is a freer access for me to the ear of the Catholic King, and greater liberty for me, as a priest of the Church militant, to plead before him my own cause and that of the Roman Church."

Having explained at length to Philip, in the passage already quoted, all the circumstances under which the treatise was written, and the active part taken in it by Clement, he went on, in words instinct with his fervent devotion to the Holy See, to vindicate his own action in the matter: "All this occurred while Clement was alive, but when, soon after the publication of the volume, that holy Pontiff was taken from us, all weapons were turned upon me, left to stand alone without his protection. ... But in this time of adversity great confidence was begotten in me, and my sense of security was increased by the consciousness that, having been commanded by Peter and approved by Peter, my treatise had gone forth from Peter, and would, therefore, endure for ever. He who, according to the words of our Lord, will build his house upon a rock must build it on Peter, for thus only will it be stable and impregnable. I stand upon a rock which has never yet been broken by any form of persecution, but which, on the contrary, breaks those who incautiously strike against it, and grinds to powder those on whom it falls. Let, then, its adversaries beware how they strike against it, lest perchance that rock fall upon them with power from on high, and crush them utterly. Let secular powers learn even now, though it be late, how perilous it is to condemn and proscribe writings which have been approved by the Holy See; and let them learn how unbecoming and offensive it is for princes to lay hold of the key of knowledge which the Church declares to belong to Peter alone, and to judge those things which have been said by command of the Roman Pontiff, to whom alone belongs the authority to judge, approve and condemn.

"Although Clement has been taken from us, his authority, his spirit and his desires still live in Paul, whose administration is as admirable as was his election. He is the last man to suffer the laws of God to be imperilled, or the immunities of the Church to be violated, or, in a word, to permit anything to be snatched from him who has a right to hold it; for he is a most stanch upholder of all the rights of the Church. ... What Christian prince will despise the monitions of him on whom, as the pivot and head of ecclesiastical unity, the whole Catholic world turns? Now, by the necessity of circumstances, I have sometimes to perform the office of ears, eyes and even mouth to that head; and it was solely in that capacity that I wrote the treatise."

Baronius concluded his letter by pointing out to the King the little likelihood of his being influenced by malice in the authorship of the tract, for, as his born subject, he had always considered it one of his first duties to pray for his welfare. He had, in fact, always taken special interest in Philip III When the latter was a boy, he used to send the Annals, volume by volume, to the young prince's tutor, Garcia Loaisa, begging him to bring up his charge in the principles they involved; and this Loaisa, who was a devoted admirer of Baronius and a greedy devourer of the Annals, undertook to do.

Cesare's interest in the King was further increased by his marriage with a young Archduchess of Austria, contracted when he ascended the throne of Spain. The marriage was celebrated by proxy at Ferrara while the papal court was there; and Baronius, being presented to the young Queen, was very enthusiastic about her piety and charm, and related his introduction to her in a letter to Talpa, full of graphic and characteristic touches.

"The espousals were celebrated very devoutly," he wrote. "The Archduchess, mother of the Queen, having heard about me, sent for me three times. I went yesterday evening, and remained some time, the office of interpreter being filled by her confessor, a Jesuit father, a friend of mine. Then, without being sent for, the Queen came in, and we remained together for a long time, conversing on spiritual subjects. I, not wishing to intrude, made a move more than once, as if I wished to take my departure, as it was already two hours after sunset but each time that I moved I was constrained to remain longer. Had it not been that their presence was expected at a representation of

330

Judith, which the Pope has arranged, they would not have let me go till supper. But why do I tell you all this? I declare to you, my father, that the Queen is a pure dove, well brought up, of a gentle nature and of fitting beauty, which is accompanied by a majesty which, though it is a gift of nature, seemed to me something more than natural.

"The mother is a matron of rare prudence, who combines stately manners with profound piety. Her eldest son, the Archduke Ferdinand, who came this summer to visit the Pope incognito, was also visited by me by night, through the intervention of his confessor, a great friend of mine. He received me most graciously. About a month ago he drove all the heretic preachers out of his dominions, at the risk of a rebellion among his people, for all the nobles are heretics. However, God protected him. He is a large-hearted youth, and full of zeal for the Catholic faith. I write all this to you from no spirit of frivolity—far from me be such a thing—but because I promised to pray for the happy estate of the royal couple; and I beg of you not to fail to do so likewise, for I believe that all prayers offered up for them are well bestowed."

It is to be hoped that this favourable opinion of the young King and Queen was well founded. It is certainly to the credit of Philip III that, when he received Baronius's letter he read it and re-read it several times. Not only did he openly profess his admiration for it, but owned himself convinced by it of the absence of all malicious intention in the tract against the Sicilian monarchy.

CHAPTER XXVI
The Two Conclaves

T HE vow taken by Cesare after he was made Cardinal, to do all in his power to avoid being raised to the Chair of Peter, was seldom out of his mind, and often renewed during the nine years that Clement VIII lived. Each month that passed showed him more plainly that his vow might have to be kept under difficulties for he was not blind to the high position he held in the Sacred College, or to the imminence of his danger should he live to take part in the next conclave. As Clement's age and infirmities increased, muttered rumours were rife as to his probable successor and an influential section of the Cardinals made no secret of their intention to further the election of Baronius. Some of these Cardinals were Cesare's close friends, but as soon as he became aware of their project he withdrew from their intimacy, and his relations with them became strained. The end justified these precautions, for had it not been, on the one hand, for his ingenious diplomacy, and, on the other, for his fearlessness about offending the adherents of Spain, he could not have escaped the event so dreaded by him.

At length the apprehended danger became a reality, for Clement, after months of ill-health, died on March 3, 1605. To make matters worse for Baronius, Cardinal Aldobrandini, who, from his energy and abilities, as well as from his relationship to the late Pontiff, held a position of exceptional influence in the Sacred College, set his heart on his election, and even confided to Cesare that he was working his very utmost to get all the Cardinals created by his uncle to promise him their votes. He had not, he added, the slightest doubt of success, for the only candidate whom he regarded as even a possible rival was Cardinal Alessandro de' Medici. Little did the astute Aldobrandini suspect that, by thus indiscreetly taking Cesare into his confidence, he was planning the overthrow of his pet scheme. Baronius diplomatically kept silence, though Cardinal Pietro's words filled him with dismay, and increased the fears already raised by the general rumours floating about Rome that he was to be the next Pope. He did not sit idle, but, as soon as his visitor had departed, sent his confidential secretary to interview Cardinal Sforza, whom he knew to be at the head of the party promoting the cause of de' Medici, and inform him of Aldobrandini's purpose, and urge him at the same time to do his best to further the election of his own candidate.

Meanwhile he himself called on all the Cardinals whom he suspected of being favourable to himself, and implored them for the love of God to put no hindrances in the way of de' Medici's election. To his prayers be added menaces, and assured them that if their choice fell on himself they would live to repent of it. He reminded them of his excessive rigour on some points, which as Pope would make him extremely disagreeable to them. Nor were they to elect him in the hopes of getting rid of him by a short pontificate, for they would be building on false expectations, as he belonged to a very long-lived family. This was the only occasion on which he allowed himself to ignore his presentiments of approaching death, or argue in favour of his probabilities of longevity.

All these precautions met with no immediate success, as, the very day before the conclave, a Cardinal, one of Aldobrandini's warmest adherents, sent a special messenger to Baronius to assure him that there was no doubt of his obtaining the necessary majority of votes. "I admire his courage in sending me such a message," replied Cesare indignantly. "I do not wish to be Pope. I am a nobody; I am inexperienced; and I am totally ignorant of my own or family's antecedents. Tell the Cardinal that if he interferes any more I shall be furious with him; and if he persists in going on in the same way, I will never say another prayer for him as long as I live!" "But," replied the envoy, who was a man of high position, pointing as he spoke to a crucifix, "if God has decreed that you are to be the Chief Pastor of His Church, how could you resist His will?" "If God were to ordain this," replied Cesar vehemently, "I would turn to Him and say: Govern, O Lord, Thy Church as Thou wilt, I beseech Thee, but do not impose this burden on me!"

In a letter written to Talpa immediately after the election which placed Cardinal de' Medici on the Chair of Peter, Baronius himself relates the successful issue of his machinations. "Were I to write down all the particulars of what took place," he says, "many sheets would be required. Moreover, I have not the time to tell you everything, though to speak the truth I am rather restrained by scruple, for it is a dangerous thing to write about oneself, even though the glory be given to God in all things. If we are together some day I might perhaps, as a pastime, tell you everything. At present all I will do is to ask your help in rendering thanks to God. As to the choice of our new and holy Pastor, I will extol myself in God the Author of all good, that, before we went into conclave,

335

and when my election was ardently expected, I, by a secret way, and, as it were, by a countermine, began to put forward the claims of the Cardinal of Florence, so as to create a diversion from myself; and I managed affairs so successfully that they reached the desired end. By God's grace it fell to me to put the finishing stroke to the business by extinguishing the resistance of Cardinal Aldobrandini, who still hesitated. God willed, however, that he should suddenly make up his mind, and that finished the affair. I feel moved to tell you this. Let us return thanks to God, for, according to my judgment and that of the whole College, we could not have made a better choice, for he whom we have elected combines in himself many qualities not easy to be found. May God be praised in all things."

As soon as the conclave was over, and Cardinal de' Medici elected Pope under the name of Leo XI, Baronius, full of joy, returned to his rooms, and throwing himself on his knees, poured out the most heartfelt thanks to our Lady, to whose care he had entrusted the success of his endeavour to escape the papal dignity. While his words of thanksgiving were still on his lips, one of the Cardinals, coming in to condole with him on the result of the Conclave, and exhort him to be resigned under the disappointment, was amazed to find him so jubilant. For all answer to his visitor's condolences Baronius pointed to the image of our Lady with the words, " She will some day give me a true and supreme pontificate!"

While he was doing his utmost to turn from him the highest dignity on earth, Baronius—probably in reward for his humility—obtained so great a contempt for the things of this world that, after the danger was over, he affirmed that he was ready to set not only the papal throne, but

336

every other position or possible possession at the value of a few farthings. At the same time he wrote to Talpa; "I thank you for the prayers you have been offering up for me in these troublous times. Indeed, I have all throughout felt the sensible aid of God, enabling me to despise, abhor and avoid that which many might regard as the zenith of human happiness. To God be the glory, for I know that this has not been of my own strength, but entirely His gift and grace."

Baronius had good reason to rejoice in the election of Leo XI Not only was the new Pope distinguished for the holiness of his life and his zeal for the interests of the Church, but he was bound to the Oratory by the closest ties. Among all St. Philip's penitents and disciples few can be found more devoted to him than Alessandro de' Medici. He used to spend hours in the Saint's room, often without speaking a word, for it was a consolation to him merely to breathe the same air as St. Philip, and when he left his company he declared that the hours he had been with him had seemed like so many minutes. "Say what you will," he replied to the remonstrances of certain friends about what they considered waste of time, "Philip's room is to me a paradise." Now that he found himself called to the Holy See, he bethought himself of testifying to his love and gratitude in a way now in his power. Among the many points of sympathy between the new Pontiff and Baronius was the desire to see those raised to the altars of the Church who were, by evident tokens, reigning with God in heaven. During the few days of their communication on earth after the Conclave Cesare urgently pleaded the cause of the beatification not only of his own holy father, but also of St. Charles and St. Ignatius. "Yes," replied Leo,

"I have been thinking of them; but above all I will not forget Philip Neri."

The Pope did not live to carry out his pious intentions; and his unexpected death less than a month after his election destroyed Baronius's peace of mind by re-opening the question of the succession to the apostolic see. Leo, though advanced in years, was under seventy, and in good health and sound of mind; so that all men had hoped to enjoy his wise and holy rule for at least a few years. But the cares and responsibilities of the papacy shattered his health and brought him to the grave. He himself had good cause to believe that his time on the papal throne would be short, for, though others had forgotten it, certain words spoken to him by St. Philip twenty years before were fresh in his memory. "Well, Alessandro," the Saint had said, "I can tell you that you will be both Cardinal and Pope, but you will not last long." How constantly this prophecy dwelt in his memory can be shown by almost the first words pronounced by Leo after his election. When Cardinal Ludovisio, afterwards Gregory XV, approached to pay him the accustomed homage, he gently replied: "We shall not give you much trouble, for we shall not last long."

Leo's death renewed all Baronius's anxiety about his possible election to the See of Peter; and this time there was no convenient member of the Sacred College whose cause he could promote in opposition to his own. All he could do was to storm heaven with fervent prayers. The short interval between Leo's death and the assembling of a new conclave was spent by him in real agony of mind; and the terrors of the papacy, and the dangers it would bring to his soul were impressed upon his mind by a series of awful dreams, which he unhesitatingly interpreted as a sign, vouchsafed to him by God, that he was to strain every nerve to avoid the dignity. One night he would imagine himself to be on the summit of a mountain peak, from which he fell into empty space; another time he seemed to be crossing crumbling ruins on a narrow and slippery plank; and, again, he saw himself walking on a pleasant hill decked with flowers, when a mighty flood arose which surged and swelled until the hill was covered, and he was surrounded by and sucked into the waters with nothing to cling to. These horrible visions of the night were related by him in confidence to Father Zazzara of the Congregation, with the expressed conviction that they had been sent to him in warning.

When the assembling of the conclave approached, a large section of the Cardinals, who were bent on having Baronius as Pope, came to him and urged him most strongly to change certain passages in his tract on the Sicilian monarchy, which were likely to raise the prejudices of the Cardinals of Spanish sympathies, who, his friends doubted not, had influenced the result of the last election. Not one word, however, could he be induced to alter. All that he had written, he said, had been in the interests of truth and by command of the Pope. He would rejoice, moreover, if his treatise should prove itself an obstacle to his election, and he would turn it to the same account as Elias did the water with which he drenched the sacrifice which he called for fire from heaven to consume. All the same, he added, he placed himself entirely at God's disposal, for the Spirit breatheth where He will, and the hearts of kings are in God's hand.

In spite of the entire submission to the will of God apparent in the last sentence Baronius took all possible measures to avert the blow. As once before, previous to his elevation to the Sacred College, he seriously thought of seeking safety in flight, and reluctantly abandoned the idea when convinced by his friends of its obvious futility. His personal shrinking from the responsibility of the burden was only the partial cause of his almost violent antipathy to the thought of the papacy. It is evident from his own words, that he was actuated in his struggle to escape by the conviction that he would not fill the Holy See to the glory of God. He speaks of himself as a man of contention, and it is possible that, knowing the fixedness of his principles and his impetuous nature, he foresaw that his elevation to the papacy might cast a fire upon the earth which would conduce neither to the salvation of souls nor the welfare of the Church.

Some such thought as this was in his mind when he published the reasons of his reluctance in the twelfth volume of his Annals, with the completion of which he was struggling painfully all the time that he was experiencing such varied emotions about the papacy. "I asked myself anxiously," he there says, "whether by giving myself to the waves, like another Jonas, I might save others from harm. But according to the judgment of certain wise brethren this course was considered inexpedient, seeing that I was not fleeing from the face of the Lord, as did the prophet, and ought, rather, to stand before the house of Isræl like a wall of defence. With all hope of escape thus frustrated by my brethren's verdict, and being weighed down more than most men by the burden of life, I broke forth with Jeremias into this lamentation: 'Woe is me, my mother! Why hast thou borne me a man of strife, a man of contention to all the earth?'"

Once shut up in conclave, Baronius's zeal for the interests of God and His Church made him contend for other matters besides his own escape from the perils of the papacy; and by this self-forgetfulness nearly brought about the end he so much dreaded. There was one Cardinal on whom the votes of a large faction centred, but to whose election Baronius was vehemently opposed. It is expressly stated that this candidate for the papacy was a man of blameless life, so it is to be presumed that Cesare's objection to him lay in the fact that he was too much under the influence of the King of Spain, and, if raised to the See of Peter, might replace the papacy in that state of servitude from which Clement VIII had freed it. So strong was the faction in favour of this Cardinal that his partizans sought to secure his election by illegal means, and tried to hail him as Pope before a proper scrutiny of votes had been taken. This Baronius resisted, and declared with a loud voice that he would never give his consent, and that he would withstand the election to the very end, even if there remained only his one vote to oppose it. He insisted on matters proceeding in the ordinary way, and, meanwhile, betook himself to prayer. Casting himself on his knees he cried aloud to St. Gregory Thaumaturgus, appealing to him with that instinct which always made him turn to the early fathers of the Church as his familiar friends. "O Gregory," he prayed aloud, "worker of miracles, show forth thy power now and obtain for me that strength and constancy necessary to resist this election, which would, I know, find no favour with thee. Strengthen me, O Lord, in this hour. Look on me that Thou mayest raise up Jerusalem Thy city, and that I may bring to pass what I have purposed."

In these and other words of Scripture did he pray, till even his friends in the Sacred College reproved him, and tried to raise him from his knees, saying that it was too late to struggle against what was evidently the will of God; but all the more fervently did he pray. His action turned the danger on to himself, for a large number of the Cardinals, seeing him thus inflamed with an almost inspired zeal, like unto that of the prophets of old, were filled with admiration and said one to the other: "Come; let us have this man as our Pontiff!" A great commotion followed, and Baronius was, in his turn, dragged against his will and in spite of his struggles into the Pauline Chapel, and his friends hailed him as Pope in the same way that the other faction had done by the Cardinal whom he opposed. Amidst the fierce contention and Babel of tongues Baronius at length obtained a hearing, and implored that there should be one more scrutiny, made in the accustomed and appointed manner. When at length this desire was complied with—Cesare praying aloud all the while—the result, unexpected by all, was that instead of Baronius or the other candidate against whose election he had so fiercely struggled, the requisite majority of votes centred on Cardinal Borghese, a man in the prime of his strength, full of zeal for the liberties of the Church, and a man therefore, after Baronius's own heart.

Cardinal Joyeuse, who wrote an account of this conclave, paid his testimony to the part taken at it by Baronius, and the holy fearlessness displayed by him. "While all this was going on, the great Baronius—for thus I can and must designate him on account of his action at the conclave—whose fervent zeal for God's honour is known to all men, was the only Cardinal who—O memorable example—in that crucial moment of electing the future Pontiff dared to speak out with holy liberty."

Cesare was, indeed, safe, but the sense of the dangers through which he had passed terrified him as he looked back on them, and he could not refrain from describing his experiences to the readers of the twelfth volume of the Annals, published two years after the conclave, and dedicated to Paul V "as a perpetual thanksgiving to the immortal God for his deliverance from the great peril." "So nearly was this volume brought to nought by the trials of its parent," he wrote, "that I would have called it *Benoni*, the son of my sorrow, but owing to the sudden change of circumstances I will henceforth call it Benjamin, the son of my right hand. All things were terrible, and the winds and the waves were roaring, when, behold, the Church was shaken as by an earthquake, and the minds of men were moved and overturned. Though I was impelled by friendly breezes, yet they bore me into the midst of a whirlpool from which it was not easy to escape; but, so that I might learn to seek assistance and support from God, Who is alone Omnipotent, the face of affairs was most admirably changed in a moment as though by a convulsion. It was as if once again the Lord was roused from His sleep by the cries of those who were toiling at the oars, and rising up commanded the winds and the waves to cease; for behold, there was a great calm, and by universal consent Paul was set in Peter's Chair."

The life of this holy man, who had toiled all the day and borne its burden and heats, was drawing to its close, but, though the goal was nearly in sight, the time for rest had not yet come; and during the last two years of his life he bent his back to his daily task as faithfully, though more painfully, than he had done in his earlier years. He was not sixty-seven at the time of the conclaves, but, worn out by his gigantic labours, he was an older man then than his holy Father had been at eighty. He was slowly dying of a painful disease, and his powers daily decreased while his yet unfinished task lay before him. But God meted out the necessary strength, not indeed in full measure, but just sufficient for his needs; and the twelfth volume of the Annals was finished and given to the world with its dedication to the reigning Pontiff barely a week before Baronius was seized by his last illness.

To pain, weakness and weariness, solitude was added to the burdens of his last years. His life was changed. Clement, with whom, in spite of his deep reverence for him as the Vicar of Christ, he had been on such familiar terms, and who had been to him at once friend and father, was no longer in the adjoining apartments. No longer was he called at all moments from his studies by the too familiar summons of the Holy Father, causing interruptions in his work which were not all pain. No longer, either, could he of his own accord seek him out, and find his wise and ever ready interest in any detail of the Annals which affected Catholic truth. A stranger dwelt in his place. Baronius firmly believed that Paul's election was the direct work of the Holy Ghost but maybe the new Pope's intense conviction of the same thing had too much fierceness in it to be restful. Though Cesare thanked God from the bottom of his heart for raising to the Holy See one so imbued with the principles for which he himself was ready to lay down his life, perchance the rigour with which Paul V enforced his regulations, and the relentless inflexibility with which he punished offenders, added to the sufferings of Baronius's last days.

CHAPTER XXVII
The Return to the Oratory

T HERE had always been a tacit understanding on the part of Baronius, both with the Pope and the fathers of the Oratory, that he should end his days at the Vallicella, whither Tarugi on the strength of a similar understanding, had already retired. This arrangement, as far as Cesare was concerned, presented few obstacles now that Clement had gone to his reward. The fathers gave over to his use certain rooms near the church, which included his former room, with the key of which he had never parted. This apartment he fitted up in a way to suit his present position, and, little by little, even before he occupied them, he drifted back into closer connection with the Oratory, and preached there frequently. At the time that he was seized with his last illness he was giving a series of familiar discourses on the Dialogues of St. Gregory.

When the year 1606 was drawing to a close Baronius exhibited an almost feverish urgency with the workmen who were arranging his rooms for him; and, do what they would, they could not work with speed enough to satisfy him. The fact is that he felt inwardly convinced that at last the end was near, and this not only on account of his rapidly failing health, but for reasons entirely of the nature of presentiment. All through his life, as has been noted, he was powerfully influenced by such manifestations as visions, dreams and interior voices; and the very fact that he had almost completed the twelfth volume—the last of the "other two" with which an inward monitor had commanded him to proceed—might have been taken by him as a token of approaching death. No doubt this affected him, though he allowed no such considerations to stay his pen or hinder him from beginning a fresh volume and his presentiments of approaching death had other and stronger foundations.

He need not have looked for death from natural causes. He was only in his sixty-ninth year, and, in spite of his weak and suffering health, there was, humanly speaking, no reason why he should not live some time longer, and even reach the fourscore years of his holy father, already passed by Tarugi. It was, however, precisely because he was in his sixty-ninth year that he was convinced of the approach of his last hour, and anxious to move to the Oratory before it was too late.

When he was taken ill some months later, both fathers and doctors refused to consider his state hopeless. Baronius, however, took a different view, and confided to Father Manni his reasons for refusing to listen to any suggestions of probable recovery. Many years before, previous to his elevation to the purple, he had had a dream which, he was convinced, had been sent to him by God. He was very ill at the time—so ill that he had prepared himself solemnly for death. As he lay on his bed, awaiting his last hour, he saw, on the wall opposite, the number LXIX in large black Roman numerals. He was greatly perturbed by this writing on the wall and earnestly implored God, if it were good for him to know, to show him its meaning. When he turned from prayer and opened his eyes he saw before him again the same numerals, looking this time as though cut out of white marble. As he gazed, the conviction forced itself on his mind that the number referred to the years of his earthly pilgrimage, and that therefore he was not to die of his present illness.

"Truly," he went on to say to Father Manni, "I refused to yield full faith to this vision, for I know how often the devil seeks to deceive us in such ways, and this might have been one of his devices to turn me from penance and good works by the lying promise of a long life before me. Nevertheless, this number has always remained fixed in my mind, even though I refused to rest my faith on it, and the effect of thus remembering it has been to keep the thought of death constantly before me, and make me take greater pains to prepare for it. Now that, by the slow march of time, my years have attained that number which I beheld in vision, and at the same time I find myself reduced to nearly the lowest ebb of bodily weakness, I can scarcely fail to comprehend that this is indeed the year appointed for me to die, and that I shall very soon lay aside my earthly tabernacle." Having said these words, he asked Father Manni to write this number in Roman figures, as he had seen it on the wall, in all the books and papers in his room.

As soon as his rooms at the Oratory were ready for him—which was not until towards the end of the spring of 1607—Baronius supped with the fathers preparatory to taking up his abode with them. During the meal the twenty-ninth chapter of the book of Job was read; and later in the evening he rose to his feet in the midst of the assembled fathers, and addressed them by paraphrasing the chapter to which they had just been listening. "Most wonderfully," said he, "do I find these words to apply to myself when I call to mind those early days in which God kept me in the Congregation; when over my head there shined His lamp, namely Blessed Philip; when I walked by

347

his light in the darkness of my youth, when God was secretly in my tabernacle, when the Almighty was with me, and you, my brothers, were round about me; when I washed my feet with butter, namely the abundance of heavenly consolations which inundated my soul in the performance of our spiritual exercises. And from that rock were poured forth to me rivers of oil, that rock I mean from which we are hewn, namely our Blessed Father, from whose sweet mouth there flowed lessons unto salvation, and from whose breast we drew copious streams of charity. Then I said to myself, 'I shall die in my nest, and as a palm shall multiply my days.' But I was violently torn from my nest, and sent forth like the dove from the ark, exposed to the turbulent floods of the world. Nowhere could I find rest for my feet. All day long have I desired to return to the ark, and behold now at this the last hour of evening, when the sun of my life is setting, I long for it more than ever. It is my one hope to die by God's mercy in the Congregation as in my nest. Therefore, O my fathers, do you who have always borne me such affection, receive me now when, after struggling all day with the flood, I have by God's grace returned to the haven. Nothing on earth that you could do for me would equal this boon that I crave." Then, broken down by his emotion, Baronius, without another word, went away and shut himself in his old room.

Only a few days after he had established himself at the Oratory, Cesare was seized by the illness destined to bring him to the grave. Suffering as he had done for years from the weakest and most painful of digestions, his symptoms now took an aggravated form; he could swallow nothing but a few spoonfuls of liquid, and his strength failed visibly. The physicians who were called in pronounced him to be in a critical though by no means dangerous condition, and said that his best hope of recovery lay in his removal from the heats of Rome to the fine air of Frascati. Baronius received this verdict as a sentence of death. "I know that the change of air will do me no good," he said to Father Manni, "for I am convinced that my last hour is nigh. But as it is always good to obey, I will do as the physicians tell me. But I would fain have stayed here, to be near you all, for you could have helped me in the event of my sudden death."

From that moment Cesare had no thought but for the care of his soul. Though, as he told Sixtus V seventeen years previously, the history of the Church hung together in his mind as such a united whole that he could not write one volume of the Annals without the one to follow evolving itself in his brain in such a way as to make him long to be at work on it; and though he had actually begun to write a thirteenth volume, he now entirely put aside what he was doing. Even the memory of it did not remain as a distracting element to be driven away from his thoughts, but dropped from his mind as if it had never existed and left no room except for the things of God. St. Philip's ways of dealing with him, which Cesare had found so hard to understand, had indeed borne their fruit. As death, the great destroyer of illusions, approached, Baronius proved unmistakably that the absorbing interest he had always taken in his history and the great questions with which it brought him in contact was a very secondary consideration, and that he had spent his strength on his work for God and God only. The moment it was made clear to him that it was not the divine will that he should go on writing, he ceased to write as simply and whole-heartedly as if it had not been his

349

monopolizing occupation for more than twenty years. For God he had taken up his pen; for God he laid it down.

This simple fidelity was richly rewarded, for few deaths have been more full of childlike joy than that of this holy man who, to use his own words, having borne the burden and heats of the day from the first hour, now, being broken down by toil, lay down and rested in the shade for which he had longed the whole day through. Like the labourers of the parable, he hoped that he might receive his penny in the evening, though, considering the justice of God and his own sins, he ought to feel some misgivings. His longing to go into the presence of God was intense, and his favourite words, *"Eternitas, eternitas,"* were more than ever on his lips. When Father Manni talked to him about heaven, he could scarcely contain himself for the joy which the very word kindled in his soul. "O blessed they who enter into Thy glory," he cried. "I desire to see Thee, O Jesus my Lord. O love, love, O Jesus my Love. How good a thing it is to do the will of God!"

The doctor who attended Baronius at Frascati, full of the responsibility of having such an eminent patient in his care, begged him earnestly to moderate the fervour of his ejaculations, lest he should aggravate his malady and, perhaps, hasten death. "Hasten death?" exclaimed Cesare. "And why should I fear death, which all these years has been to me as a sister, with whom I have held sweet converse every day?" When left alone after the doctor's warning, he burst out into prayer more fervently than ever. "Why should I fear Thee, O Lord my God? Dost Thou not love me? I thank Thee, Lord, for all things. I thank Thee for having given me my blessed father Philip. I thank Thee, I thank Thee!"

After Baronius had been a little while at Frascati, tended by Father Manni and Father Pateri, the fever which was already on him increased in violence, and, thinking death might be at hand, he begged to return to the Oratory. "See how this fever takes possession of me," he said to Manni. "Let me go and die in Rome. It is not fitting that a Cardinal should die out of Rome." And after a pause he added, "I wish to die in the midst of the Congregation." A litter, the best that could at the moment be procured though rough and short, was borrowed in haste, and the doctor, now thoroughly alive to the imminence of his patient's danger, accompanied him to Rome, fearing that he might die on the road. Cesare was in great pain, and the heat of the June sun and the jolting of the litter tried him much; but he never uttered a word of complaint either then or at any time throughout his illness.

When Baronius arrived at the Oratory, it was evident to all that death could not be far off. Tarugi, hearing in his own rooms that his friend had been brought back in a dying state, wished to go to him, but age and infirmity forbade it, and there is no record of any parting interview between those two sons of St. Philip whom he loved so especially. In the early morning Cesare roused himself from the state of semi-coma in which he had been lying, and, before fully conscious, called out to receive Communion. "Where is He?" he cried, "where is He? Why do you not bring Him to me?" When the Blessed Sacrament, which had been reserved through the night in his private chapel, was brought into his room, Baronius, raising himself exclaimed, "I renounce Satan and all his works; I cleave to Thee alone, O Lord Jesus!" and made acts of love and contrition aloud. And after his

351

Communion, with the help of one of the fathers, he recited the *Nunc dimittis*, thinking the end was at hand.

We cannot refrain from dwelling thus in detail on these last days of Baronius's life, and recording the broken words of prayer which, as they fell from his lips, were written down and treasured by the fathers.

In a measure they raise the veil which his humble reserve habitually threw over his interior life, and reveal to our view the inner sanctuary of his soul, wherein lay that haven of rest in God to which he returned when the strain of exterior work relaxed its tension. It required the unbending effects of mortal illness, or the breaking down of reticence consequent on semi-delirium, to induce him to betray the secrets of his soul. His habitual silence about his interior life now took its revenge by these fervent outpourings made regardless of the presence of bystanders, which revealed the intensity of his personal love of our Blessed Lord, as the one Object of his life. Over and over again, in loving, longing accents, did he repeat the Holy Name, and sometimes he burst forth into more prolonged ejaculations. "I want my Lord," he would say when his mind was in a half wandering state. "Where is He? My Lord Jesus, I want Thee. I desire to be with Him O how gladly will I go to Him. O Lord Jesus, how good Thou art!" The day after Cesare's return to the Oratory he rallied, and next morning, bidding his attendants open the windows, he tried to get up and dress to say Mass, but could not stand. He was, however, supported into the chapel, where he was present at the Holy Sacrifice for the last time. Later in the day he sent for all the members of his household, blessed them, bade them farewell, and said some parting words to each. A great-nephew of his, Camillo Baldino, came to see him, and Baronius thus addressed him: "My son, behold I am going the way of all flesh. All I leave and bequeath to you is what my father left to me, namely poverty. Beware of too great a devotion to learning, and rather incline to mortification. There is no knowledge greater than that of how to be humble. Think little of all that belongs to this world." And with these words he dismissed him.

Then turning to the fathers who were standing round his bed, he said to Father Angelo Saluzio, with whom he was on intimate terms: "Listen to what I say. Nothing in life has given me greater pain than being made a Cardinal. I wish all men to know it. It fills me with shame to think that I, so unworthy, should have been raised to so high a dignity. O miserable wretch that I am. Let us seek God only."

Meanwhile, the forty hours exposition was going on in the church, which was thronged with worshippers praying for the prolongation of the precious life of the great historian. When Baronius heard of the prayers that were being offered up for his recovery, he protested. "Take no thought for my body," he said; "pray rather for the salvation of my soul. The only boon I ask connected with this earth is the Holy Father's blessing." One other wish he had, which, however, was destined to be ungranted, and one last sacrifice, cheerfully offered, was asked of him. When he restored his titular church, he had prepared a place of burial for himself in it; and now he expressed his wish to be buried there. When, however, Father Zazzara, on behalf of the Congregation, gave him to understand that there would be great difficulties in the way, he yielded the point without a moment's hesitation.

While the faithful were storming heaven for Cesare's recovery, the physicians attending on him did their best in

353

their own way to effect the same end, and tortured his last days in order to keep him a few hours longer in this world. They forced food down his throat, though every morsel he tried to swallow caused him real agony and produced the most violent retching. Under this treatment his fortitude nearly failed him. "I can no more," he said, turning appealingly from the physician to the fathers. "Listen to poor Cesare's prayer. He only asks this one small thing of your charity." But Angelo Vellono, the doctor, still insisted. "It is necessary," he said, "absolutely necessary for you to take food, even if you suffer, for so only can you gain strength to carry out God's will." Then Baronius quietly submitted, assuring Vellono the while that there was no slightest chance of keeping him alive.

Of all the fathers he had the greatest affection for Father Flaminio Ricci, who had for some years been his confessor. This father, who was at the time superior, happened to be away from Rome when Cesare was taken ill. As soon, however, as he heard of his danger, he hastened home, and went straight to the dying man's bedside. Cesare's human heart was filled with joy at seeing him, but he was by that time too weak to say much, or give any ordinary sign of pleasure; but, taking hold of a little bell which had been placed beside him, he tried to ring it as an expression of his feeling of delight.

On June 27 Baronius received Holy Viaticum in presence of the assembled fathers. "Now in truth is it my sixty-ninth year," he murmured, as our Lord approached. "*Dei sum! Dei sum!* Pray for me," he then said turning to the fathers. "Help me to die well, for to this end did I come here." After he had received Viaticum, he was anointed, and by that time his strength had failed so completely that he believed himself to be dying. "Pray for me—for my eternal salvation, nothing else," he whispered. "*O quam bonus Deus Israel!*"

But the joyous confidence with which he welcomed death did not prevent his being full of holy fear. When a friend who visited him said indiscreetly that such a one as he ought to feel but very slight tremor at the prospect of death, but should rather be filled with elation by the hope of receiving at the hands of God the reward of his great labours in His service, Baronius rebuked the speaker with humble indignation. "You speak foolishly," he said. "We must all look forward to the judgment with fear and trembling prostration of spirit; for our hope is in God alone." Thus did he speak with the full deliberation of his reason; nevertheless, all his instincts were those of joy and desire.

Baronius lingered on for three days after he received the last sacraments, and celebrated one more feast of St. Peter on earth. He asked on that day to have a picture of the holy Apostles placed before his eyes, and, though he could not speak or utter a prayer, he kept his gaze fixed on it. It was evident to all that his thoughts were dwelling on those who had been his patrons and intercessors during his long years of labour for the cause of the Church.

Next day, June 30, his soul was set free from its worn out tenement. The Congregation was summoned in haste, and Father Ricci recited the commendation of the departing soul—so often rehearsed by Baronius in the days of his strength, and repeated over his own body. His last distinguishable words were eminently characteristic. Raising his voice with a final flicker of strength, he exclaimed in Latin: *Ergo, ecce nunc tempus exultationis et lætitiæ. Moriamur.*[29] Then unaided he crossed his arms on his breast, composed himself, and so died, with joy on his lips and in his heart.

The learned, humble and self-denying life of the great son of St. Philip was known to all in Rome; and when the news of his death was spread abroad, all classes flocked to the Oratory where his body lay exposed. Pieces of his clothes were cut off and kept and many of the more enthusiastic touched his remains with their rosaries and other pious objects, regardless of the efforts made by the fathers to check such marks of devotion. But after a while these popular demonstrations ceased of themselves, and for a time Cesare's body was suffered to rest quietly before St. Philip's tomb, where, when alive, he had so often lain prostrate in prayer. Then he was buried to the left of the high altar, where, about a year after, that other great son of St. Philip, Tarugi, was laid by his side.

Thus was it given to Cesare to return to die and await the resurrection in the house of his holy Father. Time passes and eternity remains. The cruel wrench which severed him from the Oratory was forgotten like an evil vision of the night. The purple robes, heavier than chains of iron, fell from him like mouldering rags which crumble into dust when exposed to the light of heaven. Only one thing that had appertained to him in this transitory life remained, namely his vocation and the character of a son of St. Philip.

Finis

---

[29] "Behold, now is the time of exultation and joy. We die." -Editor.

The Tomb of Cesare Cardinal Baronius
Santa Maria in Vallicella, Rome.

Other Great Books from Mediatrix Press

The Life of St. Philip Neri
by Lady Anne Hope

The Life of the Venerable Anne of Jesus
by a Sister of Notre Dame de Namur

The Life of St. Francis of Assisi
by Candide Challipe, OFM

St. Therese and the Faithful
A book for those living in the world
by Benedict Williamson

A Small Catechism for Catholics
by St. Peter Canisius, S.J.

On the Marks of the Church
by St. Robert Bellarmine, S. J.

On the Roman Pontiff, vol. 1
By St. Robert Bellarmine, S.J.

CPSIA information can be obtained
at www.ICGtesting.com
Printed in the USA
BVHW030753180620
581361BV00005B/54